REVIVING LOCAL DEMOCRACY

Related titles from The Policy Press

What works? Evidence-based policy and practice in public services
Edited by Huw T.O. Davies, Sandra M. Nutley and Peter C. Smith
ISBN 1 86134 191 1 £17.99 pbk 216x148 mm July 2000
    1 86134 192 X £45.00 hdbk

Local political leadership
Steve Leach and David Wilson
ISBN 1 86134 154 7 £17.99 pbk 216x148 mm February 2000
    1 86134 206 3 £45.00 hdbk

The dynamics of public service contracting: The British experience
Young-Chool Chi
ISBN 1 86134 139 3 £18.99 pbk 216x148 mm February 1999
    1 86134 140 7 £45.00 hdbk

Trust and contracts: Relationships in local government, health and public services
Edited by Andrew Coulson
ISBN 1 86134 086 9 £16.99 pbk 216x148 mm August 1998
    1 86134 107 5 £40.00 hdbk

Moving pictures: Realities of voluntary action
Duncan Scott, Pete Alcock, Lynne Russell and Rob Macmillan
ISBN 1 86134 233 0 £13.95 pbk 297x210 mm May 2000

REVIVING LOCAL DEMOCRACY

New Labour, new politics?

Nirmala Rao

The POLICY

PP

PRESS

First published in Great Britain in September 2000 by

The Policy Press
34 Tyndall's Park Road
Bristol BS8 1PY
UK

Tel +44 (0)117 954 6800
Fax +44 (0)117 973 7308
e-mail tpp@bristol.ac.uk
www.policypress.org.uk

British Library Cataloguing in Publication Data

A catalogue record for this book is available from the British Library

ISBN 1 86134 218 7
A hardback version is also available

Nirmala Rao is Senior Lecturer in Politics at Goldsmiths College, London.

Cover design by Qube Design Associates, Bristol.

Illustration on front cover (Belfast City Hall) supplied by kind permission of Rodney Miller Associates, Belfast.

Printed and bound in Great Britain by Hobbs the Printers Ltd, Southampton.

Contents

List of tables

Acknowledgements

This work has benefited from the generosity of a number of people and organisations. I thank Dr Stephen Almond for undertaking the multivariate analysis reported in Chapter Five and Appendix A, and Steven Finch, of the National Centre for Social Research, for carrying out the second stage of the survey of non-working councillors. I am grateful to the Nuffield Foundation, which funded this latter study, and to the National Centre for Social Research (formerly SCPR) for giving me the opportunity to report the results of several of the surveys on which I was invited to collaborate. I owe a special debt of gratitude to the Research Committee of Goldsmiths College for supporting my national survey of councillors – the results of which are reported in Chapter Eight. Of course, the survey would not have been possible without the support and kind cooperation of the large number of councillors who gave up their time to contribute their views to the ongoing debate on the 'modernisation' of local government. It has been a pleasure to work with all the individuals involved in these various surveys and studies.

This book owes much to the encouragement of Ken Young, whose sustaining friendship and intellectual stimulation prompted me to embark on this project. Michael Hill introduced me to The Policy Press, where Dawn Louise Rushen's enthusiasm and crisp organisation gave the project its much-needed momentum. My thanks to them. The eventual manuscript would not have taken the form it did had it not been for the painstaking efforts of the anonymous reviewers – lest their contributions go unmarked, I take this opportunity to express my gratitude to them.

Nirmala Rao
July 2000

ONE

New times for local democracy

This book is about New Labour's plan for the modernisation of local democracy. The election of the Blair government in May 1997 precipitated an intense debate about local government: local authorities, it was said, had failed to adapt themselves to the challenges of the late 20th century. Public indifference, voter apathy and declining trust in the institutions of representative government justified urgent measures to reform the ways in which councils connected with their communities. Behind this programme lay a more fundamental critique of a deeper process of mismatch between popular expectations and governmental performance. The 19th century institutions of representative democracy had outlived their usefulness, not just in Britain but worldwide. The need for renewal was comprehensive, and local government provided a useful point of entry for the 'democratisation of democracy'.

In terms of concrete proposals, however, there was much that was familiar in the package put forward in the 1998 White Paper, *Modern local government: In touch with the people*. Proposals for enhancing public participation through local forums, and through changes in electoral procedures, had an element of novelty about them. However, other parts of the package – notably the transformation of decision-making structures through the creation of separate local executives or elected mayors – covered ground already well-trodden during the previous 40 years. The distinctiveness of New Labour's proposals lay less in their substance than in the passion with which they were advocated and the political commitment with which they were enacted.

Bringing passion into politics is risky: one may become beguiled by one's own rhetoric, pursuing policies that are strong on symbolism and weak on actual achievement. New Labour was not immune to this risk. 'Modernisation' became a slogan: an assertion that change is needed. That need cannot be assumed, but must be demonstrated. Widespread ignorance and apathy cannot be reconciled with the democratic health of a nation. Few would dispute that low turnouts in local elections signify a weakness in the democratic process and bringing councils more closely in touch with local people through new mechanisms for participation can be readily justified. To that extent, reforms of the type proposed may be defensible.

It is less clear that changing the ways in which local authorities make their decisions by creating a special class of 'executive' councillors is necessary to improve the efficiency of local government. The fact that the committee system of decision making has existed for more than a century does not, in itself, warrant its abolition. It may well be the most inclusive and the most flexible of all possible systems.

Has the world changed so radically that institutions are now in dire need of adjustment, as the proponents of the 'third way' maintain? Has so wide a gap opened up between people and their local governments as to demand comprehensive reform? If so, do New Labour's proposals address the problem in a realistic fashion? And how acceptable – how workable – are they likely to prove?

Reviving local democracy

'Democratic renewal' is the catch-phrase of New Labour's programme for local government. As an aspiration it commands wide assent, if only by virtue of its ambiguity: it can be interpreted more or less as one wishes. In fact, at least three distinct usages are discernible in the government's use of the term.

First, it may be used to describe a set of practical responses to clearly identifiable problems, such as low levels of electoral turnout. To deal with such problems, the government proposes changes to election procedures and practices, such as electoral registration processes. At this level, the changes proposed amount to little more than attempts to improve the current system. The problems are not attributed to any deep-seated malaise, but rather to the inflexibility and inconvenience of present arrangements. The timing and frequency of elections, and the accessibility of the polling station are key issues. Making voting easier – holding elections at the weekends, providing for rolling registration and placing polling booths in shops or railway stations – should improve turnout, perhaps to the levels of the past.

Second, the term 'democratic renewal' illuminates the presence of deeper failings in the practice of local democracy. Loss of faith in the institutions of modern government and declining trust in the people who run them, rather than the inadequacies of the particular mechanisms, are the true causes of public indifference and lack of involvement. Democratic renewal in this sense does not refer to failures of local government as such, but to inherent weaknesses in the culture of democracy. The diagnosis is clear enough. What is less clear is what measures can be proposed to remedy such deficiencies.

Third, the term 'democratic renewal' may be used to describe a new type of political system in which "different components of representative, deliberative and direct democracy are combined to create a more open, participative and responsive polity at the local level" (Pratchett, 1999, p 2). The intention is to create a new democracy by involving people in a wide variety of ways alongside the existing structures of elective representation. Revitalising local democracy becomes a feasible ambition if steps are taken to involve local people in decision making, perhaps through citizens' panels or juries, or focus groups. An element of direct democracy can be introduced through more widespread use of referenda. Taken together, more responsive and attentive local councillors, widespread use of consultative forums and placing key issues directly to popular vote promise a reinvigoration of local political life. The government's agenda for 'democratic renewal' seeks to promote just such initiatives.

While each of these positions is entirely coherent in itself, it is far from clear how they relate to each other. The first and the third are mutually reinforcing: reducing the barriers to participation at elections and more direct engagement will encourage greater involvement. But can a revived local politics really inculcate the civic virtues on such a scale as to reverse the adverse cultural changes of the past few decades? To expect it to do so may be to place an unrealistic burden on the otherwise sensible steps taken to improve the politics of local government. It is to confuse modest improvements in turnout with actual shifts in beliefs, motivations and outlook on political life.

New Labour, new politics?

New Labour puts changing social values – 'cultural change' – central to its mission. Institutions express cultures, and the 19th-century institutions of local democracy reflect that century's preoccupation with representative democracy. Therefore, Chapter Two – 'Local democracy and after' – traces the origins of contemporary local government to the 19th-century reforms of both town and countryside. It shows how the demands of governmental growth and the building of the welfare state eclipsed the realisation of those values. These developments satisfied municipal ambitions, but raised the question of what local government, in serving a national agenda, was for.

This question came into sharper focus as the increasing scope and complexity created a mounting overload on local authorities. The structures no longer appeared adequate, while the people required to run the system well were in short supply. By the 1960s, official concern led to a series of high-level inquiries into whether local government was capable of attracting the best talents. Chapter Three – 'The failed promise of reform' – shows that the absence of real change provoked a gathering crisis of confidence. Governments found reform to be less easily attained than they had supposed. Thenceforth, they were to bypass local authorities, rather than seeking to strengthen them. The stage was set for Britain to turn away from local democracy after 1979.

This, then, was the institutional problem: to reform local government or to accept its relegation to the margins of the political constitution. It would not be solved without an understanding of the deep cultural changes that had occurred in the postwar period. Chapter Four – 'Civic-minded Britain?' – explores Britain's cultural revolution in its larger global context. This revolution, which might be characterised as the collapse of the civic culture, raised fundamental questions about the utility and significance of local elections, the value of local autonomy and the standing of elected representatives.

This loss of faith in political institutions was expressed most vividly in public non-participation in elections – low turnout is an international phenomenon. Variations in turnout, and the propensity of some groups of people not to exercise their right to vote in council elections, have long troubled those who see full participation as the hallmark of democracy. Chapter Five – 'The reluctant voter' – presents an analysis of the factors that affect local voting and identifies the key issues which successful reforms must address.

Chapter Six – 'The third way and democratic reform' – introduces New Labour's reform programme as a key aspect of the much-vaunted third way. The new politics manifests itself across the developed world as a move to bring government closer to the people, to promote accountability and transparency, and create a more open style of governance. New initiatives to transform education, promote regeneration, tackle social exclusion and modernise political structures are presented in this chapter as expressions of the third way.

The two chapters that follow look in depth at New Labour's modernisation of local government. Chapter Seven – 'The modernising agenda: enhancing participation – deals with enhancing participation, and outlines the government's critique of the present state of local democracy. It considers the initiatives already taken to bring local government closer to the people and rehearses some of the problems to be overcome to achieve participation in local affairs beyond the ballot box. Encouraging people to vote in local elections is another matter, and here the government's proposals are put to the test of public opinion. Do people support the proposed changes? More importantly, would they be more likely to vote under New Labour's electoral reforms?

The second instalment of the modernising agenda, to develop new political leadership, is the subject of Chapter Eight – 'New forms of political leadership'. The government's critique stresses the need to achieve greater representativeness and attract a wider range of people to serve on councils. New forms of political decision making are proposed, with separate executive and scrutiny roles, enabling councillors to spend their time more effectively. Radical options for change include directly-elected mayors with executive responsibilities, or 'cabinets' based on the Westminster model. Again, these proposals can be tested against the views of those most affected: councillors themselves and the wider public. How much support do these proposals command? How likely are they to be adopted?

This book both sets out the context and background of the problems that New Labour's programme seeks to address and tests the modernisation proposals against the evidence.

TWO

Local democracy and after

Britain's system of local government is rightly said to be a 19th-century creation. As such, its origins are inseparable from the rise of popular politics, with all the passions that they inspired. 'The representation of the people' – a stirring phrase still used today for statutes dealing with electoral matters – was to be achieved at both the parliamentary and the local level. Local councils were seen as the mechanism by which ordinary people could participate in the politics and governance of their own local communities. As such, they were to provide a training ground for participation in the wider world of political life. Although the new county, district and parish councils fell short of expectations – few working men were elected, and the new authorities tended to be dominated by the old order – they nevertheless succeeded in providing a platform for popular participation. In the towns, on the other hand, political contests could be fierce.

As the 20th century progressed, it proved difficult to sustain popular interest and participation in local politics. Although around half the electors voted in most contested elections, many rural areas often produced no contest, with prominent people – sitting councillors in particular – being returned unopposed. The system settled into stasis, with long service the norm and some well-established councillors serving for virtually the whole of their adult lives. Politics in the towns also gradually settled. During the 1920s and 1930s, many Conservative voters moved out to the growing suburbs, while the rise of Labour secured the industrial cities as fiefdoms for that party. Local politics came to be a closed shop, with social leaders and their networks on the one hand, and suspicious party officials on the other, controlling entry to the representative process. The great hopes of the 19th-century reformers were as dust.

But if local *politics* was withering, local *government* was thriving – especially after 1945. Local authorities were the natural vehicles for delivering the greatly expanded services of the welfare state. Some local services – particularly those concerned with the urban infrastructure – were lost to national or regional bodies, but many more were developed under new legislation, and these new services tended to be people-oriented or 'human' services. Only where national consistency was paramount, as in the vexed area of monetary benefits, was local discretion seen as undesirable. The provision of public housing and community health was hugely expanded as slums were cleared and war damage made good by replacement. Welfare services were rapidly developed and new services for children at risk introduced. Education became the subject of a great expansionist drive, while councils gained powers for the first time to plan and control physical development. Local expenditure soared, driven by government grants designed to achieve expansion. But central control was the price of this service growth, for local discretion was diminished both relatively and also, through tightening controls, in absolute terms. By the 1960s, local government was in danger of becoming the agent of central government, a convenient implementation agency for ministers' plans and programmes. Had the attraction of new powers and new money proved a poisoned chalice for local democracy?

This chapter traces the roots of present-day revivalism to the aspirations of the founders of local democracy. It provides a benchmark for the present-day movement, seeking, as it does, to transcend 'reform' and take local democracy back to its origins. The first sections of the chapter show local representative democracy coming of age with, by the end of the century, the completion of an institutional structure of elective government for the whole country. The focus then shifts to the development of the administrative machinery of local government in the interwar period – development made necessary by the strains of reconstruction, mass unemployment and uneven growth. In this way, the foundation was laid for the post-1945 expansion of services, which, together with the problems it brought in its train, is the subject of the latter sections of this chapter.

The origins of local democracy

Today's concern with reform carries distant echoes of the origins of local representative democracy. In the early 19th century, the government of towns was vested in bodies that were unquestionably undemocratic, exclusive and unrepresentative. The borough councils – established mainly in the established towns, but joined mid-century by the rapidly-developing industrial areas – enjoyed a measure of autonomy and self-government under Royal Charters granted, in some cases, as far back as the 12th century. The older boroughs, some of which gained their charters in return for financial support or other acts of loyalty to the King, won control of local trade and markets, appointed their own justices and achieved parliamentary representation (Finlayson, 1963).

For many years before the appointment of the 1833 Royal Commission to Inquire into the Municipal Corporations, the ruling bodies in the boroughs had come under criticism for their unrepresentative character and their exclusivity. Some corporations were so decayed as to be virtually non-existent and many did nothing of value for the local inhabitants. Only some were 'real democracies'; others, by far the greatest number,

> had degenerated into closed bodies, into whose hands the freemen had tacitly resigned their rights, and whose members acted as Justices of the Peace within the limits of the corporation, these *ex officio* magistrates being, of course, quite a different body of men from those who sat on the Bench of the county quarter sessions. (Halevy, 1935, p 19)

The predominantly oligarchic character of the boroughs, based on the principle of self-election, provided few opportunities for free election by the citizens. As the report of the Royal Commission observed of one corporation, "no contest amongst the candidates has ever taken place in common hall, and no instance has ever occurred in which the candidate recommended by the common council was not elected". Other evidence showed that, in one corporation, the largest number of electors who had gone to the polls in any election during the preceding 30 years had been nine. The consequence of a system such as this, based on self-election, was an almost universal practice of bribery, corruption and misuse of public funds. *The Times* in 1833 noted that:

> The most active spring of election bribery and villainy everywhere is known to be the corporation system. The members of the corporation throughout England are for the most part self-elected, and wholly irresponsible but to themselves alone.... They have abused for base purposes the patronage which they usurped, and confiscated to their own benefit the funds of which they were lawfully but trustees.... (Finlayson, 1963, pp 37–8)

Few corporations could claim that their members were men of "station, education and substance" or respectable and "persons of property and station in life" (Hennock, 1973, p 309). There remained deep distrust among the inhabitants of the self-elected municipal councils, whose powers remained, for the large part, unchecked. Such defects could only be eliminated through reform. One of the landmarks of the 'Age of Reform' – the 1835 Municipal Corporations Act – swept aside this old regime, creating elected councils and transferring to them all the functions and property of the existing corporations. The local franchise was extended to all ratepayers of at least three years' standing. Truly the beginning of modern local government, its effects were limited to the existing boroughs, and to those growing towns that subsequently achieved incorporation.

Successive extensions of the right to vote provided a major impetus to the development of representative institutions throughout the 19th century. Although in the early years voting was restricted to some ratepayers, and the number of votes each enjoyed varied from one to six, depending on the rateable value of their property, by the end of the 19th century each ratepayer had one vote. Following the 1835 Act, the borough councillors were to be elected by a standard franchise. Every man who was an inhabitant householder within a borough or within seven miles thereof, and who had occupied any property within the borough for the previous two-and-a-half years, could vote. No serious challenge to the form of franchise was proposed, and the working classes as a whole were excluded by the fact that their cottages were not rated at all. The passage of the 1850 Small Tenements Rating Act resulted in great increases in the number of voters in those boroughs where it was adopted. Yet the borough franchise was still limited and was only extended to working men in 1867, when the borough franchise was extended to all householders. Overnight, the borough electorate was increased by 90%, with working-class voters forming the majority in many towns.

Democracy in the boroughs

Access to public office was, in many towns, controlled by party managers. Party alignments in local politics had been present before the 1835 reforms, and were intensified by them. Councils were served by tiny staffs compared to modern standards, but it was not unknown for the dominant group of councillors to appoint a clerk sympathetic to their own political views. A change of political control could bring such positions to an abrupt end, as occured in Stockport in 1835 and Bolton in 1847. After 1850, a tradition of political neutrality came gradually to be established.

Radicals had made great gains in borough elections in the 1830s; the Conservatives enjoying a brief revival in the next decade until the party split. There followed a long period in which party conflict was more subdued, and "a quiescent aldermanic Liberalism held sway" (Hanham,

1959, p 387). The 1867 reforms had the effect of reinvigorating party conflict and ensured that local contests reflected, to varying degrees, the standing of the national parties. They also brought to the fore a new political phenomenon – the high-profile local leader who personified his city on the national stage. One such leader, and the most prominent, was Joseph Chamberlain of Birmingham, who became mayor of that city in 1873. By this time, national party managers were taking local elections seriously. A man of Chamberlain's stature could build a significant power base around his mayoralty, with implications for parliamentary politics across the city. The municipal ward was the recognised basis of electioneering and to neglect organisation at the local level was to risk parliamentary losses. Local politics had become the nursery school of modern electioneering and local elections a barometer of national party strengths.

While the desire for party supremacy, and the need to keep the party organisation active between general elections was a common factor, political issues and party alignments on them were a kaleidoscope of local circumstances and traditions (Hennock, 1973). Birmingham was again at the leading edge of change, with Chamberlain's exploitation of seemingly mundane issues of urban infrastructure leading to the politicisation of almost all local issues, an example which was followed in Leeds and a number of the other great industrial cities.

The extension of the right to vote did not always produce the desired outcome. Apart from enhancing "treating, bribery and canvassing" in some towns, "the character and dignity of the corporation" were "lowered by the intrusion of unworthy members, and by the introduction of personal squabbles, tending to impair the decorum of its proceedings" (Keith-Lucas, 1952, p 69). Whether based on party divisions or personal rivalries, town politics could present an unedifying spectacle, and reformers began to switch their concern for extending democracy to finding ways to temper its excesses in order to achieve local government that was both responsible and effective.

Preaching the doctrine of local self-government, John Stuart Mill argued the need for creating a class of able, qualified and intelligent men worthy of their share in local administration (Redlich and Hirst, 1972, pp 182-90). Although he saw the value of democracy as being based on the widest suffrage, he remained cautious of the universal franchise advocated by Bentham. Chadwick also regarded local self-government as a potential vehicle for corruption, and supervision from the centre as essential (Redlich and Hirst, 1972, pp 140-50). Leaving local ratepayers to decide how to spend on services could clash with attempts to impose national standards. The wider the electoral participation, the more likely clashes were to occur. Central control was a necessary check on local enthusiasms.

The advocates of representative government were not necessarily entirely in favour of unbridled democracy. Rather, they favoured a 'ratepayer democracy', and argued that those who contributed to the local rate should control the spending of the money raised. Mill pressed for a single elected board for every county to act as a "representative sub-parliament for local affairs, supervising the administration of all local business". From this body, all ex officio members were to be excluded and the franchise for election to the ratepayers alone to be restricted, even allowing greater weight in voting to those who contributed most to the rates. Although Mill argued that participation in the process of government was a valuable education in public affairs which helped to stimulate local leadership, the dangers were all too clear: giving the vote to all implied that policy might be controlled by the wishes of uneducated people and people who contributed little or nothing to the rates but still derived the benefits. In his *Considerations on representative government* (1861), Mill modified the utilitarian doctrine, accepting the need to work with and through educated local opinion.

Rural democracies?

Despite the dangers of popular participation, the extension of franchise was inevitable, for the restriction of the right to vote became not only politically indefensible, but also administratively difficult. As local government reform gained ground, the need to apply representative principles to county government could no longer be delayed. County structure was the most 'aristocratic' of all institutions, according to Mill, "at variance with all the principles which are the foundations of representative government" (Mill, 1861, p 380). Certainly, there was nothing representative about county government, yet, by the second half of the century, deference to the aristocracy and gentry was already in decline. In those counties that were being suburbanised by the growth of the great manufacturing cities, a new type of councillor was emerging whose power and authority owed more to position on the county council than to social standing outside it:

> ... government by country gentlemen was transformed between 1840 and 1880.... The landed gentry were displaced from their monopoly of

local politics by new social leaders ... who had made their wealth out of the expansion of urban industry.... By the end of the Second World War, the county society of social leaders was replaced by a community of public persons.... The noblemen and squires were slowly replaced by the new businessmen.... (Lee, 1963, pp 4-5, 212-13)

Early attempts in 1836 by Joseph Hume to introduce a bill to establish elected county councils achieved no success, and half a century passed before county reform was seriously established on the political agenda in 1880. There were three reasons for this extended lapse of time in the extension of local democracy from town to country. First, county administration, vested in the hands of the justices, was not corrupt in the manner of the unreformed boroughs and there was little demand to displace the gentry on 'reform' grounds. Second, the mid-century growth of government was, in the counties, accommodated by the growth of *ad hoc* bodies, thus spreading the administrative load that would otherwise have fallen on elected authorities and tested their abilities. Third, prior to the 1884 Reform Act and the redistribution of parliamentary seats that followed, the House of Commons was dominated by rural interests with a blocking majority (Young, 1989).

When county reform at last came, it had a radical temper. As in the towns, reform focused largely on the need to create responsible institutions accountable to the ratepayers. The 1884 Representation of the People Act extended the household suffrage already existing in the boroughs to the counties, thereby enfranchising the agricultural labourers. The lack of elected local government in the counties was now glaring and Chamberlainite Liberals seized the opportunity to capture the new mood of political expectancy. The mould-breaking 'Radical Programme' provided a manifesto for representative democracy, arguing for elected county councils and subordinate district councils as part of a total package of popular reforms.

Although the Local Government Bill introduced in 1888 restricted change to the county level alone, it was particularly threatening to the ancient borough councils. While throughout their history they had been administered separately from the counties, they were now to be subordinated to the county councils in whose area they were located. The government conceded only that the 10 largest borough councils were strong enough to administer all local services. This was not enough to assuage municipal pride and ambition. Local pressures, applied in the House of Lords, managed to reduce the qualifying size to 50,000, leading to the immediate exemption of as many as 59 borough councils from county government with the independent status of 'counties of boroughs' or, as they became more commonly known, county boroughs.

Between 1889 and 1894 county councils were the sole local government body for the areas of countryside outside the boroughs. But in 1894 the Liberal government introduced a new second-tier of local government – the district council – alongside the boroughs. Areas of relatively recent urban growth that had not been incorporated as boroughs by Royal Charter were now granted their own urban district council, with powers and duties broadly similar to those of the non-county boroughs. The remainder of the county's area, where there were no towns of any size, was dealt with by the creation of similarly-constituted rural district councils. The old non-county boroughs retained minor powers of their own, but the principal difference between them and the new district councils was ceremonial.

Councillors in the older towns – whether 'county' or 'non-county' boroughs – enjoyed a focal point of civic loyalty in their mayor, could confer honour on local notables (or defeated council candidates) by electing them as aldermen, and were entitled to wear ceremonial robes. The district councils enjoyed no such titles or privileges and were presided over by mere chairmen. Many argued that the status of a local authority determined how successful it would be in recruiting people of standing and ability as councillors, as the dignities and privileges of a borough were attractive to potential candidates. This benefit was often cited by district councils seeking incorporation, and most potently in the demand for borough councils to be established within London, something which was achieved only in 1899 (Davis, 1988).

The 1894 Local Government Act, which created the new district councils, also introduced a new, grass-roots level of local government in the parish council that could only be formed within a rural district area. The parish was the smallest unit of church administration, which, from the 16th century onward, began to develop civil responsibilities in relation to the upkeep of roads and the care of the poor. Prior to the reform of the counties, parishes were considered too small and weak to carry the burden of additional duties, and the growth of government in the mid-19th century was largely achieved through a combination of the extension of justices' administrative powers and the creation of special purpose authorities. After 1894, it was the county and, to a lesser extent, the district councils that profited from the growth of public services, but the parish councils remained as representative bodies with limited statutory powers.

During the period leading to the creation of the county councils 10 years before 1894, radical opinion had begun to shift in favour of local, village-level structures, based on the parish, as being closer to the people. The National Liberal Federation, which had agitated for the democratisation of the parishes since the 1870s, was disappointed that Goschen's parish reform bill of 1871 had been dropped. In 1882 and subsequent years, the National Liberation Foundation urged that:

> ...policy and justice alike demand that the local government of counties and rural divisions should be based upon representative principles, so that the people of such districts as well as those in towns may have constitutional control over the expenditure of the funds to which they contribute, and over the laws and regulations to which they are subject. (Redlich and Hirst, 1972, p 214)

When the Conservatives created the county councils in 1888, Gladstone called for local government to "go still nearer to the door of the masses of the people" and:

> avail ourselves of the old parochial division of the country, and to carry home to the mind of the peasants and the agricultural labourers the principles and the obligations, and to secure fully to them the benefits of local government. (Redlich and Hirst, 1972, p 215)

The success of the landed classes in retaining control of the counties in the first round of elections had strengthened the argument in favour of more local institutions in which, it was hoped, the newly enfranchised labourers could develop political experience. This was very much Gladstone's programme. His last speech in the Commons was in support of the Parish and District Councils Bill, through which he completed the final extension of the principles of the 1835 Municipal Corporations Act to the smallest units of local government. The parishes were, then, from the outset an experiment in political, rather than administrative development and, as such, central to the local democracy programme of a century before (Horn, 1984). Even so, the early expectations of the political impact of parish councils – just as those of the county councils before them – were not fulfilled, and they aroused little interest then, nor have they done since.

Through this succession of developments, the 19th century witnessed the extension of the elective principle to a range of public bodies, giving rise to the belief that England was progressing towards popular government. It is tempting to ask to what extent the election of new councils succeeded in establishing a system of administration responsible to, and representative of, its inhabitants. But it can be misleading to view 19th-century developments in representative government through modern eyes. The expectations of 'representativeness' were different from those of today. 'Responsible' – that is, accountable – government was the most keenly-felt need, to the extent that,

> Free election of representatives by all adult citizens came indeed to be almost completely identified with democracy.... The movement toward universal suffrage, without legal constraints on the social origins of candidates, constituted such a manifest advance of political equality that the possible persistence of inegalitarian or aristocratic effects appeared simply irrelevant. (Manin, 1997, p 132)

The removal of barriers to inclusion was judged to be a sufficient concession to ensuring that those who held office bore some resemblance to their electors. The problem of 'representation of the people' was solved by progressively extending the franchise, rather than by seeking correspondence between electors and the elected.

Representation in practice

The impact of reform varied widely from place to place. The boroughs had been the first to feel it, and half a century passed before local government in the county areas was on anything like the same basis as that in the incorporated urban areas. The age of reform was also the age of burgeoning urban growth, soon to be followed by a rippling out to the suburbs – a movement which, in time, polarised city politics between the Labour heartlands and the outlying Conservative districts. Many of the older boroughs remained small throughout the 19th century and beyond. Their precedence as historic areas was rapidly eclipsed as industrial growth led to the rise of new unincorporated towns based on the coal and iron-ore fields. In these new towns, local interests successfully sought their own charters, for example Birmingham grew rapidly over 150 years, from a small manufacturing centre to a chartered borough in 1889 (Briggs, 1952). Some of the oldest boroughs were ecclesiastical centres and, as the seat of a diocese, had a resident bishop, a cathedral and the title of 'City'. But population growth, driven by industrialisation, prompted the Church to develop its own diocesan structures in response, enabling those new large industrial towns which formed the centre of metropolitan regions to eventually achieve their own diocese and City status.

The mid-century also saw the rise of a new middle class that was largely urban based – men drawing their income from commerce, industry and the professions. City politics thus came to be polarised between traditional landed power and the rising middle class, whose ascendancy in local politics confirmed their new-found social position. The professions secured greater representation in London than in the provinces, with professionals the largest single group on the London County Council (LCC) throughout its life, followed, after the turn of the century, by administrators and managers. Working men were few, even when the Progressives (Liberals) and Labour dominated the council. Only a handful of skilled and semi-skilled workers feature in the early LCC membership, and just one unskilled labourer was present in the 1950s and 1960s (Clifton, 1989, p 6). Even in Birmingham, professionals constituted up to a quarter of the council's membership in the interwar years, while working men – including trade union officials – peaked at around 18% in the 1950s (Hennock, 1973, pp 48-52).

Outside London, the large landowners came to terms where they could with these new social forces and reached an accommodation with them (Cannadine, 1982). New alliances in favour of the Conservative Party were formed in this way, while radical and working class pressures for the development of publicly-financed urban services drew the Liberal party into a closer relationship with collectivist politics. The question of *who* represented *whom* began to loom. Chamberlain claimed that the Corporation of the City of Birmingham "represents the authority of the people" (Fraser, 1979, p 110): a claim that was not based on simple resemblance, but on common membership of the local polity.

When the new county councils were finally created under the 1888 Local Government Act, there was an expectation – and, for some, a fear – that they would, in a real sense, be representative of the newly enfranchised rural labourer. The expectation was not fulfilled. From the outset, the men who administered county affairs "were almost all men of fortune, some by birth, some by inheritance, some by sheer effort" (Moylan, 1978, p 30). Certainly, if the combination of franchise extension and the creation of county councils was expected to bring the agricultural labourer into political prominence, that expectation was also disappointed. In Lancashire it was judged that "throughout the county the best of the magistrates have offered their services as elected representatives, and many of them have been elected, and by so acting have secured for themselves more influence than they previously possessed". What was true of Lancashire was true of most of the rural counties, namely that "the advance of democracy had brought only the strength and the rule of the magistracy, and ... the new county authority was doing much the same thing as the old" (Marshall, 1977, p 5).

In Kent, the Act had brought about some change in the representativeness of county government, but the change was barely noticeable: no labourers were elected before 1913 (Moylan, 1978, p 29). The new authorities continued to be dominated by the old order – the influential men and landed-owning classes. In some counties the landowners and squires were returned unopposed, while in most the "distances that councillors would have to travel from their homes to the county town for council and committee meetings excluded all but the leisured carriage-owning gentry" (Keith-Lucas, 1952, p 114). Perhaps the most significant change was the incorporation of the non-county boroughs into the county area, which brought townsmen onto the new councils alongside the gentry. Thereafter, they were the growing class, favoured by continuing urbanisation and by boundary adjustments, so that, in Kent between 1889 and 1914, the number of merchants and manufacturers on the county council increased from 23 to 75 (Moylan, 1978, p 31). Similarly, in Lancashire the proportion of gentry and landowners on the county council remained stable from 1889 to 1928, although among their number was a rising proportion of "successful urban businessmen who had made their fortune in manufacturing and had acquired country estates" (Denver and Hands, 1977a, p 58).

Overall, the patterns of representation established in 1889 remained remarkably stable and as such, were shaped irredeemably by that first county election. The major landowners had converted their appointed office into an elective one, to the point that "it would almost seem as if the House of Lords, in despair of finding any adequate opportunity for work at Westminster, had determined to seek it in the provinces" (cited in Game and Leach, 1989, p 30). They were the more secure for it:

> There were in total no less than 131 peers (as well as 87 MPs) on those
> 1889 English and Welsh county councils – with the Southern English
> counties, as might be expected, having at least their fair share of the
> social and the military elite. Bell's history of the East Sussex county

council, for example, records that the elected membership of the first council included three peers, a peer's son, and a baronet, in addition to four gentlemen of leisure, six farmers, two brewers, two physicians, two solicitors, a publisher, two auctioneers and four merchants. No dukes, though - unlike neighbouring West Sussex. That county's first elected council was able to boast two dukes (Richmond and Gordon, its first chairman, and Norfolk), two 'other Lords', three baronets (two of whom were MPs), one knight, a major general, three lieutenant colonels, a captain, and four clergymen. (Game and Leach, 1989, p 31)

West Sussex was presided over by some of the largest and the most powerful landowners in the country. Wiltshire, too, had its share of nobility:

> Chaired for no less than forty years of its 20th-century history by the fifth Marquess of Bath (1906-46), the 1889 council elected the fourth Marquess as its first chairman, and numbered amongst its membership three other peers, three baronets, 24 landed proprietors, 11 farmers, three clergy-men and five lawyers, as well as 23 manufacturers and traders. (Game and Leach, 1989, p 31)

The tone of politics in the counties was markedly different from that of the towns, not least in respect of political conflict. Challenging the traditional leaders required persistence and dedication. There were widespread party 'understandings' in Kent, as elsewhere, to avoid contests. These understandings "worked in favour of the traditional leaders of society, regardless of the party to which they belong". In this way, elections became a rarity in many county divisions, and "the gentlemen who ran the county did, for the most part, find it easy to ignore the electorate, and the electorate was, for the most part, content to be ignored" (Moylan, 1978, p 29). So it remained, for much of the life of the original county councils, until their merger with the county boroughs or their incorporation into the new metropolitan areas in 1974.

Despite falling short of expectations, the emergence of numerous elected bodies in the 19th century created a platform for popular participation, especially in the urban areas. This led to the development of local services and, in turn, of an administrative class of professional local government officials. Taking stock of the 100 years that had passed since the 1835 Municipal Corporations Act, Lord Snell concluded:

The influence of English local government upon the life of the nation during the past hundred years has been profound; it has been a precious nursery of the civic virtues, the fruitful training ground for the national and imperial service; and it has helped to produce a reserve of administrative capacity on which British civilisation may continue to draw. (Snell, 1935, p 81)

20th-century developments

Throughout the 20th century, the newly-created county borough and county councils were given responsibility for an expanding range of social and personal services. Previously, they had been mainly concerned to establish the basic infrastructure, and provide the fabric of modern life: sanitary services, police, highway maintenance and, in some areas, water, gas, electricity, buses, trams, docks and libraries. Personal services to meet the needs of individuals had been the responsibility of ad hoc authorities which operated outside the local authority sector – the School Boards, which provided elementary education, and the Boards of Guardians which dealt with the relief of poverty.

Both were elected bodies, and School Board and Board of Guardians elections were often bitterly contested partisan contests. When they were brought under local authority control – education in 1902 and poor relief in 1929 – the greater part of their duties was transferred to county boroughs and county councils. One effect of this change was to import into local council politics something of the intensity of passion with which elections to these ad hoc bodies had been fought. The issues raised by the provision of personal services proved to be more divisive by far than those that attend the provision of infrastructure.

The growth of services

One of the most contentious services in the 20th century would prove to be public housing, as county borough and district councils became the leading providers of social housing after 1919. At the end of the 19th century, local authority housing activities had centred on slum clearance, as the problems that needed to be addressed were seen in terms of public health. Public health is, as the term suggests, everybody's business and healthy towns are for everybody's benefit. However, by the time of the First World War, the general shortage of houses and problems of overcrowding had become more apparent. The morale of the public, and of the troops in particular, was sustained by extravagant promises of 'homes for heroes' – promises which were not kept when postwar depression hit the public purse.

The 1919 Housing and Town Planning Act nonetheless established that the provision of homes was a social responsibility, and central government provided financial assistance toward the costs of council building. Local authorities began extensive house-building programmes and, by 1939, had built over a million homes. Generally, these programmes brought credit to local government and, for much of the interwar period, local authorities were rewarded with progressive increases in their powers and in the esteem in which they were held. That is not to say that conflict was absent. The question of where council housing was to be provided could be deeply divisive and new developments in the less dense outer areas of towns were sometimes bitterly opposed. It was safer, if more expensive, to build dense flat-type developments in the urban centre, keeping working-class tenants away from their semi-detached fellow townsmen. The second issue of contention, which was to grow in significance throughout the interwar and postwar periods, was financing social housing: put bluntly, working-class housing meant affordable rents, which required an element of subsidy. Insofar as this subsidy was locally provided from the pockets of other ratepayers, it set local citizens against one another and politicised the provision of local housing.

It was in this context, of national need and local politics, that central government came increasingly to steer local housing provision, in this case through the provision of subsidies in the form of percentage grants. Changes in the grant system, or in the sums available, were expected to encourage local authorities in the direction that ministers wanted them to go, while insulating them from local ratepayer resistance. Thus, local authorities were inescapably the agents of central policy. However, there was another model based on working partnership between Whitehall and town or county hall, operating within a policy consensus engineered by central government. This was the model used for education, where 1944 marked a watershed between benevolent oversight by the Board of Education, and firm policy steered by the far more powerful Ministry of Education which succeeded it.

Previously, county councils and county boroughs had the duty to provide both elementary and secondary education, but non-county boroughs were primarily responsible for elementary education. A new and complex structure of primary, secondary and technical education developed, and between the beginning of the century and the outbreak of war in 1939, revenue expenditure on education increased six-fold (Keith-Lucas and Richards, 1978, p 41). The Board of Education had been charged with the supervision of the public system of education and, after 1904, it became the senior and predominant partner while the new local education authorities (LEAs) learned their job. When the LEAs found their feet, the Board's influence declined and came to depend only on its prestige. The balance of power and the initiative passed to the LEAs and there was a tendency for the Board to leave the field to them (Gosden, 1976, p 239-40).

Not until the Second World War, when bodies such as the Trades' Union Congress (TUC), with their well-established education agenda, were drawn into policy making, did the Board of Education's officials retake the lead in education policy, with a view to bringing about a new settlement for the postwar world. In early 1941 the Board produced a series of proposals for reform, incorporated in a single document, which came to be known as the 'Green Book'. In this they took a forward-looking stance, accommodating the longstanding commitments of the Labour party. The Board's officials expected Labour ministers to play the lead role in planning for postwar reconstruction, for they imagined that the postwar government would be 'national' in character and "prepared to face radical changes in our social and economic system" (Addison, 1975, p 172).

'Rab' Butler, wartime President of the Board of Education, confident of the support of other coalition ministers, took the Green Book proposals forward in his 1943 White Paper and in the Education Act that followed a year later. Importantly, the 1944 Act espoused a new doctrine of partnership in education, in which the central ministry would assert itself and lead from the front. There was a growing recognition that differences in provision between the various LEAs were no longer acceptable and that far more emphasis needed to be placed on national policy. Only greater centralisation of control could redress the inequalities and would provide for more purposeful national planning in education.

The 1994 Education Act was to provide just that framework, creating a new Ministry of Education, widening the duties of LEAs in a number of ways and giving them responsibility for reorganising their secondary education. In reconstructing the school system, the Act also changed the pattern of LEAs by rationalising and reducing their number. By those means, a strong and stable partnership was established between central and local government that was to last for the two decades that led to the very different world of the 1960s. But, if the LEAs looked like equal partners, it was only because officials at both levels of government basked in the new consensus. When put to the test, the Ministry would prove the stronger partner.

The drift to the centre

The Local Government Boundary Commission of 1945-49, had noted that in the second half of the 19th century,

> ... legislation was content to leave local authorities with a wide measure of discretion in the exercise of their functions.... Since the close of the century a sharp reversal of this policy has been apparent.... The later pattern of legislation dictates it [the local authority] to prepare and submit to the appropriate Minister a scheme of arrangements for making the service available and empowers the Minister to accept, modify, or reject the scheme as he thinks fit. (Maud, 1967a, p 70)

The freedoms that local authorities enjoyed in exercising their powers was becoming a thing of the past. By the 1960s, powers given to local authorities were usually balanced by specific, countervailing responsibilities granted to ministers to oversee that exercise and intervene where they judged it proper − or expedient.

Throughout the interwar period local government expenditure had steadily risen, from £131 million in 1918/19 to £366 million in 1938/39. The extent to which spending was financed from local rates could not keep pace. The rating system was insufficiently buoyant to support such growth and the balance was met by grants from the Exchequer, with the percentage met by grants rising from 23% to 39% over this period (Rhodes, 1976, p 154). Grant aid to local expenditure mainly took the form of assigned revenues or percentage-specific grants, but from 1929 the system moved toward one in which an aggregate sum was distributed to local authorities on the basis of a formula, reflecting their different needs and conditions. The introduction of such a scheme − which necessarily involved central judgement about the relevant indicators − had to be made gradually, and not until after 1945 was the formula-based distribution fully phased in.

Greater central funding implied greater central control. This might, in theory, be a matter of regret, but only by funding a range of locally-devised and centrally-approved schemes could the Attlee government bring about the expansion of public services for which the electorate had voted. Under Attlee, the building of the welfare state both withdrew functions from local authorities and, at the same time, compensated for their loss by giving them new duties. After 1945 in particular, local authorities played a key role in the development of the welfare state. 'Building Jerusalem' required the full participation of local authorities as partners in that enterprise. Councillors and officers worked harmoniously together and, with central officials, toward widely-agreed goals of social renewal. However, the initiative was central government's.

One means by which postwar aims were to be achieved was through a gradual shift of responsibility for services to the higher levels of local government, to the larger authorities, or to joint arrangements and pooled resources that brought together counties and county boroughs. Town and country planning was the subject of a typical transfer of functions to the upper tier of local authorities. Legislation between 1909 and 1932 had allowed boroughs and districts to devise and introduce local planning schemes, but the plethora of planning authorities made it difficult to control overall development. The 1947 Town and Country Planning Act centralised responsibility to counties and county boroughs and introduced a comprehensive system for the control of development. The police and the fire services provide further examples of the transfer of functions to fewer and larger units of operation, the latter being transferred back to local authority control after 1945. After the 1946 Police Act, the remaining non-county borough forces were absorbed into the county police; subsequently, the process continued with the amalgamation of county and county borough forces. Counties also became the authority responsible for the fire services under the 1947 Fire Brigades Act. The 1948 Children Act further concentrated responsibility for children in need to counties and county boroughs (this service became the core of the postwar growth in local authority personal services, and would merge with welfare departments in 1974 to form the new social services departments called for in the Seebohm report).

In acting as the instruments of the national government in building the welfare state, local authorities necessarily forfeited a degree of independence. An elaborate system of financial incentives and controls, arrangements shifted the balance of expenditure on local services, and enhanced the prerogatives of central government. In time, this shift came to be seen – belatedly, but correctly – as threatening the freedoms of the local authorities and, thereby, the realities of local democracy. However, it was only by such means that the aims of postwar social policy were to be achieved and few carped, or even considered the longer-term implications.

Yet the fact was that from 1945 to 1969 the proportion of local expenditure met by the central government never fell below 40% and would later reach far higher proportions. Local authorities' expenditure would grow from £949 million in 1949-50 to £10,733 million in 1973-74 (Minogue, 1977, p 301). Financial instruments – incentives, subsidies and controls – were the principal means by which central government steered local provision: through them local authorities became the service delivery agents of the centre. The mechanism of percentage grants was to be found, prior to 1958, across a wide range of services where government had accorded local development high priority. Policy proceeded, in broad terms, on a simple stimulus–response model: grant offered, service developed. In this way, the business of local government had become more important and demanding, despite the loss of some services to the centre, and its national economic significance was greatly enhanced. As a result, the spirit of partnership between central and local government that had characterised the early postwar period would come under increasing strain after 1960.

Central government ministers had understandably come to regard all local financial activities as a matter of national concern. The expenditure and borrowing of local authorities were, for them, convenient instruments of macro-economic control. This evolving arrangement between central and local government continued to be described as 'partnership', but it was not a stable partnership. Ministers increasingly sought to manipulate local expenditure in the national economic interest. Such central presumption (as it seemed to them) irritated the local authorities and they responded by pressing for change. Local authorities sought a new departure in local finance, new sources of local revenue and a new deal for local government. The tension inherent within the partnership prompted a search – a fruitless search as it turned out – for a healthier balance between central control and local initiative.

Any concern about the need for a new settlement in the relationship between central and local government, while of philosophical interest to a minority of ministers, was overshadowed by electoral considerations. As local authority expenditure (and local rates) climbed steadily in the 1950s and 1960s, governments sought to cushion their impact upon households (Rhodes, 1976). As a result, the burdens shifted onto industry and onto the national taxpayer. The search for new sources of local revenue became an increasing preoccupation as the realisation dawned that local 'government' was becoming a transparent fiction.

The loss of autonomy was not just a matter of financial control, however. After 1945, there was a marked willingness on the part of local councillors to accept a degree of central direction in policy development. The Maud Committee warned of:

> ... a dangerous complacency amongst local government members and officers in their acceptance of the way in which the initiative of local authorities is sapped and in their acquiescence in growing government interference through regulations, directions and exhortations. We see this leading to a general impatience with the democratic element in local government, and to pressure for local administration to be performed by organs untrammelled by popular representation, more amenable to central control and fitting tidily into a unified structure of public administration. (Maud, 1967a, p 76)

Democratic local government, they counselled, would be undermined if local authorities were to be reduced to complete dependence on the central government and "regarded as mere agents of the will of the central government with no life of their own" (Maud, 1967a, p 76).

The twilight of local democracy

The 30-year period following the war was a period of expansion in the provision of local services, punctuated only by periodic economic crises. Both major parties were committed to growth and consensus on the desirability of the provision of public services characterised an entire political generation. It was a received belief in the political class prior to 1980 that,

> palpable injustices and differences in the life-chances of the well-to-do and of the poor could be diminished by public expenditure and redistributive taxation: and that the agents to bring about change were the bureaucracies of central and local government, under the control of elected ministers and councillors. (Annan, 1990, p 12)

Sustained by this powerful consensus, local government had become the deliverer – rather than the originator – of a wide range of services, from public infrastructure and housing, to education and social welfare (Lowe,

1993). The consequence was a period of continuous expansion in services, expenditure and employment – much of it in the local authority sector.

By the mid-1960s, the central–local partnership had come under strain as ministers increasingly used their powers instrumentally, with little regard for local autonomy. The foremost focus of concern for both parties' local government policies was local government finance. Labour had taken office in 1964 under Harold Wilson with a clear and unambiguous commitment to relieving the ratepayer. But in doing so, a ratchet effect was established, whereby each year a greater proportion of local expenditure would be met from the centre. Not only did this weaken local authorities' sensitivity to the fiscal burdens imposed by their decisions, shifting the burden from the ratepayer to the taxpayer actually exacerbated an underlying problem: the weakening link between those who supported spending in a particular locality, and those who would foot the bill across the country. After "13 wasted years", Labour supporters were looking for big results from their government: local authorities would be looked to for the implementation of nationally-formulated policies and programmes.

The Committee on the Management of Local Government reported unanimity in their evidence on the weaknesses in central–local relations and for the need to give greater freedom to local authorities:

> We are clear that there is tendency for control and direction by the central government to increase, and for the financial independence of local authorities to decline still further, and that both these tendencies weaken local government as an organ of government and detract from its effectiveness ... *ultra vires* as it operates at present has a deleterious effect on local government.... The specific nature of legislation discourages enterprise, handicaps developments, robs the community of services which the local authority might render.... (Maud, 1967a, pp 76-9)

Growth did not come cheap and, from around 1960 onward, successive governments found themselves torn between wishing to expand local services and containing expansion in the national economic interest. The conflict almost always took the form of a contest between Treasury ministers and those responsible for the major local government services, with the Minister for Housing and Local Government, and later the Secretary of State for the Environment, acting as the principal spokesman for local authority expansion. Expansionism reached its zenith in the decade that followed the election of a Labour government in 1964.

Thereafter, while both parties continued to pay homage to public services, they became increasingly uneasy about paying for growth. By 1975, when Anthony Crosland foreclosed on expansion with his brutal warning "the party's over", there were already stirrings on the right of a new approach, foreshadowed in a series of speeches by Sir Keith Joseph in 1974. The consensus crumbled as Conservatives turned their backs on the spirit of 1945.

None of this could have been foreseen when Labour won the general election in October 1964. The party's appeal was characterised by a breezy optimism – a young, technocratic approach that mirrored the new leader himself. The new mood of institutional reform turned the spotlight on local government and, with the example of the creation of the Greater London Council before them, politicians of both parties embraced a new programme of enforced restructuring.

At the same time, it was becoming increasingly apparent that central government control was stepped up with each new initiative. Ministers were not especially fastidious about local discretion; in that respect too, the mood had changed since the postwar Attlee and Churchill governments. In both housing and education, the Wilson/Callaghan period, and the Conservative interlude under Heath, were marked by ministers looking for results. They were not notably successful. Labour's lack of success in pursuing its social policy aims was dispiriting to its supporters, while the similar failures of the Heath government produced a brisker reaction (in 1975 Heath was deposed as Conservative leader by Margaret Thatcher). Few at the time could have foreseen that the victor – a youngish woman who had featured so far only as a rather ineffectual education secretary – would transform the political landscape and, by 1990, write local government out of the political constitution.

THREE

The failed promise of reform

By the mid-1960s, astute observers had come to see local government as the victim of its own success. Services had expanded and expenditure risen, to the great satisfaction of many councillors and officials, but at the price of local authorities becoming the agents of central government. The gradual rise of central control and the corresponding loss of local autonomy had been neither anticipated nor desired. Recognition of the problem prompted a series of White Papers, published during the 1950s, and their culmination in the 1958 Local Government Act. However, these measures were too little, too late. Some commentators were convinced that the decline of local government's standing would be irreversible in the absence of more radical reform.

Thus, debates on wholesale reform came to dominate the 1960s. They focused on the need to renew local democracy by drawing on the services of community-conscious people who, until that point, had stood aloof from local affairs. A number of obstacles lay in that path, including social change, the increasing intrusion of party politics, the time demands of council service and the debilitating effects of centralisation itself. Most, although not all of these, could be addressed by structural change, accompanied by reform of the methods by which local authorities conducted their business.

So arose a new orthodoxy: that fewer, larger and more powerful local authorities would attract greater public interest and reverse the declining respect paid to councils and their councillors. Likewise, speedier and more effective decision making, conducted along business lines, would make local authorities more accountable and effective, and perhaps more attractive too. But more than structural change was required. If local democracy was to be renewed, the wider public had to become involved. Recognition of this point spawned a series of participatory initiatives designed to involve local people in the affairs of their councils. These initiatives, taken together, were intended to restore public confidence which, it was imagined, had been lost at some point between the 19th century and the present.

Whatever the effectiveness of these successive attempts to kick-start a revival of local democracy (generally limited, in most observers' opinion), by the 1980s they were seen as irrelevant. Britain had entered an age of strident confrontation between central and local government, and between the contesting parties within local authorities. Local politics had become so highly politicised, and attracted such hostile press, that well-meaning attempts to sustain public interest and the recruitment of public-spirited individuals seemed futile.

The Conservative government of the mid-1980s sought to moderate the conflicts and restore standards in local government by restraining the worst effects of this politicisation. But their larger programme of public service reforms itself sparked conflict, for it diminished the traditional role of local authorities as providers by creating new appointed bodies alongside them, severely restricting their financial freedoms. Centralisation in the interests of the ratepayer – who needed to be protected from his or her local authority – became the new orthodoxy. It was an all-time low point in the fortunes of local government. So extreme was this subjugation of local government that it eventually evoked its own antithesis, in the form of a popular campaign to revive and renew local democracy. By the time New Labour formed a government in 1997, revival, through radical change and the restoration of powers, had become the key plank in the party's local government platform.

Finding the right people

The central problem of the local government system in Britain by 1960 was that it had not moved with the times. With its roots in 19th-century respect for democratic forms, and in the old tradition of local leaders' direct and detailed responsibility for local affairs, local government seemed an anomaly. Its ethos and modes of working were at odds with the realities of central direction of a wide range of activities, and the employment of large numbers of professional staff (Maud, 1967a, para 126). The Ministry of Housing and Local Government's civil servants urged action:

> The functions of government are increasing in scope, and in several directions, are becoming more 'positive' in character; this is reflected in the demands made, and in the demands that should be made, on local government. Unless local government is able to play a full and effective part in the developing role of government, its influence and power will become progressively weaker. (HLG, 1964a)

There was a need for adjustment if these new challenges were to be met.

The problem was readily dramatised as one of the 'quality' of local government's decision makers. Modernising local democracy in the 1960s was seen as a matter of bringing in higher 'quality' people, principally, although not exclusively, as councillors:

> It is important that the quality of local government should be the highest possible and to this end it is worth considering whether anything needs to be done to ensure that local authorities are able to attract, and will continue to attract, both as elected representatives and as officers, sufficient men and women of the calibre that they ought to have. No study has ever been made of the kinds of people who become councillors and question of what obstacles might exist to deter other suitable people from seeking to become members.... The competition both in the public and private sector for able people is so great today that this question would repay further study. (HLG, 1964)

The local authority associations agreed the need for such an investigation, and took the initiative to prompt the Ministry of Housing and Local Government to establish two parallel committees on 'people in local government' under the chairmanship of Sir John Maud and Sir George Mallaby, respectively.

This switch of emphasis from structures to people was entirely novel. Since the 1940s, the 'problem' of local government had been seen as pre-eminently one of structures, functions and boundaries, and it was through restructuring that the key values of efficiency and effectiveness were to be realised. This now seemed too simplistic, for while "reorganisation would give a better framework" it would achieve little "unless we can get better councillors, better management [and] better officers" (HLG, 1963).

Some thought restructuring a prerequisite of recruiting good people; others that no new structure would work well unless the best people were attracted to it. For the first half of the 1960s, with a Conservative government in office and Dame Evelyn Sharp dominant as permanent secretary at the Ministry of Housing and Local Government, this latter view held sway. Under its influence, the Maud Committee became the principal vehicle for exploring the reasons why people of ability eschewed the office of councillor.

It was an unquestioned assumption at the time that there was a pool of talent in modern Britain, on which local authorities could draw if only their powers and authority were sufficient to attract them. Essentially, the number of people with leisure and public spirit was limited, and men of initiative and intelligence could only be attracted in proportion to the powers an authority possessed, because, to such men, responsibility is itself an attraction (see Dearlove, 1979, pp 15, 67, 79-80). This argument implied a reversal of some of the long-term trends towards the centralisation of local government, for it was commonly believed that the removal of functions from local councils had left insufficient authority to attract ambitious people as councillors, while the growth of professionally-driven services had made councillors secondary figures, with titular responsibility but little real power.

So far-reaching was the centralisation of local decision making, and so great the dependence on Whitehall, that little incentive remained for anyone to put their talents to use in this particular way. The long-criticised regime of *ultra vires*, which constrained local authorities from doing anything for which they did not have a specific statutory power, was held to discourage enterprise, handicap development and deprive the community of services that the local authority might provide. Accordingly, it did little to encourage individuals from participating in public affairs. Similarly, the transfer of executive powers from local authorities to centrally-appointed ad hoc bodies in the immediate postwar period exacerbated the appearance that local government was a poor relation of more significant bodies.

Revitalising local government by strengthening its power base was widely seen as prerequisite for drawing in people who could be considered natural community leaders. But where were they to be found? Just as social, economic and political change had transformed the nature of local government, so too did it diminish this notional pool of talent from which councillors might be drawn:

> [T]he economic pressures on commerce and industry now make it very difficult for the directors and senior executives of companies to find time for local government work [and so] the standard of the elected representative has declined in recent years ... because the conduct of a successful business *and* active participation in local affairs take up more time than they did 50 years ago. (cited in Dearlove, 1979, p 186)

Moreover,

> [W]hereas in the past a young businessman would go into his father's firm and stay in his home town, in which he had roots, now-a-days he

would go to University and from there into a big firm, move about the country, and never put down any local roots. Moreover, there were far too few employers who encouraged their executives to go into local government. (HLG, 1964b)

As *The Times* commented in 1961, "many professional men and business executives nowadays never strike deep local roots" (cited in Reads, 1964, p 240) as they move up their firms' national career structures. That this was so was due to changes in corporate structures, whereby career progression had become possible only through geographical mobility. The days of the locally- or regionally-based business were drawing to a close.

This lack of candidates was not simply a matter of changes in the industrial structure, with large, multi-plant firms displacing locally-based concerns. Population mobility, suburbanisation and the growth of communications all contributed to the loss of that quality of local community identity and involvement that provided the base for participation in local affairs. The principal motive for taking part in local politics is a felt need to serve the local community and the desire to gain prestige within it (Birch, 1959, p 115). As 'community' itself became less meaningful, so too did the spirit of attachment and local service atrophy, and with it the willingness of people to stand for election. Meanwhile, these social changes were compounded by two other factors specific to local government itself: the growing influence of party politics and the steady increase in the time demands of council service.

Party politics

The intrusion into local government of party politics could well have exercised an increasing deterrent effect on potential councillors in a number of ways. In the first place, even without the presence of party alignments, the requirement for election itself discouraged many local notables from accepting nomination and exposing themselves to competition and potential conflict. According to Hennock, in the 19th century "elections frequently proved an obstacle to the recruitment of the leading citizens of the borough" whose social standing was such as not to admit the idea of a contest (Hennock, 1973, p 13). This would have been less of a problem in those areas where an individual could count on not being opposed, in which case recruitment to the council was really a matter of accepting an invitation from the existing leaders.

By the mid-1960s, unopposed elections were still common in a large part of rural England, especially on the Scottish and Welsh borders.

Any reluctance to expose oneself to a contest would be exacerbated under party elections, with the consequence that "a number of good men [were] permanently kept out of local administration" (Hasluck, 1936, p 35; see also Hennock, 1973, p 13). The selection of candidates through party organisation left the choice in the hands of few leading activists, which, in a small community, could well discourage 'the right sort of people' from seeking council candidacy (Grant, 1977, p 89; see also Gyford, 1984, p 53). Moreover, a party label tied a councillor's fate to that of his party, and in the 1960s some councillors complained of the negative effects of electoral uncertainty. Sir Thomas Bland of the County Councils Association argued that in many places "a man would build up a body of knowledge about a subject of which he might be committee chairman, and then find that the swing of the pendulum would put him out of office" (HLG, 1964a). That the tide of opinion, rather than personal performance, might determine one's fate was not calculated to appeal to middle-class men.

Second, many people refused to identify themselves with a party, and harboured a distaste for partisan politics with its subjugation of individual judgement to collective decision making and discipline. Those in business and the professions – the very people whose contributions were the most keenly sought – were the most likely to find party politics abhorrent to them, since, in its partisan form, "it undermines the moral integrity ... [and] corrodes the quality of their intellectual processes" (Clements, 1969, p 52). It could also lead to "the adoption of doctrinaire policies regardless of individual circumstances" (Grant, 1973, p 249). Those who disliked the implications of party discipline believed that partisanship entailed "inefficiency, time-wasting, wrong-decisions and dishonesty" (Clements, 1969, p 60). These widely expressed sentiments were endorsed by the Maud Committee's research, which indicated that "party politics deter independent candidates from standing" and that "professional men in particular are deterred from offering themselves for service when it means seeking the support of a political party" (Maud, 1967a, p 109). Of ex-members in the social survey carried out for the Committee, 71% thought that the work of local authorities could be done better if party politics did not intrude (Maud, 1967a, p 110).

Such reactions on the part of councillors, potential councillors and ex-councillors were reflected in the views of the wider public. Then – as now – many people felt local government to be an inappropriate arena for party politics. The Maud Committee's opinion survey indicated that for a large proportion of the electorate, party politics in local government were unwelcome, and their presence was the most commonly cited criticism of the working of the democratic process in local government (Maud, 1967c, p 69). Most important, only a tiny minority of people were willing to join a political party, and thus accept the basic prerequisite of local political life – for without that membership, there was no chance of being selected as a candidate with any chance of election to a council in most parts of Britain. Under a party system, only the partisan-inclined can be considered to comprise the pool of potential councillors. But in any case, few people actually expressed a desire for public office either in 1965 or subsequently. No more than 8% of the respondents in the Maud Committee survey of electors intended to stand for election, or felt that they might stand if an opportunity arose, and while 6% had considered doing so, only 2% had actually stood.

If party politics was an important factor in the mid-1960s, when many authorities outside London and the metropolitan areas were politically quiescent and a good proportion of seats uncontested, it was to increase sharply in importance after 1974. The first elections to the re-organised system held the previous year, saw the parties contesting territory for the first time in many years. Merging counties and county boroughs wiped away the comfortable spheres of influence that the two major parties had formerly enjoyed. Outside the cities, Conservatives could no longer afford to hold back from contesting local elections, secure in the knowledge that anti-Labour independents would represent their interest. Throwing themselves into the contest, Conservative party candidates brought about the overnight exclusion of many independent councillors.

It could be expected that the exclusionary effects of a party-dominated system outlined above would have become more acute in the late 1970s and 1980s. The evidence is consistent with this. A study of electors in 1994 found that only about 1% had stood for election, and a further 4% had considered standing but had not done so (Young and Rao, 1995). The categories are not exactly comparable but, taken together with the great reduction in the number of council seats – that is, in the number of opportunities to stand – these figures suggest that, since the mid-1960s, there has been a falling off in people's willingness to stand for election. Only a handful of people will consider becoming a councillor, and the pervasiveness of party politics has much to do with this.

Time demands and compensation

If the politicisation of local government played its part in deterring people from seeking office, in all probability, so too have the increasing time demands of council service. A survey of economic and social notables in Bristol in the 1960s – a time when local government was less demanding than today – showed that the "reason most frequently given ... for not becoming councillors is that council membership levies too heavy a toll upon time, which respondents cannot afford to give" (Clements, 1969, p 54). The Maud Committee also noted that "lack of time is the main reason for not wanting to become member ... given by employers, managers, professionals and farmers", and saw the "time factor ... as the most serious deterrent to service and a major reason for members declining to stand again for election" (Maud, 1967a, pp 141, 144) – a claim subsequently repeated by the Working Group on Local Authority Management Structures set up to advise on the management of the new authorities (Bains, 1972, p 30).

However, this claim is not sustainable as, on Maud's evidence, lack of confidence in their ability to take on the role of councillor was the most widely cited reason for people not wishing to put themselves forward for election (32%). Insufficient time, although important, was cited by only a quarter of Maud's respondents. (At that time, the average councillor devoted some 52 hours per month to council business – a figure which increased after reorganisation in the 1970s to around 75 hours.) Leading councillors spent, and continue to spend, much more time than this, giving a commitment that few people, whatever their interest in local affairs, would be able to match (Table 1). This remains true, and has possibly become more true, as the amount of time the average councillor gives has risen over the years.

Table 1: Councillors' time commitments in 1997

	Average monthly hours spent
Council leaders	152
Deputy leaders	105
Council chairs/mayors	118
Committee chairs	107
All councillors	88

Source: Rao (2000a)

Two, somewhat contradictory, approaches have been adopted in response to the deterrent effect of council time demands. The first was to recognise the time commitment required and seek to compensate it adequately. The second was to deny its necessity by promoting reforms to decision-making structures so as to make the business of being a councillor a less time-consuming activity.

Compensation has long been a contentious issue. In a competitive world, in which there was no longer a leisured class, it became increasingly difficult to find sufficient candidates of good quality and from all walks of life to stand for election. Work claimed the time of a far higher proportion of eligible candidates than in the 19th century, and in the 1960s even employed councillors generally gave their job higher priority and derived greater satisfaction from it. To allow local council service effectively to 'buy out' part of that working life by compensating for loss of income raised important issues about the professionalisation of the office of councillor.

Nonetheless, Maud argued that a more generous system of allowances would attract a better 'calibre' of councillor, with payments to members related to the duties they performed (something which varied widely according to the office held). The 1933 Local Government Act had provided that counties and county boroughs could pay their chairs and mayors such salaries as they thought reasonable. During the period of the postwar Labour government, the position of councillors was comprehensively dealt with. The 1948 Local Government Act enabled local authorities to pay members travelling expenses, subsistence allowances and to compensate them for any financial loss incurred while performing an approved duty. Limits to expenses and allowances were to be prescribed by regulation and a series of Acts in the early 1960s extended these provisions in light of subsequent experience.

The Maud Committee, in their interim report of May 1966, recommended against the payment of salaries, other than to the council and committee chairs. They proposed that local authorities should be free to prescribe an annual flat rate expense allowance, payable quarterly, for the remaining councillors. The reason for this was, in part, that the Committee found that many members would not benefit from financial loss allowance, as they would be unable to demonstrate specific loss of earnings. Their main report, 12 months later, proposed the creation of executive management boards, with payment of salaries restricted to management board members, thus linking remuneration to the scope of a councillor's responsibilities.

The 1972 Local Government Act introduced an attendance allowance for councillors, subject to a daily maximum prescribed by the Secretary of State for the Environment. Authorities retained a good deal of flexibility in deciding which 'approved duties' qualified for payment – some regarding party group meetings as properly qualifying and some not. The Act also enabled councillors to continue to opt for the financial loss allowance in lieu of attendance allowance, which was now subject to a higher daily maximum and (unlike the attendance allowance) was tax free. Finally, the 1972 Act introduced an additional special responsibility allowance, payable to councillors in leading positions and subject to maxima set for both the authority and for any individual councillor. These maxima, revised from time to time by the Secretary of State, varied according to the size of the authority, with larger authorities having more generous limits.

These arrangements were all based on the assumption that any working person should be able to serve as a councillor without making either financial gain or suffering financial loss. The 1969 report of the (Wheatley) Royal Commission on Local Government in Scotland argued a radically different case for the professionalisation of council service. The key issue – whether councillors should be full time and paid, or serve on a part-time voluntary basis – was now brought into sharp focus. Wheatley found:

> no virtue in making elected membership painful and sacrificial or in arguing that the service given ought to be its own reward.... To keep using [this] argument is a way of keeping people out of local government, not bringing them in. There is a job to be done, and the labourer is worthy of his hire. (Wheatley, 1969, p 224)

The Commission went on to suggest that those holding special responsibilities should get up to 50% more than the basic salary and council chairs up to 100% more, and concluded that:

> ... to pay a salary is the simplest, least invidious and generally most satisfactory way of dealing with a real problem. It removes any tendency which may exist under the present system to stretch out or multiply meetings. It puts the emphasis where it belongs, namely on the work that a councillor is called upon to do. It will not solve the problem of financial loss completely for every councillor: but if the salary is fixed at an appropriate level, it ought to go a long way towards making

membership possible to a much wider section of the community. If it is felt that the salary is tending to attract the wrong sort of people for the wrong reasons, or that an individual councillor is not earning his salary because he is failing to give his council duties the attention they deserve, then the remedy lies in the hands of the electorate themselves. (Wheatley, 1969, p 225)

It was not, however, a view that commanded support south of the border, where decisions were made. Labour's 1970 White Paper announced that despite the arguments which had been put forward for paying councillors, or councillors with specially heavy responsibilities,

> [a salary] would raise a major issue of principle, on which there is no agreement within local government, the political parties or public opinion generally. The traditional arguments for local government being unpaid carry great weight: and the government would not propose a change until and unless public opinion crystallised or it became clear that the proposed new system was likely to impose a wholly new burden on the time of councillors. (DLGRP, 1970)

The incoming Conservative government in 1971 reopened the question but eventually came to the same conclusion, that "local government should not become a salaried occupation" (DoE, 1971). In the mid-1980s the Widdicombe Committee reconsidered and reinforced this view, reluctant as it was to countenance making it easier in any way for councillors to devote themselves full-time to council affairs.

Despite all this ambivalence, the remuneration of councillors remained a reflection of the traditional assumption that council service was a form of lay voluntary service to the community, the conduct of which should be financially neutral in its consequences. Local government required 'the best people' in the late 20th century just as much as it had in the late 19th century, but they were not to be bought. Attention accordingly turned to finding other means of widening recruitment: the reform of structures and processes to reduce time demands and give greater decision-making opportunities in order to increase the attractiveness of council service.

Reforming structure and internal management

Since the 1940s, a firm consensus had developed about the practical problems of local government and the reforms which would lead to a better system. The system had become increasingly inefficient because it was out of step with modern age – numerous, small authorities could neither reap the economies of scale nor attract people of calibre as officers and members. In 1942 the Labour Party claimed:

> There are too many local authorities, the majority of which are too small ... too many authorities lack the population and rate revenue necessary to provide essential services. (Labour Party, 1942, pp 5-6)

Likewise, calling for larger authorities on the ground that they provided greater scope, Dame Evelyn Sharp argued that,

> part of the trouble in getting good enough people to serve arises ... from the fact that the areas and status of local authorities are often too cramped or too small to enable a satisfactory job to be done. (Sharp, 1962, p 383)

The solution was to enlarge the areas and powers of local authorities to make them sufficiently attractive. What the 1960s added to this prescription was the idea that local authorities would be best run along business lines by a small number of councillors carrying executive authority (Dearlove, 1979). A combination of these two types of reform – to structure and to management – would attract the best people.

Structural reform

The wartime period saw the first recognition of the need to reorganise local authorities into fewer, larger units. The Local Government Boundary Commission of 1945 was set up to achieve just this, but fell foul of the Labour government and was stood down amid vehement protests. There followed a lengthy period of argument within Whitehall about how best to achieve reorganisation, before Conservative ministers engaged the local authority associations in discussions from which a grudging 'concordat' emerged. The result was a new Local Government Commission, set up in 1958, working its way across the country in a series of local reviews, resolving anomalies and promoting rationalisation.

This was a gradualist approach and one which, at first, seemed well able to produce the desired results. "We are", advised Permanent Secretary Dame Evelyn Sharp, "at the moment in the throes of reorganisation":

> The object of [which] is to match local authorities to the present distribution of population and to the demands now being made on local government; to produce authorities of adequate resources to tackle the increasingly difficult and costly responsibilities falling to local authorities; and generally to ensure the maintenance of a strong and independent local government system. We believe that if we can improve the present structure it should help in encouraging people to feel that the job of local government is worthwhile, and so in securing a good supply of strong candidates for election – and also in encouraging first class people to enter the local government service. (HLG, 1963)

However, experience showed that the new Local Government Commission was a haphazard and uncertain vehicle for achieving reform. Its procedures, founded as they were on extensive consultation and local hearings, moved slowly, while its recommendations were often unwelcome to ministers.

An alternative, and indeed parallel model, existed in the form of the Royal Commission on Local Government in Greater London. Briefed to bring about a complete rationalisation of metropolitan government to revitalise local democracy, the Herbert Commission stressed in its report the need to increase the size and scope of local authorities:

> If we are to encourage a sufficient supply of councillors of ability, the scope and size of the authority on which they serve must be such that the arena in which their talents are displayed is wide enough to require (and indeed to stimulate) their qualities and to satisfy their ambitions; there does seem to be some relationship between the size and scope of the authority and the capacity of the councillor and official attracted. (Herbert, 1960, p 63)

Indeed, "a certain minimum size and scope of authority seems to be needed to attract councillors and officers of the right calibre" (Herbert, 1960, p 63). However, the Herbert Commission departed from the Whitehall consensus (which favoured very large authorities) by postulating an optimum size, beyond which the risk arose of creating 'outsize' jobs without sufficient 'outsize' people to fill them.

The report on London, and the Act which followed in 1963, set an example, showing that clear radical proposals could be taken from a small Royal Commission and imposed on even the most recalcitrant local authority through general legislation. It seemed the most certain route to the agreed end, and one which held particular attractions for Richard Crossman, the new Labour administration's Minister of Housing and Local Government. Against the opposition of his permanent secretary, Crossman set up a Royal Commission on Local Government under Sir John Maud (later Lord Redcliffe-Maud, and still chair of the committee which bore his name) to consider the structure of local government in England outside Greater London and to make recommendations,

> for authorities and boundaries, and for functions and their division, having regard to their size and character of areas in which these can be most effectively exercised and the need to sustain a viable system of local democracy. (Redcliffe-Maud, 1969, p iii)

After an exhaustive inquiry lasting three years, and backed by a large number of commissioned research studies, Redcliffe-Maud eventually produced the expected radical redrawing of the map of England based on the 'unitary' principle. Yet, despite the time expended, the research commissioned, and even despite the generally laudatory press and public reception, Redcliffe-Maud's brave new England came to naught. The episode was memorable less for the Royal Commission's proposals themselves than for their abrupt rejection by the incoming Conservative government and their replacement by a more limited reorganisation aimed at preserving the existing counties (Alexander, 1982).

The Commission's 1969 report had argued that far-reaching changes were necessary in traditional organisation and methods of work. The Labour government's White Paper on the reform of local government shared the view of the Royal Commission and reaffirmed that:

> unless local government is organised to meet the needs of the future, and in particular is organised in units large enough to meet the technical and administrative requirements of the services which it administers, its powers must diminish, and with it the power of local democracy.... Radical change is overdue. And only if such change occurs, and local government is organised in strong units with powers to take major decisions, will present trends towards centralisation be reversed, and local democracy secure its place as a major part of our democratic system. (DLGRP, 1970, para 10, 97)

The Conservative government, which took office before Labour could implement its proposals, put in place less far-reaching reorganisation under the 1972 Local Government Act, but accepted the basic premise that a reformed system would be more democratic, as well as more efficient and effective. The most frequently voiced criticism of the pre-1972 system had been that many of the units were too small for efficiency (Table 2) and that the existence of so many small authorities meant that it was difficult to secure the services of councillors or officers of high calibre (Dearlove, 1979). The new local authorities – larger and fewer in number, even under the Conservatives' scheme – would therefore gain much of their benefits from their larger size and more impressive powers which, it was claimed, would attract better people into local government.

But there was no consensus on the question of size. Too large an authority would make it difficult to ensure control by elected representatives and councils would be "ineffective talking shops offering little scope for people at the local level" (Jones, 1973, p 158). Furthermore, the bigger the unit, the more doubtful it became whether the individual citizen could have a real sense of belonging to it. Little could be done about this last point, for the Redcliffe-Maud Commission's own research suggested that people identified only with their most local areas. It was a blind alley. Convoluted arguments had earlier been advanced to the effect that local democracy would be enhanced by the creation of fewer, stronger authorities. By 1972 the pretence that the circle could ever be squared was largely abandoned and it was conceded that the size of authority would be determined on efficiency grounds. The problem remained one of creating meaningful and effective tasks for elected representatives on those authorities, thus maximising democratic values.

With the 1972 Act in place (Table 3), it would have been reasonable to suppose that the restless search for something better would come to a

Table 2: English local government in 1972

Type	Number	Smallest	Largest
Counties	45	29,680	2,428,040
County boroughs	79	32,790	1,074,940
Boroughs, urban and rural districts	1,086	1,490	100,470
London boroughs*	32	134,000	318,000

*The 32 London borough councils were established by the 1963 London Government Act.

Table 3: English local government after 1972

Type	Number	Smallest	Largest
Counties	39	337,000	1,396,000
Metropolitan counties*	7	1,142,000	425,000
'Shire' districts	296	24,000	425,000
London boroughs	32	134,000	318,000
Metropolitan boroughs	36	174,000	1,096,000

* Including the Greater London Council which, together with the six metropolitan county councils, was abolished by the 1985 Local Government Act.

pause, if not to an end; but it was not to be. Even before the structure imposed by Peter Walker started to come apart at the seams, the urge to reform had begun to gnaw at the local government system once more. The 'settlement' of the 1972 Local Government Act proved to be no such thing. Within three years the former county boroughs were straining to break out of the constraints of county government. The next Labour government seriously contemplated undoing the structure again and taking the major cities – Labour strongholds – out of the counties but there was never a realistic chance of making such contentious changes after such a short interval (Young and Rao, 1997b).

Internal structures

Contained within the structure of every local authority is a process of local decision making within which national priorities are roughly reconciled with local preferences, budgets set and services managed. Prior to the 1960s, central government had not thought of venturing into that territory with proposals for reform, although from 1940 there were many private critiques of the quality of councillors and how they made their decisions (Rao, 1994). But, by 1960, the notion was gaining ground that the 'modernisation' of these internal structures and processes – of the *political management* of local government – was worth attempting. The events which followed reflected an apparent desire to create local government which operated more like the private sector, with a clear concentration of responsibility facilitating speedy decision making.

First, an authoritative committee (Maud) was established, whose deliberations were supposed to settle the matter with some sensible reforms. Nothing happened. Twenty years of frustration and allegation passed before another committee (Widdicombe) was established, only to dismiss radical reform. After scarcely a decent interval, Conservative ministers blithely reopened the issues with their own favoured solutions, in this case holding up the prospects of Westminster-style cabinet government or Chicago-style mayoral government for Britain's local authorities (DoE, 1991). Their enthusiastic advocacy fell on deaf ears as local authorities showed no interest in making the changes suggested. Nevertheless, somehow an orthodoxy was established that local government, faced with the pressing need to embody just such internal structures, was too conservative to reform itself. That was the issue to which New Labour would, in time, address itself.

Maud's Committee on the Management of Local Government, had sought to define attractive roles for councillors in terms of new executive responsibilities. Maud had been given the task of investigating the running of councils, the roles of their members and considering "how local government might best continue to attract and retain people of the calibre necessary to ensure its maximum effectiveness" (Maud, 1967a, p 1). Maud's analysis concentrated on the deficiencies of the committee system, the heart of local decision making and the basis of the English system of local government. To that extent, their critique was a radical one. The virtues of committees, maximising the opportunities for councillors of all types to contribute to policy discussion, were seen as limited in comparison with the failures and inadequacies of the committee system as a whole. Further, the number of committees had grown with the addition of new services for which local authorities were responsible, leading to problems of coordination. Moreover,

> It becomes increasingly difficult for committees to supervise the work of the departments because of the growth of business, lack of time and the technical complexity of many of the problems.... The system does not encourage discrimination between major objectives and the means to attain them, and the chain of consequential decisions and action required. (Maud, 1967a, p 35)

This cumbersome system prevented councillors from putting their time to good use, for "the system wastes time, results in delays and causes frustration by involving committees in matters of administrative detail". Time wasting and dilatory, it was an unlikely system to attract good people as councillors:

> ... the larger the committee, the more difficult the task of producing an adequate level of comprehension when issues of any complexity are to

be decided: there is a tendency for committees to spend their time talking about small matters because they come easily within the reach of their understanding and to avoid discussion of major questions because of the difficulties which they involve. (Maud, 1967a, p 31)

In recommending a new structure for their internal organisation, Maud jettisoned the committee system altogether, basing the proposals on three principles: effective and efficient management under the direction and control of the members; clear leadership and responsibility among both members and officers; and an organisation which presents to the public an intelligible and responsive system of government. These principles could be achieved by concentrating decision-making power in the hands of a few – presumed to be the most able – members. The Committee's report accordingly proposed a small management board of five to nine members which would formulate the principal objectives for the authority and control and direct all its work. Council committees were to be deliberative and representative bodies only. Accordingly, real power would be vested in a handful of members, who would need to have the "capacity to understand increasingly complex technical, economic and sociological problems" and the "ability to innovate, to manage and direct; the personality to lead and guide public opinion and other members; and a capacity to accept responsibility for the policies of the authority" (Maud, 1967a, p 143).

Maud's proposals, presented as a means of finding attractive opportunities for able people, were widely attacked by commentators. Streamlining the decision-making process by involving fewer people and concentrating executive authority might bring its own dangers, and examples abounded of the corruption which followed when power was exercised without corresponding accountability. Generally, it was thought that the proposals would have the contrary effect to that intended. A committee member with a dissenting opinion even argued that proposals which privileged a minority of decision makers would necessarily exclude the participation of many councillors. Instead, members as a whole must be given a worthwhile part to play.

The response to the report from local authorities was equally negative. Many councillors rejected the proposals for a management board on the grounds of their impracticability. The most trenchant criticism came from D.N. Chester, the Warden of Nuffield College, who showed persuasively that the proposals would fail to meet their basic objective of renewing local democracy by attracting into council service many able people who presently stand aside. Instead, committees and their chairs would be made completely ineffective and indeed "so useless as to wonder who would serve on them". He argued that, in these circumstances, fewer, not more, able people would be attracted onto local councils (Chester, 1968, pp 287-98).

Involving local people

The proposals of the Maud Committee were overtaken by the Redcliffe-Maud Royal Commission, which, while abandoning the small executive management board in the face of such criticisms, largely reiterated the earlier committee's broad proposals for streamlining decision making. It was soon apparent that both structural reform and the reorganisation of internal management would not be able to revitalise local democracy by attracting a new type of councillor: neither programme could overcome the lack of public confidence and willingness to participate in community life. That few people chose to consider standing as councillors was no more than an indication of the deeper problem of public disengagement from local affairs.

A crisis of confidence

During the 1960s, the high level of ignorance and confusion that existed among the general public about their local authorities was implausibly attributed to the complexity of the local authority system itself. Maud regarded it as a "matter for concern that there should be an indefinable gulf between local authorities and the communities which they serve" (Maud, 1967a, p 94) – revealed in their finding that:

> ... nearly a quarter of the survey's informants suggest that they have a feeling of 'alienation' from the local authority in the sense that the members do not care about the electorate or are not known to it, or that the electorate is not told enough about what is going on. (Maud, 1967a, p 92)

The problems were real enough but the account of their origins was scarcely adequate. 'Defects' and 'complications' in the overall structure of local government structure were the cause of the 'fatalism', 'ignorance' and 'indifference' that the public displayed to their local authorities. The solution proposed was a "clarification of the local government system", whereby "the public would then become more aware of local government and more interested in it" (Redcliffe-Maud, 1969, pp 28-9; see also Herbert, 1960, p 180).

Nonetheless, Redcliffe-Maud acknowledged that, in itself, local government reorganisation was unlikely to increase awareness. For that, reliance would have to be put on educational development. The best-educated people were the most aware; therefore, as the standard of education continued to rise, so should interest in local government. The Commission was content to look to the 'hopeful sign' that,

> on the fairly safe assumption that more people will reach a higher level of education in the future, we may expect that interest in local government will steadily increase rather than fall off. (p 59)

However, not knowledge, but involvement was the key to reviving local democracy, and there was no good reason to suppose that increased knowledge would in itself promote greater participation. At the same time,

> no amount of potential administrative efficiency can make up for the loss of active participation in the work by capable, public-spirited people, elected by, responsible to, and in touch with those who elected them. (Redcliffe-Maud, 1969, p 59)

The gulf between rhetoric and reality had never been so great. Government – central and local – had to win back confidence from a "grudging electorate" (Royal Commission on Standards in Public Life, 1976, p 117). A survey undertaken for the Royal Commission on the Constitution pointed to a 'we' and 'they' situation and a 'sense of grievance' in which people tended to feel powerless in the face of government and cut off from it (Royal Commission on the Constitution, 1973, pp 18-21). Further evidence of public distrust and governmental concern was provided in 1976 by the Committee on Financial Aid to Political parties and by independent surveys. In Marsh's survey of 1974, as many as half of all respondents voiced a lack of confidence in the British system of government, and agreed that there was need for improvement (Marsh, 1977). Politicians were seen as placing their own interests over and above the wider public interest, with nearly six out of 10 respondents 'never' or 'only some of the time' trusting the government. The subsequent 25 years has seen a steady decline in these figures, with today fewer than one in four displaying trust in British institutions.

With illusions of local government reform fading, the answer to the problem of alienation was to shift power downwards to the people themselves and restore confidence and trust through programmes designed to promote direct participation in local affairs. The idea and practice of participation began to gain popularity, with "a sudden upsurge of interest in the idea that ordinary citizens might have a part to play in the decision-making process" (Richardson, 1983, p 3).

Promoting participation

Interest in popular participation had been stimulated by experiments in the US, where President Johnson's Great Society Programme (aimed at rebuilding urban communities and accommodating civil rights protests) promoted a range of schemes to involve local people in decision making, while directing resources to their neighbourhoods. The novelty of the Great Society Programme was its recognition that:

> A policy of institutional reform ... could not depend for its mandate only on the support of the institutions to be reformed, however powerful their influence. Mayors, school superintendents, public spirited bankers, representatives of organised labour, pastors of churches, were not the accredited spokesmen of the poor. They stood rather for that established power whose rivalries and mutual accommodations has always vitiated the good faith of the concern they expressed. Some countervailing authority was needed to protect the programmes against the encroachment of institutional self-interest upon genuine service.... Thus the programmes were not only to be dispassionately rational, and endorsed by community leaders, but also an authentic expression of the wishes of the programmes constituents. (Marris and Rein, 1967, p 164)

In Britain something of the same trend was discernible, much of it openly imitative of the US programmes. The Educational Priority Areas (EPA) of 1967/68 pumped money into schools in deprived areas, as did the Housing Action Areas and Urban Programme Priority Areas the following year. The Community Development Programme of 1969, followed by the Comprehensive Community Programmes in 1974, emphasised community self-help in attempting to reverse the cycle of deprivation in poor neighbourhoods. These were central government initiatives, but one of their more important effects was to encourage individual local authorities to pioneer new ways of drawing people into a closer engagement with local service provision. Schemes, such as area-based management, were adopted to provide opportunities for local people to exercise some control over their lives at a neighbourhood level.

However, most initiatives were developed in the context of specific services. In 1968, the Seebohm Committee report recommended local authorities create new departments for coordinating social services which it urged to consider how clients might become more directly involved in decision making and the delivery of services. These changes coincided with a trend towards community work in social services departments, which aimed at helping local communities to develop the skills and confidence to overcome apathy and learn to represent their own interests to authority.

This trend struck a chord with the Skeffington Report on Town Planning in 1969 which, having recognised the changing structures of representative government, observed that:

> There is a growing demand by many groups for more opportunity to contribute and for more say in the working out of policies which affect people not merely at election time, but continuously.... Life ... is becoming more complex, and one cannot leave all problems to one's representatives. (Skeffington, 1969, para 7)

Moreover, as people lost faith in the judgement of professionals, the planning process was becoming fraught with difficulty. If those people directly affected could be involved in the policy process and persuaded to give their support, planning might regain its effectiveness.

In 1977 the Taylor Committee recommended greater parental presence on the governing boards of schools, while the housing review conducted by the Department of the Environment promoted tenant participation in the management of council housing. However, creating participatory structures was not confined to local government services. In the 1970s, Community Health Councils were established to ensure that consumers were better represented in health service administration – although their effect was limited to that of pressure groups. Overall, participation was indirect rather than direct, but the general thrust was toward finding ways of achieving greater direct involvement on the part of the consumers.

Some initiatives in community consultation centred on finding ways to open dialogue with ethnic minority communities in inner-city areas. Early developments in Lambeth, south London, were rapidly emulated in a number of other areas, spurred by the urban disorders of 1981. Several variants of community forum emerged, but the high expectations placed on them were not generally realised (Prashar and Nicolas, 1986). In some localities these moves to widen consultation ran into difficulties from long-established mechanisms – often based on the community relations councils who had a presence in most areas of major ethnic minority settlement – whose privileged channels of consultation and claims to 'representativeness' were increasingly contested.

A number of linked themes run through the generation of these initiatives. First, concern about the increasing centralisation of British government. Second, functional specialisation, leading to concern about fragmentation of uncoordinated service provision. Third, the creeping professionalisation of local services, which distanced providers still further from those to whom they provided. Fourth, rising demands from minority communities, which left many public agencies uncertain how to respond. The overall effect was to make government, both central and local, appear remote, and it was in response to this perceived remoteness that participation initiatives were developed to provide a popular counterweight (Boaden et al, 1982, pp 17-34).

It is dangerously tempting to see the surge in public participation during the 1960s purely in terms of government's compensatory initiatives. In fact, participation schemes were driven as much by the demands of local residents as by bureaucratic largesse. A report on the role of volunteers in the social services noted the growing sense of dissatisfaction with the bureaucratic state and argued that:

> ... the degree of control over parts of our lives and the loss of some of the personal element, particularly at work, have produced a desire to counteract these effects by undertaking activities which give scope for spontaneity, initiative and contact with other people. (Aves, 1969, para 210)

The basis for this new assertiveness was to be found in the erosion of the old simple lines of division and the development of a more pluralistic and differentiated society, in which it was much easier for people to strike common cause together in respect of specific issues.

This diversification was perhaps the most profound change to occur in the second half of 20th century and it permeated all aspects of social life: the economy, employment, gender relations and the family:

> Economically, the increased diversity of society is reflected in the growth of specialists shops, of direct mail-targeting and of moves towards customised production rather than standardisation.... In the media special interests magazines proliferate.... Self-help and mutual aid groups arise to cater for specific problems, disabilities and disadvantage amongst particular sections of the community. Taken together these changes amount to a move away from a society with a large degree of consensus on interests and values towards a more diverse and fragmented society within which there are asserted a plurality of sectional interests and values. (Gyford, 1986, p 110)

From this growing diversity of sectional interests emerged a greater inclination to challenge the old established ways in which local authorities operated and a more critical view of 'official participation' initiatives. Local government had been slow to respond to the growing demand for real participation: opinion surveys carried out in the mid-1970s concluded that:

> Local authorities have failed to convince the public of the credibility of the participation process. There is a widespread feeling that they do not do enough to find out. Worse though, these attitudes have not changed over time. (Henney, 1984, p 309)

The 1970s created the conditions and climate in which voluntary action and self-help could be celebrated anew. Their strengths lay in the opportunities that they gave to individual initiative and participation in what were, for the most part, self-governing societies of a mutual aid or charitable nature, formed or joined from free choice – voluntary action releasing energies which otherwise might well have remained dormant. The Conservatives – traditionally the party most closely associated with these qualities – were well placed to capitalise upon this changing spirit. Not so much participation in government sponsored schemes, but spontaneous self-help activity was to be celebrated. It was, according to Margaret Thatcher,

Time to change the approach from what governments can do for people to what people can do for themselves: time to shake off the self-doubt induced by decades of dependence on the State as master, not as servant. (Loney et al, 1983, p 54)

Giving up on local government

By 1979, a series of attempts had been made to revitalise local democracy. Structural reform had been imposed, but was unpopular and increasingly seen as having distanced local government from the people. It had narrowed the social groups from which councillors were drawn by making the councillors' job – representing many more electors – more exacting by far. The increased time commitment demanded excluded still more people from the opportunity of serving their community as councillors. The attempt to provide potential councillors with exciting management prospects through the abolition of the committee system had been decisively rejected, and the decision-making process remained in its 19th-century mould. In many ways, the world of the councillor was probably not fundamentally different in 1979 to that which existed in 1900. Public participation had proved to be less controllable and predictable than had been imagined and yet, at the same time, of negligible general impact. Meanwhile, local authorities had lost much of the respect, trust and support that once they enjoyed.

Whereas previous governments – Labour and Conservative – had agonised over the quality of local democracy, those led by Margaret Thatcher and her successor shifted the emphasis towards defining a new and lesser role for local government in modern Britain. After 1979, centralism was the new orthodoxy and the following years saw local government relegated to the margins of the constitution as a wave of legislation brought a transformation of their role. For the first time, local authorities were seen not as a solution to Britain's problems, but as the source of many of them. Britain, it seemed, had given up on local government. With the advent of Mrs Thatcher, began the long period of Conservative reconstruction of local democracy, which was carried over into the Major years.

The election of the Conservatives in 1979 marked the beginning of a period of radical change in the internal workings of local authorities, in their role as service providers, and in their relationship with central government. For the first time since 1945, the assumptions of the postwar settlement were decisively repudiated and policy came to be driven by different assumptions. The new government rejected the idea that worthwhile social ends could be achieved by a wide and increasing role for government, and asserted – with greater confidence than in 1970 – the primacy of the market. Margaret Thatcher and her mentor, Sir Keith Joseph, articulated this difference in terms drawn directly from Friedrich von Hayek: markets and bureaucracies are in fundamental opposition. Markets operate with a plurality of players, and in a free market a multitude of individual decisions are made by people judging how best to provide for themselves and their families; they are the precondition of a free society. In contrast, bureaucracies provide for decisions to be taken by the few, on behalf of the many; their tendency is to extinguish freedom.

Mrs Thatcher's aim was to move decisively away from bureaucratic decision making and allocation towards a freer market and thus (as she saw it) a freer society. This inescapably involved a shift of power *outward* – opening up markets by bringing in competition to challenge the hitherto monopolistic position of public agencies – and *downward* – to enfranchise or empower the individual consumer of public services. The problem was that these shifts of power required strong central intervention to achieve them, leading to a period of relentless centralisation. This gave Mrs Thatcher no pause. Unusually for a Conservative, she harboured a strong distaste for local government and was unabashed by the prospect of central intervention to liberate people from their local authorities. A new framework of accountability was sought, with due regard for cost and competitiveness in the delivery of services.

Streamlining the structure

The 'un-Conservative' reforms of local government structure carried through by Peter Walker in 1972 excited little admiration from Mrs Thatcher. To her, the new metropolitan authorities and the Greater London Councils (GLC) were wasteful and politically distasteful. When Labour won control of these – some of the largest local authorities in the world – the scene was set for a tumultuous confrontation. Three months after Mrs Thatcher's second election victory in 1983, the White Paper, *Streamlining the cities*, was published to a hostile reception (see, for example Flynn et al, 1985, pp 1-18). In the face of the fiercest opposition, the 1985 Local Government Act abolished the GLC and all six metropolitan authorities, leaving local government in the hands of the London boroughs and metropolitan districts, working, for many key purposes, through complex joint arrangements.

Mrs Thatcher had been persistently opposed to unnecessary levels of local government and under her premiership the search began for stronger mechanisms of financial accountability. Some Conservatives demanded the dismantling of the 1972 Local Government Act in favour of a single tier of unitary authorities. What appealed to Mrs Thatcher was that unitary local government – the pattern now found in London and the metropolitan areas – offered clear accountability compared to the county/district system. There, the division between revenue collection (at the district level) and the greater proportion of spending (through precepting, at the county level) was said to confuse the electorate. Mrs Thatcher took no steps toward bringing about these changes, but when she was replaced by John Major, the issue gained a new momentum with a new review process entrusted to a new local Government Commission.

The presumption was in favour of a unitary structure, so that,

> people can identify one authority which secures services in their area. Having a single tier should reduce bureaucracy and improve the co-ordination of services, increasing quality and reducing costs.... Such a structure is also important for proper financial accountability on the part of local authorities to local taxpayers: people must know who is responsible for setting a budget and achieving value for money in services in their area, and how the size of their local tax bills relates to what is spent on local public services. (DoE, 1991a)

The result was a patchwork. Local government in England would now be a mixture of new unitaries, existing unitaries (in London and the metropolitan areas) and the older two-tier structure.

The problem of achieving local financial responsibility remained. It was in order to re-establish a direct link between voting for, and paying for, local services, that the Poll Tax (or Community Charge) had been introduced on the basis that those who benefit should pay. The Poll Tax had been the last of Mrs Thatcher's many attempts to control local expenditure; in this case by exposing councils to greater electoral accountability. Its introduction was a confession of two failures, rather than one: the failure to find an acceptable replacement for the rates and the failure to find a workable means of controlling expenditure from the centre. With few winners and many losers, the Poll Tax was deeply unpopular and threatened almost certain defeat at the coming general election. It was to be a major factor in Mrs Thatcher's downfall. The solution imposed by her nemesis, Michael Heseltine, shifted the burden of local expenditure still further from local to central sources.

Competing in the market place

Of all the changes in British local government brought about by the Thatcher and Major governments, perhaps the most important was the subjection of local authority services to the disciplines of the market place. The advocates of competitive tendering pointed to the inefficiencies of public sector 'in-house' monopolies, with their restrictive labour practices and low productivity. In housing construction and building maintenance, where a hard-pressed private sector alternative existed, the criticism from industry was continuous. Regular recontracting would allow for a review of both the quality and cost of the service on offer, leading to better value for money and greater accountability for public spending. Both Mrs Thatcher and her succession of environment secretaries were drawn to competition as an alternative means of securing public sector service delivery, and applied it progressively within local and central government and the National Health Service (Hartley and Huby, 1986; Ascher, 1987).

After a slow start and a prolonged period of manoeuvring by Labour councils seeking to evade the new requirements, compulsory competitive tendering (CCT) began to bite in the late 1980s and early 1990s. It first appeared in the 1980 Local Government, Planning and Land Act, which introduced limited CCT in local authority building construction and maintenance and highways maintenance work, and required these services to be subject to competitive tender. Local authorities were permitted to carry out the work themselves, through their Direct Labour Organisations (DLOs), only if they won the right to do so through successful competition against private tenderers. Subsequent regulations lowered the thresholds at which items of work had to be exposed to competition (Flynn, 1985).

The Act was aimed initially at Labour local authorities' direct labour departments, to tackle feather-bedding and to break the power of the blue-collar unions. It also sought managerial benefits from separating out client and contractor functions and introducing commercial disciplines into public services. Managers would be liberated from the constraints of democratic and bureaucratic controls, while councillors could revert to setting objectives and determining service standards, leaving service delivery to be determined by the tendering and contract processes. By

1987 CCT had acquired doctrinal trappings, with Nicholas Ridley's claim that a new 'enabling' role had been defined by the adoption of competition and contracting out (Ridley, 1988).

Labour local authorities fiercely opposed this new regime. As a result, they resisted calls to adapt to the new requirements, their very reluctance making it less likely that their in-house services would survive. Although enforced competition brought about the unwelcome depression of pay and conditions, there was enough evidence to show that where a service had been subject to the tendering procedure it resulted in a significant improvement in efficiency and savings (IPF, 1986). Such improvements encouraged Conservatives to progressively tighten government regulation of the competitive process, culminating in the 1988 Local Government Act. This milestone legislation extended the competition requirement to services such as building cleaning, grounds maintenance, schools and welfare catering, street cleaning, vehicle maintenance and refuse collection. The Act also permitted the Secretary of State to add to the list of defined activities and in 1989 sport and leisure management was included.

The replacement of Mrs Thatcher by John Major produced no let-up in the pressures to subject local authorities to this new market accountability; quite the reverse. The new Prime Minister had earlier gone on record with his belief that those who work in the public services should become:

> ... full participants in the more competitive and demanding economy which now surrounds them. They will have less insulation from economic risk and uncertainty. But to the greatest extent possible in services with a strong monopoly element, they will have the same opportunities and incentives and the same responsibilities for efficiency and success as elsewhere in the economy. (Audit Commission, 1989, p 8)

In November 1991 the government published the consultation paper, *Competing for quality in the provision of local services* (DoE, 1991), proposing the extension of CCT beyond manual work into professional and technical activities. *Competing for quality* estimated the market for these activities to be worth between £5 billion and £6 billion. The proposals were substantially enacted by the 1992 Local Government Act, which not only extended CCT to finance, computing, personnel, and architectural, library and construction services, but also required local councils to publish information about the standards of performance of their services.

The 1992 Act required all authorities to provide full statements of the gross costs of their operations in a Statement of Support Services Costs so as to enhance the transparency of central service provision. In November 1993 the government announced proposals defining the activities to be exposed to competition, the timetable for implementation and the sizes of contracts. By the summer of 1992, housing management was also in the frame with the publication of *Competing for quality in housing* (DoE, 1992), the government's consultation paper on the introduction of CCT into the management of council housing, on which modified proposals were incorporated in the 1992 Act. The Major government continued to view contracting out as an integral part of the new management of local government. Indeed, it pushed the competition regime forward, far beyond the limits seriously envisaged in Mrs Thatcher's time.

CCT introduced a new dynamic into local authority management and service provision; it was the most controversial of all the Thatcher/Major governments' local government measures. The boundaries between public and private provision were transformed by the competition regime, so too, it seemed, was the ethos of 'the public' itself and, thus, the motivating spirit of postwar local government. In this respect, exposing local authorities to market disciplines was perhaps the most significant un-making of the postwar settlement.

Providing for choice

Two main themes of choice and independence predominated the reform of public service delivery under the Thatcher and Major governments. The 1989 White Paper, *Caring for people* (DHSS, 1989), aimed at giving people a better opportunity to secure the services that they needed and would stimulate public agencies to tailor services to individuals' needs. Local authorities were cast largely in the role of an enabling authority which would stimulate non-statutory service providers. Social services would move toward a mixed economy of care, involving local authorities, voluntary organisations, health authorities and private sector providers alike.

Until 1979, local authorities had played a central role in the provision of social housing in Britain, but their role and their relationship with central government was to be changed dramatically by the 1979 election. The underlying aims of government policy after 1979 were to curtail the role of local authorities, to increase the contribution of housing associations and to revive the private rented sector, while continuing to encourage the expansion of owner-occupation. These changes could only be made at the expense of local government, where they would be directed to breaking the grip of the Labour party on the political allegiances of council tenants. For political and other reasons, it was imperative "to get local authorities out of managing and owning housing" (Thatcher, 1993, p 606).

In time, this strategy would be encapsulated in a new vision of local government, based on a shift from 'providing' to 'enabling' (Malpass, 1992, pp 10-28). Local authorities were to see themselves as enablers – ensuring that everyone in their area was adequately housed, but not necessarily by them. Their function as providers of housing was to be substantially reduced, as it was no longer for them to take direct action to meet new and increasing demands (DoE, 1987, para 5.1); their role remained a strategic one – "protecting the public interest in services provided by others, and seeing fair play". This was to be the new function of government, both national and local.

Only in Mrs Thatcher's third term did the pace of change accelerate. The 1988 Housing Act sought to achieve diversity in social housing: it encouraged local authorities to transfer their housing stock to housing associations and required them to offer tenants the option to choose their own landlord, and so opt out of municipal control. Central control of local housing was expressed through the Housing Action Trusts designated for some run down housing estates, under which private developers would take over the estates for improvement and refurbishment. None of the planks in the Conservatives' post-1979 platform – which included deregulation of the private rented sector, as well as disposal of council houses to tenants, housing associations or other landlords – were designed to meet raw housing needs. Their underlying aim was simpler: to restructure the tenure patterns of British housing to the disadvantage of the local authority role, so breaking what Conservatives had long seen as the politically incestuous relationship between Labour councils and their tenants (Ridley, 1991, pp 86-92).

The new regime was applied to education with great promptitude: the Thatcher government's first Education Act was passed immediately in 1979, a limited measure designed to repeal the statutory obligation on local education authorities (LEAs) to submit comprehensive schemes. This removed an element of compulsion, but the larger agenda was to increase the range of parental choice and school autonomy at the expense of local authorities. The subsequent 1980 Act required at least two representatives from the parents of registered pupils to be included among the governors appointed by the local authority. Such provisions were further enhanced in the 1986 Education (No 2) Act which advanced the representation and power of parent governors on governing bodies (DES, 1985, p 13). Another strand in the Conservative aim to create an education market was to require the publication of information on school performance.

The government strengthened its own influence over the curriculum in 1984 by abolishing the teacher-dominated Schools Council, and establishing the new Secondary Examinations Council and the School Curriculum Development Committee, the members of which were nominated by the Department of Education and Science (DES). As education secretary, Sir Keith Joseph took an interventionist role, conceiving his mission as being to root out opposition to the enterprise culture where it was most deeply embedded – in the schools and teacher training colleges. The latter he addressed in his White Paper, *Teaching quality*, in 1983, and in the following year he introduced a system of specific grants to be paid to LEAs in respect of expenditure incurred on certain training programmes initiated by the Secretary of State (DES, 1983). In the years that followed, central government assumed further powers, but not until Kenneth Baker replaced Sir Keith Joseph in 1986 was there any attempt to push the counter-revolution beyond the relatively limited achievements of the first two Thatcher governments.

Baker's contribution was an Education Reform Act which did indeed reverse the postwar trends, described as "the most important and far-reaching piece of educational law-making in England and Wales since the Education Act of 1944" (Maclure, 1988, p ix). It restored to central government powers over the curriculum, which had been effectively surrendered between the wars, and set up formal machinery for exercising power at the centre. It introduced limits on the functions of LEAs while giving greater autonomy to schools and governing bodies. New schemes of financial management were to be adopted by schools, which achieved a greater degree of autonomy at the expense of the LEA. Parents were given the right to seek admission for their child to any school and were no longer constrained by catchment areas, raising the prospect of schools competing against one another for the best pupils. Most radically, parents were given the right to ballot to take their children's school out of local authority control into 'grant maintained' status. Education policy under the Conservatives thus articulated a new view of education management, the essence of which was to dismantle the old power structures and redistribute power downwards from the LEA to schools and parents, and upwards to the Department of Education.

John Major had little of Margaret Thatcher's overt hostility towards local government, nevertheless, the centralising trends continued with the further extension of CCT to white-collar services. The Poll Tax was replaced by the less objectionable Council Tax, but the price was a major shift towards greater central funding of local expenditure. The loss of autonomy was seen as near-fatal. As the Labour party began to rethink all its policy positions after losing the 1992 general election, the advocates of local democracy began their fight back.

Local democracy fights back

The social policies of the period 1979-97 sought to redraw the map of British public administration, to the detriment of local authorities and the public sector in general. Yet for all the rhetoric about 'choice' or 'rolling back the frontiers of the state', the statutory sector under the Conservative administrations of Margaret Thatcher and John Major remained largely intact. Within it, power had shifted from town and county hall to Whitehall. Significantly, where new functions had to be developed, or existing ones expanded through new initiatives, it was not to local authorities, but to single-purpose appointed bodies that the government looked. Thus began 'the quango state'.

Since the mid-1970s, quangos (quasi non-governmental organisations) and the patronage involved in appointments to their boards became central to debates about democratic accountability. Extensive media interest in the trend towards government by quango was expressed in such titles as 'The patronage explosion', 'How the new system of patronage in government scatters the confetti of privilege', and 'Quango, the name for Whitehall's latest gravy train' (Stott, 1995, pp 148-9). These non-elected bodies had been created for a variety of administrative, managerial, policy and political reasons and have been a continuing feature of the administrative structure of Britain. Nevertheless, it was only since that time that much notice was taken of them, and this despite their 'growth' being more illusion than reality (Hogwood, 1995).

In the 1970s, new quangos were a Labour government creation, and it was Conservatives who attacked such quasi-state bodies as the Manpower Services Commission as "a symptom of a rapidly developing corporatist state and thus a danger to the power of elected governments and the sovereignty of Parliament" (Hirst, 1995, p 163). The publication of *The quango explosion* by the Conservative Political Centre (1978) and of *Quango quango quango* by the Adam Smith Institute (1979) positioned the Conservatives as the anti-quango party and, by implication, as the friends of elected local government.

Nevertheless, it was under the Thatcher governments that local quangos (known briefly as 'qualgos') flourished, and it was the persuant displacement of elected local authorities that excited the most intense opposition from Labour. In particular, the early creation of Urban Development Corporations (UDCs) to take the responsibility for the regeneration of run-down areas away from local authorities, and of Training and Enterprise Councils (TECs) to move forward the labour market policies which they had only recently begun to develop, seemed ominous. The Housing Action Trusts reflected similar organisational principles of private sector-led appointed bodies with weak accountability. By the mid-1990s, the expenditure of local appointed bodies had overtaken that of local authorities. In England alone, some 50,000 appointed people served on such bodies, compared to some 20,000 councillors. The concern was that:

> ... most quangos operate less openly than do most local authorities. They often meet in secret and are subject to few publicity requirements. Criteria for appointment are vague or non-existent. There is no provision for surcharge, nor are most of them subject to overt parliamentary scrutiny. There are too many of them and their work too local for the House of Commons to monitor in any meaningful way. (CLD, 1995, p 9)

Nor could this 'new magistracy' be held to account locally (Stewart, 1995b).

The prospect of a system of local democracy so severely attenuated was a bleak one, but it reflected the profound distrust with which the Prime Minister and her closest colleagues regarded local authorities. For Mrs Thatcher, the duty of the national government was to protect ratepayers from their rapacious local authorities. Moving functions out of their control into that of appointed agencies was one means of doing so, and she had considerable enthusiasm for the creation of new bodies at the expense of local authorities. Equally threatening was the development of the 'contract culture' under CCT and the doctrine, expounded in its most extreme form by Nicholas Ridley (1988), of the *enabling* local authority, whose main activity would be to let service contracts go to private sector providers. Alongside these doctrinal measures was the whole raft of specific controls, introduced through a succession of statutes during the 1980s. Financial controls – rate capping in particular – which effectively overrode the local right to set local taxation, were just the most powerful of these.

The cumulative effect of the Thatcher years was to bring about a steady diminution – not just in the powers of local authorities, but in their public standing. After 1988, there were signs that public opinion might be moving towards gradual acceptance of a high degree of central control. The position of local government in what might be termed the 'political constitution' – itself a matter, in the absence of a written constitution, of public sentiment – was at risk of permanent relegation.

From 1979 until 1991, the concern of Labour in local government was to 'defend' local democracy through a series of 'hands off' campaigns – notable mainly for their lack of visible achievements. During the Major years something of the defensiveness faded away, as if, with the Thatcherite vehemence gone, it was safe to think critically about local government again. In beginning to do so, the new defenders of local democracy were concerned to take account of the climate of public opinion. The Commission for Local Democracy (CLD), set up in November 1993 as an independent body with financial support from the public service unions, faced up to these realities:

> Local government is seen by the centre as lacking constitutional coherence. It is seen as having developed *ad hoc* within British government, its significance rising over the past century as accidentally as it is now falling. There is little consensus among civil servants and politicians nationally about the appropriate functions for local authorities and there is no agreement about their future role. While some concern is apparently felt about the rise of quangos, and about the capping regime, local government is seen primarily as a deliverer of centrally determined services and not as part of the nation's democratic life. (CLD, 1995, p 14)

The CLD concluded that:

> ... the present system of local government in Britain is seriously inadequate to meet the requirements of a mature democracy. It obscures and distorts what should be open and lively political activity for the majority of citizens and it fails to supply clear lines of accountability.

> The system encourages political parties to continue private informal management of councils and grants them inordinate power. The basis of local administration is both secretive in itself and confusing for the bulk of local people. From that confusion arises apathy and cynicism towards democracy. (CLD, 1995, pp 16–17)

From this criticism flowed new proposals for restoring local autonomy and strengthening the democratic quality of local government.

The CLD's position was that the practice and habits of democracy at local level were the foundation of democracy at the national level. Democratic political activity rested upon,

> ... the habit of facing election, of explaining oneself in public, of meeting the arguments of opponents, of accepting scrutiny, of negotiation and compromise, of leading by consent, of acknowledging that sound administration requires leaders to take responsibility for their decisions. (CLD, 1995, p 53)

This was not just a matter of habits developed within the political class itself; democracy depended equally on lively participation, with people taking part in elections, questioning their leaders, challenging their decisions: "It is the purpose of democratic reform to encourage these habits" (CLD, 1995, p 53). The CLD argued that representative local government needed to move into the 21st century, but to do so, it would be necessary to relinquish the institutional structures inherited from the 19th century. With a significantly greater degree of autonomy, local authorities would have the capacity to "lead, represent, and act on behalf of their communities". The changes required involved not only a new approach from central government, but positive reform of the electoral process, devolution and the encouragement of participation within the community.

By 1995 the reformers of the Left had found a sponsor, when the House of Lords appointed an ad hoc Select Committee, chaired by Lord Hunt of Tanworth, to consider all aspects of the relationship between central and local government. Its report, published the following year and significantly entitled *Rebuilding trust* (House of Lords, 1996), recognised the need for better relations and recommended that councils be given a specific power of local competence to act in the interest of local communities. It also called for the establishment of a new concordat, defining the right of local authorities to be consulted on policy. The report's other recommendations included the abolition of routine capping of local authority budgets, relaxation of Treasury controls, the return of business rates to local councils and the setting up of a permanent parliamentary committee to oversee central–local relations. Its central proposal that government should sign the Council of Europe's 1985 European Charter of Local Self-Government was explicitly rejected by the government, as was the recommendation to abolish rate capping.

The election of New Labour in 1997, with its well-prepared commitment to constitutional and political reform, presented an opportunity for these proposals to be translated into action by a sympathetic House of Commons. Rather than wait for the new government to show its hand, Lord Hunt quickly introduced into Parliament a private member's bill designed to enable councils to experiment with their political structures. Although the bill was well received by local authorities and there was significant interest in the opportunities that it presented for modernisation, it did not complete its passage through Parliament; legislative change would have to wait for the government to make parliamentary time available. Whether those proposals, when they came, would succeed in strengthening local democracy would depend on their ability to draw people in, involve them and restore trust in local councils.

For some, the situation might be beyond retrieval; the right question was, "Does local politics exist at all?" (Miller, 1988, p 3). Certainly, Britain's political culture had changed dramatically since the 1960s and local democracy had been allowed to corrode through the 1980s. In 1996, Sir Charles Carter, initiator of the Joseph Rowntree Foundation's long-running research programme on the relationship between central and local government, spoke for those who sought to reverse the decline, recognising that attitudes, as well as arrangements, would have to change:

> It is often difficult to remember, as the rebukes fly between central and local government, that the policy-makers and officials in both sectors are doing their best, within severe limitations, to serve the public good. The long years of rancour and mistrust must be brought to an end through measures that strengthen democracy and allow diversity to flourish. (JRF, 1996)

Could New Labour's proposed changes bring about this revival? The Britain into which local democracy was to be restored was not the same

FOUR

Civic-minded Britain?

By the late 1960s, British political culture, with its traditional respect for government and trust in governmental authority, was showing signs of change. Much more sceptical and assertive attitudes were becoming apparent, reflected in a greater willingness to protest against any disagreeable government action. Alongside the emergence of these more assertive public attitudes towards both central and local government, came a societal shift towards greater fragmentation and diversity, fostering a new style of politics which, in its sectionalism, sat uneasily with the established mechanisms of local representative democracy. These changes were not confined to Britain. From the 1970s, the western world as a whole experienced a similar shift in modes of participation, from formal electoral politics to single issue activism. They were to prove to have great significance for the workings of local democracy.

The culture shift

Local democracy in any country crucially depends for its working on the cultural setting within which it subsists, and of which it is inescapably a creation. 'Culture' is about the attitudes, values, knowledge and propensities that are shared within a society and transmitted from generation to generation. Major changes in social conditions may bring about shifts in a culture, but generally change comes about only through the succession of one generation by another. The possibility of this fluidity in a culture will, from time to time, create problems for governmental institutions, for they themselves are the products of another time and of other values. Rigidity rather than adaptation is likely to be the norm.

The idea of political culture

Political cultures are sets of values, beliefs and emotions that give meaning to political behaviour, create dispositions for people to behave politically in particular ways and provide justifications for them (Kavanagh, 1985, p 46). They concern the manner in which social attitudes and values shape people's political conduct. The concept itself has become an indispensable element in the modern political imagination, displacing the earlier usage of national character. It offers a richer and fuller insight untrammelled by the limits and distortions that result from projecting the moral nature of the individual on to the national scene, in order to calculate the attributes of the public. As such, political culture tends to be seen in such terms as a particular distribution of political attitudes, values, feelings, information and skills. And, as people's attitudes affect what they would do, so too does "a nation's political culture affect the conduct of its citizens and leaders throughout the political system" (Almond and Powell, 1984, p 37). Political culture, therefore, is typically defined in terms of orientations to situations of political action. The absence of any such orientations results in a narrower 'parochial political culture', or a low level of political culture. Most writers employ the concept as "a mere catchword or residual category for all sorts of influences that are neither legal nor institutional, and that include both structural and orientational factors" (Jessop, 1974, p 17).

The problem with such a general formulation is that it fails to deal with those elements of political culture that are specific to governmental institutions and to the governmental process:

> Defining political culture as patterns of orientation to political action or objects side-steps the question of what is to count as political. Some insist that all action is political.... If 'political' denotes power relations, then there is nothing that is not political, from child-rearing to marriage and attending school. If culture is by definition political, then the term *political* is superfluous. To avoid this redundancy, students of political culture have attempted to define political culture as orientations towards government (as opposed to, say, the economy religion or the family). This conception includes attitudes about what government does (or should do) together with what people outside of government try to get it to do. (Thompson et al, 1990, p 216)

Ideally, the reach of the concept should be extended into the decision-making arena itself, to explain the "patterned rules of the game" that shape the political process (Clark and Hoffman-Martinot, 1998, p 16). In this context, analysts of political culture have focused on cognitive, evaluative and expressive orientations, or orientations to regimes or governments. Others, somewhat arbitrarily, have chosen attitudes to other people, cooperation and individuality as the most potent themes for understanding British political life.

The most pertinent body of work on political culture was that carried out by Gabriel Almond and Sidney Verba in 1959-60. Entitled the *Civic culture*, they characterised the concept as something in which,

> there is a substantial consensus on the legitimacy of political institutions and the direction and content of public policy, a widespread tolerance of a plurality of interests and belief in their reconcilability, and a widely distributed sense of political competence and mutual trust in the citizenry. (Almond and Verba, 1989, p 4)

Almond and Verba's study encompassed Germany, Italy, Mexico, Britain and the US, and sought, by means of contrast, to establish the cultural prerequisites of a stable democracy. Influential as it was, the concept of a *civic* culture had its limitation, in that its utility in empirical analysis was weak and it provided an inadequate framework for understanding change. Almond and Verba's analysis was based on a snapshot of five countries at a particular point in time, leading them to conclude that the Anglo-American societies were 'inherently and indelibly' more democratic than those of Germany, Italy and Mexico. Assuming stability and seeking only to explain societies that fell short of achieving it, there was nothing in *Civic culture* that dealt with movements *away* from stable democracy towards diversity, fragmentation and chaos, thus only providing an analysis of political culture that is undifferentiated and homogeneous. By conflating *civic* culture with *political* culture, Almond and Verba overlooked the possibility of the direction of change being reversed (Girvin, 1990; Inglehart, 1990). Given what was to occur in the decades which followed, this proved a major shortcoming.

A cultural revolution?

The *Civic culture* authors were impressed by the high levels of support that the British population accorded to their political system. Other evidence of the period, however, has thrown considerable light on the extent of popular disaffection with the way in which the system worked. The large-scale survey of 1970 conducted for the Royal Commission on the Constitution revealed high levels of dissatisfaction with the system of governing Britain and a widespread desire for change, with 49% favouring change and only 5% of the respondents feeling that things could not be improved. This dissatisfaction was registered regardless of the respondent's political interest, activity or social background (Kavanagh, 1989, pp 140-1).

It is now generally accepted that western societies underwent a 'cultural revolution' which Marwick dates as taking place in the period 1958-74 (Marwick, 1998). He analyses this revolution in terms of the formation of new sub-cultures and movements critical of established society, amounting to an outburst of individualism – of 'doing your own thing'. The rise of youth subculture brought young people to positions of unprecedented prestige and influence, to the point where they became the creators of, rather than being bound by social norms. Meanwhile, advances in communications technology fostered a desire for spectacle and encouraged politics of gesture, while more open immigration produced a multicultural society characterised by diversity and difference. Permissiveness and a new openness of expression emerged, together with popular forms of social analysis which encouraged a critical and 'demystifying' stance towards social institutions. Respect for centralised authority came to be replaced by "a rebirth of community spirit and individual liberty" (Marwick, 1998, pp 9, 808). The challenges to authority which followed permeated interpersonal relations, "subverting the authority of the white, the upper and middle class, the husband, the father, and the male generally" (Marwick, 1998, p 18).

The social changes of the 1960s led to political turmoil, with greater concern for civil and personal rights fostering a willingness to take risks in their defence. In some instances, violent confrontations occurred between protesters and the forces of law and order. Repression was only one possible reaction to this challenge. The viable long-term response would be to adopt a more open and tolerant stance, with institutions responding to, or anticipating, the claims of protest groups. Some western critics of the 'cultural revolution' saw these changes as an 'unravelling' – turning society into a collection of splinter groups, thereby changing the nature of politics irreversibly.

Much of the analysis of the cultural revolution focuses on social mores, pop culture and dress codes. Quite distinct is the concept, developed by Clark and his associates, of a 'new political culture' – the essence of which is a transcendence of a classic Left–Right polarity, the growth of individualism, greater concern for social issues and questioning of their resolution through the traditional welfare state machinery. This new political culture counters traditional bureaucracies, parties and leaders, challenging them with much broader-based issue-specific politics. Patterns of public participation are transformed, as "activist and intelligent citizens, who refuse treatment as docile 'subjects' or 'clients', articulate new demands" (Clark and Hoffman-Martinot, 1998, pp 12-13). The new style of politics is particularly associated with younger, more highly-educated and affluent individuals. For some commentators, they constitute a 'new class' of young, university-educated activists.

For others, it is society as a whole which is changing toward 'post-materialist' values – permissive, liberal and internationalist. Inglehart's (1990) analysis locates these changes in the spread of affluence: the transition in advanced industrial societies from state provision for economic and physical security to greater self-reliance, self-expression and increased quality of life laid the foundations for the 'culture shift'. Whereas earlier generations had been prepared to sacrifice individual autonomy for national betterment, the rising generation took this security for granted, reacted against dehumanising bureaucracies and prioritised equality and freedom in both work and political life. Thus arose a new politics. On the political Right, these changes were reflected in a return to market-orientated policy, while the parties of the Left dropped old commitments to statism in favour of devolution, decentralisation and the return of decision-making power to those directly affected.

The new politics was characterised as something of a 'participatory revolution', in which unconventional modes of political expression emerged to become "the axial principle" of modern polity (Kasse, 1984, p 300). The effect was enduring: "the social movements of the 1960s ... left a continuing, critical legacy. Indeed, the criticism today is in many ways more widespread and deeper than it was in the past" (Pateman, 1970, p 111). For radicals, the hope was that the adverse conditions of the 1980s – unemployment, attacks on welfare benefits, bolstering of men's power and the threat of nuclear war – would crystallise previous doubts and criticisms and lead people to the conclusion that radical change paved the way to a more democratic society.

While in the late 1960s participation was primarily a demand by students in universities, a broader movement for industrial democracy was to follow. The failures of the traditional parties of the Left led the democratisation movement to be extended beyond the workplace to political parties and trades unions. Recognising that democracy could not be imposed or legislated from above, there was a return to the core 19th-century ideas of political education through participation. The struggle for democratisation should itself provide an education in democracy for the participants. But this time, rather than reproduce the same undemocratic power relations and individual attitudes and values that were being fought, the process would be 'prefigurative', modelling a new and more participative social order (Pateman, 1970, pp 112-13).

Britain and the civic culture

In the late 1950s, Almond and Verba concluded that British society was an exemplary case of 'the civic culture', striking a balance between deference to authority and the established order on the one hand, and confidence in people's own ability to influence political life on the other. British citizens were active yet passive; involved, yet not too involved; influential, yet deferential. Eckstein regarded Britain as the "extreme case of a congruent society" in which "individuals are socialised into almost all authority patterns simultaneously" (cited in Marsh, 1977, p 29), while Rose concluded that Britain was "outstanding for its durable representative institutions and the allegiance that its citizens give to political authority" (Rose, 1973, p 399). In the *Civic culture* survey, a sharp contrast was drawn between the Anglo-American political culture and that of Italy, West Germany and Mexico; in the former, a viable and stable democracy was seen to rest upon a balance of self-confidence, acquiescence, consensus, trust and emotional attachment.

Deference, if taken to mean the "appreciation or derogation of one or more persons by others with whom they are involved in direct or indirect social relations", varies by society, situation and period (Jessop, 1974, p 33). The 'habit of deference' was for many years a distinctive feature of British political culture. Nowhere was this more apparent than in respect for the police, for whom Gorer found overwhelming support in his 1950 survey (Gorer, 1955). The British citizen combined "respect for authority with private dignity and an easygoing complacency that the affairs of the nation are usually in able, well-intended hands" (Marsh, 1977, p 31). The British public expected their rulers "to govern more than to represent them", making it possible to sustain the balance between respect for political institutions and private participation. There was symmetry between the government and its people; a "correspondence between the leadership's confidence that the public will defer to its wishes and the willingness of the latter to accord that deference" (Marsh, 1977, p 30). Writing in 1955, American sociologist and commentator Edward Shils noted that:

> ...scarcely anyone in Great Britain seems any longer to feel that there is
> anything fundamentally wrong.... Never before has an intellectual class
> found its society and its culture so much to its satisfaction.... [This]
> extraordinary state of collective self-satisfaction extended throughout
> society. (Shils, 1955, pp 6-7)

Shils' explanation was that the makers of culture – the educated middle
class – had been coopted into the existing ascendency by the growth of
government in wartime and the postwar years, which offered so many of
them places at the Whitehall table (Hewison, 1995).

Even so, by 1959 – the year of Almond and Verba's fieldwork for the
Civic culture study – the first stirrings of change were already apparent. A
surge of institutional criticism began to appear: the question, 'What's
wrong with Britain?' was posed by the critical elite itself. Their answer:
an inability to adjust to the end of the Empire – the civil service, public
schools, the BBC, Parliament and the Army were geared up to govern a
world now lost. Hugh Thomas wrote:

> To those who desire to see the resources and talents of Britain fully
> developed and extended, there is no doubt that the fusty establishment,
> with its Victorian views and standards of judgement, must be destroyed.
> (Thomas, 1959, p 20)

The mood of Britain was moving towards restlessness and agitation, even
anger.

By the mid-1970s, when Marsh wrote his influential *Protest and political
consciousness*, it had become clear that Britain could no longer be described
as deferential and compliant. From the perspective of the 1970s, it seemed
that the 1960s marked a watershed in British attitudes and behaviour,
providing the sharpest contrast with the immediate postwar years.
Widespread distrust and dissatisfaction with government led Marsh to
conclude that "deference is no longer a force in British political culture
but has given way to a concern for influence in the decisions of the
political community" (Marsh, 1977, pp 176-7). So marked was this change
that Marsh saw in it "the decline of deference", while others saw the
collapse of the civic culture.

Re-interpreting Britain

Many explanations have been advanced to account for this apparent recent breakdown of the civic culture in Britain. Some accord the changes in British society to its declining social class basis, and the growth of a new middle class through occupational change and upward mobility. Others point to generational change, to the emergence of a new cohort of young, educated and critical people with radically different expectations from those of their parents. At the same time, "the authority of churches and chapels declined ... schoolteachers and parents became less effective conveyors of cultural values and traditional pieties..." (Halsey, 1995, p 197). These changes – paralleled, as Marwick shows, in other western societies – destabilised British politics.

New social factors, in themselves, do not provide an adequate explanation of the new politics; political events had their own catalytic effects in shattering political trust:

> Scandals from the Profumo affair (1963) onwards dealt repeated blows to the British reputation for incorruptible government. Names like Burgess and Maclean or Blunt gradually destroyed the myth of patriotic, upright and gentlemanly rulers schooled at Eton and Cambridge. The Poulson revelations of widespread racketeering in the Labour strongholds of the north-east were especially damaging to popular respect for the authority of both the Town Hall and Whitehall. (Halsey, 1995, p 197)

Much has been made of the rise of a more challenging culture, in which governments – central and local – could no longer count on the compliance of the people. The possibility that the sheer unresponsiveness of governments themselves may have exacerbated the propensity to protest has been overlooked. If societies change in ways captured by the term 'cultural revolution', in order to dispel grounds for dissent, government needs to reform itself through consultation, openness, responsiveness and accountability. Continuing governmental stability in a changing society requires an opening up of institutions to meet more participative demands.

But responsiveness is only part of the story – governments must also be effective if they are to sustain consent. Stable democracy depends on the effectiveness with which government manages the crises it confronts, among which economic problems are paramount. Few democratic regimes can survive economic catastrophe, but in the postwar world, they had hardly to face it. Rather, the challenge to government has been one of managing sharp economic fluctuations without excessive rises in prices or unemployment. Support for government (and by extension, for the governing party) largely derives from public perceptions of national economic performance – perhaps to a greater extent than the impact on the individual's personal fortunes (Inglehart, 1990).

The recognition of these hard realities, as we shall see, is what underlies so much of the Blair project, including its revivalist approach to local democracy. Not that New Labour was the first to perceive the great gulf between government and people as a problem; Margaret Thatcher had her own distinctive solution to the same problem – attempting cultural change through inculcating the values of self-reliance and individualism. Arguably, the Thatcher project failed in its ambition to achieve cultural change. On examining the impact of the Conservative government's privatisation and liberalisation reforms on support for individualist values, John Rentoul concluded sceptically that there was little sign of an answering upsurge of individualism and that "collectivist values appear still to be deeply rooted", not least among the young (Rentoul, 1990, p 176). However, the success of New Labour in securing election and maintaining support suggests otherwise: that the Thatcher revolution laid the ground for New Labour.

Tradition and change

Such arguments about social and political change in advanced democracies are plausible and attractive. Fortunately, there is no shortage of evidence against which to test their validity. The data presented in this section enable us to test whether assertions about deference, trust and confidence, and people's willingness to assert themselves politically actually stand up. Generally, the evidence is equivocal, not least because surveys since 1959 have conflated many different issues where change, if it occurred, was not necessarily in one direction. It would, in any case, be unwise to expect dramatic changes in the measurement of cultural values. Yet even relatively modest percentage changes in whole sample responses may portend great social changes, especially if there are marked differences between people of different age groups. Cultural change, as we have seen, is very much about intergenerational change. However, deference is particularly hard to define, let alone measure. One way of looking at it would be to return to Gorer's key indicator of civility and assess the extent to which people hold attitudes which may be termed as 'moral traditionalism', and to what extent they are prepared to conform to the law.

Table 4 shows that, if there was indeed a social upheaval in the 'long 1960s', its effects continue to reverberate. Rather than finding a new equilibrium, attitudes in British society continue to change. Given that strong intergenerational differences exist with respect to many 'moral' issues, we can view change as a continuing process, sustained by generational succession. As older people pass on, those who take their place grow up in increasingly liberal regimes, which they in turn pass on, creating a new climate for their successors (see Table 4).

Table 4: Attitudes to lawbreaking (1983-96) (%)

People should...	1983	1984	1986	1989	1991	1994	1996
Obey the law without exception	53	57	55	50	52	41	41
Follow conscience on occasion	46	42	43	48	47	56	55

Source: British Social Attitudes Surveys, various years

The point can perhaps also be seen from another example. A central plank in the argument about cultural revolution is the changing relationship between the sexes, with successive generations relinquishing the old moral order of male dominance. The views of those born in different decades are strikingly different regarding the place of women (see Table 5). In 1990, 85% of those born between 1896 and 1905 agreed that a husband's job was to earn money, and that of a wife to look after the home and the family. Of those born in 1926-35 just 60% agreed; a figure which fell to 25% among those born in the decade of cultural revolution − 1956-65. Moral traditionalism was waning fast.

Table 5: Moral traditionalism and intergenerational change (1896-1972)

Birth cohort	% that agree that a husband's job is to earn money, and that of a wife to look after the home and family
1896-1905	85
1906-15	79
1916-25	68
1926-35	60
1936-45	46
1946-55	31
1956-65	25
1966-72	25
All	43

Source: Heath and Topf (1992, p 17)

Deference, conformity and trust

For a long time, deference was almost universally claimed by commentators to be the distinguishing feature of British political culture. More recently, much has been made of the apparent decline in Britain of this deferent quality. Apocalyptic images of the collapse of a civic culture have been invoked to dramatise the political aspect of a cultural shift. Almond and Verba's view that a deferential culture persisted in Britain until the 1960s has been challenged by those who point to the robust tradition of insubordination toward politicians (Heath and Topf, 1987). However, the argument that a cultural revolution has taken place has little to say about deference towards politicians and more to say about respect for institutions such as the law and the family. Where attitudes to politicians are concerned, the key factor is whether or not they are trusted.

The *Civic culture* argument rested equally on assertions about trust, confidence and the willingness to participate in politics. Almond and Verba (1963) showed that individuals' attitudes to, and interest in, political issues, and their readiness to engage in political activities were rooted in their general orientations towards self and society. They concluded that trust was a prerequisite for effective political participation. On this measure of faith, Almond and Verba found trust to be low in Germany and Italy. More recent research shows that levels of trust in political leaders and other authority figures continue to decline. In Germany, for instance, the percentage of people who said they trusted their deputy in the Federal Parliament to represent their interests fell from 55% in 1978 to 34% in 1992. The proportion of Swedish citizens who agreed with the statement that 'Parties are only interested in people's votes, not their opinions', grew from 49% in 1968 to 72% in 1994. In 1996, only 19% of Swedish citizens expressed confidence in the national Parliament (Giddens, 2000, p 60).

In Britain too, insofar as the institutions of the nation are concerned, more recent research shows political trust to run at fairly low levels; indeed, it is remarkable mainly for its stability. A survey carried out in the 1970s to assess civic dispositions and attitudes to democracy in Britain showed that the majority of those interviewed believed that governments pay little or no attention to ordinary people and that elections lead only to temporary improvements (Jessop, 1974, p 23). There has been little change in people's faith in their parliamentary representatives or in their cynicism about party interests in the past quarter of a century. The British people are unwilling to believe that governments of any party put national needs above party needs and, in that respect, appear to have become more sceptical during that period (see Table 6). However, the 1998 downswing should be noted – a sign perhaps that a new government elected after nearly two decades in the wilderness, is granted at least the benefit of the doubt.

Table 6: Trust in the government to put nation before party (1974-98) (%)

	1974	1986	1987	1991	1994	1996	1998
Just about always/most of the time	39	38	37	33	24	22	29
Only some of the time/almost never	57	57	60	63	73	75	69

Source: British Social Attitudes Surveys, various years

Table 7 suggests that the suspension of belief in the integrity of governments runs deeper than a simple distrust of those in power. Here the suspicion seems to relate to the political process, with the 1990s showing an increase in the proportion of people expressing apathy and fatalism in placing trust in politicians, because governments carry on regardless of public opinion. The election of New Labour with a landslide majority in 1997 still reverberates in the latest figures, collected one year later.

Table 7: Trust in MPs and their parties (1974-98) (%)

Strongly agree that...	1974	1986	1987	1991	1994	1996	1998
Generally speaking, those we elect as MPs lose touch with people pretty quickly	19	16	16	16	25	26	20
Parties are only interested in people's votes, not in their opinions	19	19	15	16	25	28	21

Source: British Social Attitude Surveys, various years

Participation

With the exception of voting – where Britain compares well with the US – relatively few people participate in politics. Whereas low levels of voting in American elections are compensated for by widespread involvement in other forms of conventional participation, this is not the case in Britain. Trustful or not, many are content to let their representatives get on with the job of governing. There are, however, significant minorities who actively sustain political life, and the interplay between active and passive citizenship is central to any understanding of political participation.

There is a further distinction to be made between what people do politically, and what they feel they *could* do if they chose. In a well known reconsideration of the *Civic culture*, Kavanagh argued that support for British political institutions coexists, not with widespread political passivity or deference, but with "a widespread sense of political competence" (Kavanagh, 1971, p 353). Indeed, Almond and Verba make an important distinction between taking political action on the one hand, and feeling a sense that, were one to do so, one's acts would be efficacious, on the other. The importance of this sense of personal political competence was the foundation of a working democracy:

> The subjectively competent citizen has not necessarily attempted to influence the government, but he is more likely to have made such attempts than is the citizen who does not consider himself competent. [He has] a reserve of influence. He is not the active citizen: he is the potentially active citizen. (Almond and Verba, 1963, p 481)

Seeking to assess levels of electoral competence or efficacy, Almond and Verba's original questions centred on what people would do when faced with 'an unjust law', whether they had in fact ever done any of these things, and how effective they thought they would be, were they to engage in them. Essentially, the same questions have been asked since 1983 in the British Social Attitudes (BSA) surveys, allowing changes in these indicators to be monitored.

The arena of mild political protest is one in which the majority of the British public have some experience. A study carried out in the 1980s showed nearly two thirds of those surveyed had signed a petition, 40% on more than one occasion. The authors found that this was comparable to the experience in other countries. In 1983, when the BSA data series began, British electors were more active than they were in the 1960s, but passivity was still more characteristic than protest (Young, 1984). In that year almost seven out of 10 respondents claimed never to have considered a law unjust or harmful, while among those who had done so, a substantial majority did not register their protest through any of the avenues of influence open to them. As Table 8 shows, over the years, however, the British public have displayed greater confidence in their own ability to influence political life; today, many more believe that they would participate

Table 8: Willingness to take action against an unjust law (1983-98) (%)

	1983	1986	1991	1998
Personal action				
Contact MP	46	52	48	61
Speak to influential person	10	15	17	18
Contact government department	7	12	11	15
Contact radio, TV or newspaper	14	15	14	20
Collective action				
Sign petition	54	65	78	63
Raise issue in an organisation to which I belong	9	10	9	7
Go on a protest or demonstration	8	11	14	17
Form a group of like-minded people	6	8	7	7
None of these	12	10	6	6

Source: British Social Attitudes Surveys, various years

than was the case in the 1980s. Contacting their MP and signing a petition are the two most popular courses of action, with the willingness to take more direct forms of political action showing steady increases, and the proportion who would do nothing falling.

The options for action offered in these surveys allow us to distinguish between personal and collective action. In the former, the efficacy of whatever step is taken depends on the power or persistence of the individual; in the latter, it is success in acting with others that lends weight to the action. An individual may enjoy considerable influence with their local MP; but a petition of one signature or a lone protest march is unlikely to carry much weight. With collective action, numbers matter. These differences, and the shifts within and between them over time, can be neatly expressed in two simple indices that measure the number of separate actions people report that they would take, and discount them by the number who would take no action (Young, 1984). As Table 9 shows, British society continues to change in this respect also.

Table 9: Trends in personal and collective action (1983-98)

	1983	1986	1992	1998
Personal Action Index (PAI score)	0.64	0.83	0.84	1.09
Collective Action Index (CAI score)	0.65	0.83	1.01	0.88

Source: British Social Attitudes Surveys, various years

Irrespective of this self-reported action, there is a quite separate issue of people's confidence that the steps that they might (hypothetically) take would actually prove effective. In fact, more people judge a wide range of actions as potentially effective than actually take them – either in their imagination or in reality. Nevertheless, a correlation between feelings of efficacy – the sense that one *could* participate effectively – and actual participation is well established. Equally, it is also the case, as Almond and Verba noted in the *Civic Culture*, that far more people score high on the efficacy scale than *actually* participate. The conventional response is that 'efficacious non-participants' are satisfied with the state of affairs and so feel no need to be politically active.

However, there is another way of interpreting this inactivity which provides another dimension to the explanation for the social pattern of participation offered in Pateman's *Participation and democratic theory* (1970). Individuals who lack a sense of efficacy are unlikely to participate, but those who feel competent may also remain inactive if they do not regard participation as worthwhile. Some people – notably middle-class, white males – occupy a social position and have the economic and social resources that make it rational for them to assume that their participation will be effective and so activity is worth any effort involved. Other people – women, minority ethnic groups, poorer people, for example – will evaluate participation very differently.

That there is good reason for individuals from different classes and for men and women to differ in their evaluation of the worth of participating is confirmed by Verba and Nie's study of *Participation in America* (1972). They found that "participation helps those who are already better-off" (p 338) and that "those who may need governmental assistance the least participate the most" (p 12). More recently, Goodin and Dryzek have reanalysed the data from this study and their work confirms that it is relative power rather than subjective feelings that is crucial for participation: "political participation is a more rational choice for some – those relatively rich in politically-relevant resources – than for others less advantaged" (Goodin and Dryzek, 1980, p 278).

If it is to be worthwhile for people to participate, they not only need to feel confident enough to do so, they need to act within an institutional structure that is sufficiently responsive to make it worth their effort. Exhortations to vote, or to become involved are unlikely to be effective without the democratisation of power structures and social changes that ensure that those people at present confined to the periphery of political and organisational life – especially women – become full and equal members. A participatory society is a prerequisite for a politically active citizenry and the Blair government's democratic renewal agenda seeks to achieve this by wholesale reform of the local political process. However, their initiative comes at a time when the stock of local democracy stands at what is probably an all-time low.

Losing faith in localism

It is important to consider in what ways the cultural shifts we have seen taking place at the international and national levels are discernible in local political life. There are three aspects to this question. First, do people believe that local elections matter? Second, do they consider the centralisation of decisions that affect their communities to be acceptable or unhealthy? Third, how much confidence do they have in the people they elect to represent them on their local councils?

In posing these questions, we need to bear in mind the inherent difficulty of investigating matters which have only a low salience in the minds of the public. Local politics, and the elections, personalities, parties and activities that constitute it, may be of little concern to many people. That being so, their answers to evaluative questions need to be treated with great caution, for they could be giving, in many cases, near-random responses – answers given for the sake of giving an answer or what have been dubbed 'non-attitudes'. The key to the veracity of these responses lies in their stability or continuity. In a unique panel study of attitudes to local democracy in which the same sample of respondents were re-interviewed after a passage of some months, Miller found the stability of the responses to be highly variable. In particular, knowledge of local issues and personalities, satisfaction with their local authorities and orientation to local interests ranked low; not many people gave the same answer on both occasions. A similar weakness was found in a separate measure of attitude coherence, which measured people's tendency to give similar types of response to different questions in the same interview (Miller, 1988, pp 37-56).

Do local elections matter?

In 1964 research carried out for the Maud Committee on the Management of Local Government posed a series of questions about belief in local politics. Local government at the time – just like many other British institutions – was seen to be 'in crisis' and the Committee was looking to

Table 10: Belief in local electoral politics (1964-98)

Agree/strongly agree	1964	1985	1994	1998
The way that people decide to vote in local elections is the main thing that decides how things are run in this area	77	60	54	51
The people you vote for say they'll do things for you, but once they're in they forget what they've said	56	66	–	–
There is no point in voting because in the end it makes no difference who gets in	–	–	26	18
Local council elections are sometimes so complicated I don't know who to vote for	29	34	30	32

Source: Maud (1967c); Widdicombe (1986c); British Social Attitudes Surveys for 1994 and 1998

find ways of strengthening local democracy. Their public attitudes survey was intended to uncover what people thought about local government in general and to gauge the extent of their support for it. For the first time, questions were asked about whether local elections matter and whether it was considered worth voting in them. The results were disappointing to the Committee as the answers revealed a degree of detachment from local democracy. However, Maud considered that the flood of social change sweeping across Britain, raising educational standards and improving people's well-being, would, in time, increase levels of interest and the sense of civic competence on which local democracy could thrive.

As Table 10 shows, over the years there has been a considerable long-term decline in the belief that local elections determine local affairs. In 1964, more than three quarters of the respondents agreed with this proposition; in 1985, 60%; during the 1990s, this proportion has stabilised at a little over 50%. In that first survey, almost a third found local elections 'too complicated' – a figure which might well have been expected to decline. Instead, it has remained remarkably stable.

Twenty years later, the Widdicombe Committee of Inquiry into the Conduct of Local Authority Business carried out a further public attitudes survey in which it explored similar questions. The results confounded Maud's expectation: two decades of social change had done nothing to enhance the standing of local government. If anything, as Table 11 shows, people's faith in the workings of local democracy had declined still further. Two alternative constructions could be placed on the key finding of the declining belief that local elections determined what happened in the locality. The first is that Maud's assumption that rising prosperity and

Table 11: Interest in local politics by age group (%)

Level of interest	18–24	25–34	35–44	45–54	55–59	60–64	65+
Generally speaking, those we elect as MPs lose touch with people pretty quickly	19	16	16	16	25	26	20
A great deal/quite a lot	8	5	11	11	13	13	17
Some	20	28	29	30	31	25	28
Not very much/none at all	72	67	61	60	56	61	55

Source: British Social Attitudes Survey (1998)

education would increase support for local government was ill-founded, and that the more educated a population becomes, the greater its cynicism. The second is that the growth in the scale and complexity of local government and the increased central determination of local affairs had been such that the changing public response was a reasonable assessment of the diminished standing of local authorities.

In fact, neither explanation of the change is plausible. The better off and better educated have a far stronger attachment to, and belief in, local democracy than do others. This is as true today as it was 30 years ago, and was the fact which led Maud to expect rising educational standards to strengthen support for local institutions. People in the oldest age groups are the most likely to believe local elections matter and are the least likely to believe that local elections are too complicated. The youngest are the most sceptical and the most confused.

Two important points need to be made here about the age effect. The first is that many facets of older people's views of local democracy stem less from their age than from their propensity to have lived in the same locality for a considerable number of years: settled residence brings with it a greater attachment to a neighbourhood and involvement in its affairs. Also, their greater experience brings with it more confidence in the working of their local institutions. Older people are, as we shall see, far more inclined to participate, and take an interest, in local politics.

The second point concerns the young. By far the least likely to take any interest or part in local affairs, younger people find elections more complicated and show little recognition of the importance of local affairs. Why might this be so? To some extent, the answer is to be found in what distinguishes them from older people: their lack of roots which needs to be developed over a period of many years' residence in the community. Younger people are more mobile – especially while they are building their careers. As newer electors, they cannot be expected to show the same familiarity with elections, parties and candidates as do their parents. Only when people become local stakeholders through the acquisition of property, or through having their children in local schools, are they likely to feel impelled to take an interest in their local politics and government.

Indeed, the extent to which people take an interest in local politics bears directly on these attitudes to local politics. Those with the greatest interest – and few claim to be 'very interested' – are the more likely to be knowledgeable about local affairs, curious about their foundations, confident of their ability to influence them, and more likely to display a greater faith in the institutions of local democracy. Conversely, to confess to having little interest in local politics is usually to know little of their workings – to be indifferent to them. Note that these are not matters of discontent – the discontented elector may well be knowledgeable and active. Most young people are none of these things, they are simply indifferent:

> It is of considerable significance for the infrastructure of local democracy that people in general are much more interested in national than local politics, with only one in 10 expressing a substantial degree of interest in local affairs in the 1998 BSA survey, compared with 29% in politics generally. Whereas only a third confess to having 'not very much' or 'no interest at all' in politics in general, as many as 61% take this view of local politics. Here too, there is an evident association between interest and age, with as many as 38% of the youngest electors declaring that they have no interest at all in local politics, compared with only one in five of the over-45s. Perhaps surprisingly, the proportions expressing indifference to local politics were not very different in 1985/86 – when press coverage of oppositional local authorities was at its peak – and today – when local affairs are practically banished from the media front pages. (Miller, 1988, pp 15-18)

Does local autonomy matter?

Fundamental to local democracy is popular support for keeping decisions local, rather than accepting central control over local authorities. For more than a century, there has been a consensus that centralisation is inimical to local democracy. This consensus rested its case on three basic propositions concerning local democracy: that it is associated with more responsive and efficient local service provision than central government could manage to achieve; that it promotes a desirable division of power; and that, because it is closer to the people, it is able to express the democratic process more fully. The vitality of local government is the casualty of increasing central control, and without local democracy there is little purpose in local government.

However, the last 35 years have seen the steady erosion of that local autonomy. Beginning with the election of the Wilson government in 1964, the central–local partnership came under strain as ministers increasingly used their powers instrumentally, with little regard for local autonomy. They readily assumed unprecedented responsibility for local government structure, finance and services, and the consent of local authorities was no longer a prerequisite for change. Thus, local authorities were relegated to the margins of the constitution and came to be seen, not as a solution to Britain's problems, but as the source of many of them. The period from 1979 to Margaret Thatcher's departure in 1990 exacerbated this shift to centralised power. The Major government continued this new trend and, in some respects, pushed it further.

For many it seemed that local government had faded into the twilight zone of politics, having lost the respect, trust and support that once it enjoyed. People appeared to have become less satisfied with their local authorities and the services they provide. In 1964, 90% of people questioned thought that their local council ran things 'very' or 'fairly' well (Maud, 1967c, Table 91); 20 years later, that figure had fallen to 71%, with people in the metropolitan areas much less satisfied than those in non-metropolitan areas of England and Wales (Widdicombe, 1986c, Tables 3.1, 3.2). Meanwhile, government-appointed committees from Maud to Layfield excoriated central government for its controlling tendencies and pleaded for greater freedom to be given to local government. As early as 1964, Maud warned that too close control of local authorities by central government would fatally lower their status and responsibility.

Are these concerns faithfully reflected in public opinion? Since 1983, the BSA survey has regularly asked whether local councils ought to be subject to more control or less control by central government. Responses to this question have been generally stable – seemingly unresponsive to the incessant encroachments of central control. The post-election period from 1997, however, has seen a marked shift from wanting *less* centralisation to accepting the existing relationship between central and local government. Whereas in the past substantially more people favoured a reduction in central control rather than an increase, the election of the

Table 12: Views on the central control of local councils (1983-98) (%)

Local councils should be controlled by central government...	1983	1984	1985	1986	1987	1989	1990	1994	1998
More	13	14	14	15	19	16	20	16	15
About the same	45	42	46	36	34	37	34	40	51
Less	34	36	33	37	37	38	35	39	27
Margin in favour of less control	+21	+22	+19	+22	+18	+22	+15	+23	+12

Source: British Social Attitudes Surveys, various years

Blair government saw this margin fall dramatically, from 23 percentage points in 1994 to 12 in 1998.

Why, then, has so marked a change occurred? When this question was asked in 1994, supporters of the then Conservative government were markedly more content with centralisation than their Labour and Liberal Democrat counterparts, who strongly favoured reducing central control. In 1998, the previously marked inter-party differences have all but disappeared, with Labour supporters showing a 21 percentage point drop, and Liberal Democrats a 15% drop in support for less central control.

Another frequently used measure of support for local autonomy is whether it is felt that the level of Council Tax should be left up to the local council, or should be for central government to decide. The latest available figures show the lowest level of support for local determination since 1990 (Table 13). In 1998, exactly one third of respondents thought that central government should have the final say on local tax levels, again suggesting an increase in support for centralism since the question was first asked in 1984. In this case, however, party differences are small, with Liberal Democrats the most in favour of local determination.

Table 13: Who should decide local taxation? (1984-98) (%)

	1984	1985	1986	1987	1989	1990	1994	1998
Local councils	74	72	71	68	71	56	66	60
Central government	19	20	19	24	21	35	29	36
Margin of localism	+55	+52	+52	+44	+50	+21	+37	+30

Source: British Social Attitudes Surveys, various years

What can be learned from these figures? Until the 1990s, there was a substantial margin of opinion in favour of local autonomy to set local rates of taxation. Since the introduction of the short lived Poll Tax in 1990, there has been a vast change in opinion, with falling support for localism and a stronger preference for central determination of local taxation. Two observations can be made. First, the political choice presented to those questioned is extreme: to favour central government setting local taxes is unequivocally to accept the annihilation of local democracy. What is surprising, then, is not that a majority do not favour this course, but that the margin is as small as it is and diminishing – in 1998, more than one third were prepared to see central government determine local finances. Second, the long period of centralisation under the Thatcher–Major governments may well have acclimatised people to centralism. The election of the Blair government in 1997 seems to have consolidated rather than reversed this trend; centralism is now explicit, and evokes only a muted protest.

Trusting the councillor

Another important indicator of attachment to the values of local democracy is the extent to which people feel confident in the ability of their local councillors to respond to their wishes. Two aspects of public perception about local elected representatives stand out: the first concerns how remote councillors are seen to be, and the second whether or not councillors are considered to be sympathetic and caring. There is little doubt that more people today believe their councillors to be uncaring and out of touch. In 1994, more than half agreed that 'once elected, councillors lose touch pretty quickly', and four in 10 thought that 'councillors don't care much what people like me think'. An explanation for this sense of alienation might be attributed to the local government reorganisation of 1974, which led to an increase in the number and size of local authorities. Larger local authorities clearly meant that more electors came to be represented by far fewer councillors, and a danger of such a numerical increase in the scale of representation is a lost sense of public control over elected representatives.

Why might this be? When local government in Britain was restructured to provide larger, more powerful authorities, the overall number of councillors was halved, with a resultant increase in the 'representative ratio' (the average number of electors per member). At this scale, personal knowledge became less possible and candidates bearing a party label came to possess a comparative advantage in the electoral contest (Rao et al, 1994). With increasingly large and remote local government dealing with increasingly complex issues, the presence of parties simplifies the act of electoral choice. The party label is a convenient aid to decision making for the elector. It is therefore not surprising that local voters should today be expressing their opinion on the competing national parties.

The larger consequence of this shift in scale has been the enormous strain on the relational aspect of representation itself – that is, on the link between representatives and those represented. Leoni Bruno observed that:

> the more numerous the people ... one tries to 'represent' ... and the more numerous the matters in which one tries to represent them, the less the word 'representation' has a meaning referable to the actual will of actual people other than that of the persons named as their 'representatives'. (Bruno, 1961, p 470)

Yet if representation is taken to mean 'acting for' or 'acting in the interests of', inevitably the effectiveness of the representative process is likely to suffer under the combined effects of electoral numbers and big government. In large, dense and heterogeneous areas, it becomes difficult for any single individual to make his or her wishes known, and for any one councillor to respond to the individual constituent. One cannot develop personal contacts in ways that are possible in traditional face-to-face communities. Thus, the larger and more complex the systems, the greater the difficulty in sustaining relationships based on connection, of neighbourliness and acquaintance predominant in small, rural settlements.

Perhaps this sense of slowly deepening alienation has more to do with the predominance of political parties in local government? Large-scale local government tends to generate highly politicised party systems, and the English local government reorganisation of 1974 was no exception. Partisan politics flourished once again, with well-established party organisations, intense party competition and adoption of party policies in respect of various council priorities. These developments have affected individual councillor responses as the party line increasingly comes to replace the individual member's judgement when deciding on policy matters.

In this changing climate, it might be argued that representation has lost all immediacy and the process itself can no longer be seen to be based on a simple relationship between the electors and elected. Although a councillor is entrusted with a double mandate from his constituents and from his party, in practice, the party mandate takes precedence over the electoral mandate. Over a third of the British public agreed in 1994 that councillors generally put party needs over and above those of the areas they represent. Half believed they would do so some of the time, and only 15% that they never do so, with young people by far the least trusting. As with attitudes to other aspects of local democracy, people's perceptions of what their councillors should do, or how they ought to behave, are shaped to some extent by their own personal circumstances. The more educated and well off are far more likely to express greater confidence in their councillors. People's interest in politics and, to a greater extent, the locality in which they live also bear upon their attitudes, with those living in urban areas displaying greater dissatisfaction.

Whatever the reason, people's attitudes to councillors became still more negative between 1994 and 1998. In 1994 just 36% agreed that 'councillors don't care much what people like me think' (40% in 1998), and 47% that 'those we elect as councillors lose touch with people pretty quickly' (increased to 55% in 1998). Such findings clearly have serious implications for local representative democracy.

In itself, the levels of trust expressed would give rise to some concern, but more significant by far is the contrast between how people *expect* their councillors to behave and how they would *wish* them to behave. A climate of generalised scepticism about councillor conduct coexists with what appears to be a deep-seated cultural assumption that councillors should function as faithful local representatives. As Table 14 shows, the only real division of opinion is between those who think that a councillor should represent the interests of the ward that elected him, and those who concede that the interests of the larger area should be taken into account. Other views – whether personal or party – are held to be inadmissible.

Table 14: Expectations of councillors' actions (%)

It is most important for councillors to take into account:	
His or her own views	1
The interests of the ward he or she represents	40
The interests of all the people in the council's area	52
His or her party's views	2

Source: British Social Attitudes Survey (1994)

It appears that local democracy is in poor shape and few of the 19th-century hopes for it have been borne out. One response would be simply to note the passing of the age of local government and accept that, in an age of globalisation, the distinctiveness of local political life has gone for good. The alternative is to see the health of democracy itself as resting on the vitality of local political life, and strive to create the institutional conditions in which local democracy can enjoy a revival. The current debate centres on the need to enable councillors to become more accountable and more responsive to those who elected them. A clearer separation between the representative and management roles of councillors would enable the 'backbench' councillors to give more time to their constituents and represent their views to the executive. That is the aim of the New Labour project for local government, placing, as it does, increasing public participation and a thoroughgoing renewal of local democracy at the top of the agenda. However, its success will not be judged by the extent to which attitudes or 'political culture' changes, but on a more tangible indicator: reversing the decline in people's willingness to cast their vote in a local election.

FIVE

The reluctant voter

The centralism of the Thatcher years, and of her third term in particular, received much of the blame for the loss of faith in local government and the decline in trust granted to local councillors. In fairness, the tide of centralism had been rising for many years before Thatcher. The standing of local government in the 1960s and 1970s fell in proportion to the attrition of its effective power and governments of both Conservative and Labour parties were to blame. Arguably, this erosion brought in its wake a withdrawal of public interest, expressed in absenteeism at the polls. Boredom with the ballot box seemed a reasonable response, for if local authorities did not matter, why bother voting in local elections?

The argument is too easily overstated. Many factors bear on people's willingness of vote, as many of them cultural as institutional. And while the trend of falling electoral turnout is apparent across the world and at all levels of election, it is not evident that turnout in British local elections has fallen in the way suggested, or during the period suggested, by the centralisation thesis. This chapter assesses the problem of low electoral turnout, reviews the combination of factors that bear on the decision to vote, and examines what light recent evidence can throw on people's attitudes to the electoral process and their local voting behaviour. Understanding the dynamics of local elections is a vital preliminary to considering the electoral reform proposals of the Blair government.

Low turnout as a problem

The problem of poor turnout in Britain is not new, and has long been recognised and deplored. Although voting offers the only universally available opportunity for citizens to participate in politics in a uniform and equal manner, poor participation rates have prompted the central question of why the act of voting is not itself universal: why do some vote and others not? It is useful to start by placing the problem of low turnout in its international context before looking more closely at the British experience. We can then pose the question of how that experience is to be interpreted: that is, in what ways does Britain's low turnout *matter*?

The international context

It is helpful to begin with the most general electoral phenomenon, that of voting in national elections. Here we find that there has been a worldwide trend towards decline in electoral turnout, with the world average for elections this decade dipping back to 64% (IDEA, 1998). It is no longer the case that higher turnout is largely the prerogative of the western world: there is no difference to be found between rich and poor countries; no difference between small and large countries. The only socioeconomic factor which does appear to correlate with turnout rates is the United Nation's (UN) Human Development Index (HDI): comparison with which shows that the top quintile of countries have an average voter turnout of 72%, and the bottom quintile an average of 56%.

Countries such as Malta and Seychelles now have the world's highest turnouts, with 96% of their eligible population voting; Uruguay ranks third, followed by Indonesia. Other countries from Western and Eastern Europe, Africa and Asia also figure prominently among those with high turnout levels. The IDEA database of voting in 163 countries during the 1990s shows Britain to occupy 65th place in the international league table of election turnout, with 72.4% of the electorate voting, behind Italy (90.2%), Belgium (84.1%), Australia (82.7%), Denmark (81.1%), Spain (79%) and Germany (72.7%). Of Britain's usual comparator countries, only France and the US rank lower.

Declining turnout is a typical preoccupation of the Anglo-American political culture, due not least to the expectation that American social trends are a harbinger of what might be expected to occur in Britain. Data from the US Federal Election Commission shows voting in US national elections to have fluctuated markedly, but with a downward trend between 1960 and 1996 (see Table 15). British general election turnout has been far higher in comparison, averaging at around 76% in the postwar years. This compares well with an average of 73.6% between 1922 and 1945. As in the US, turnout in the latter half of the 20th century has been falling slightly, with no election matching the 84% recorded in 1950. However, over a third of that decline has been attributed to the problems of the electoral register and it has been calculated that turnout will fall by half a per cent for every month that passes after the completion of the register in February (Butler, 1989, pp 56-7).

At the local level, comparative studies are sparse. The major international data sets held at the University of California, San Diego, are confined to elections for higher levels of government, and there is, as yet, little cross-

Table 15: Voter turnout in the US presidential elections (1960-96) (%)

Year	Turnout of voting-age population
1960	63.06
1964	61.92
1968	60.84
1972	55.21
1976	53.55
1980	52.56
1984	53.11
1988	50.11
1992	55.09
1996	49.08

Sources: Federal Election Commission; Congressional Research Service Reports; Election Data Services INC; State Election Offices

national data on local election turnout. Nevertheless, the indications are that the cross-national patterns of local election behaviour broadly reflect those at the national level, although with sources of variance exerting powerful effects on the generally lower local turnouts. Much of what has been discovered about turnout is, then, specific to the national level, and extrapolated – wisely or not – to the local level.

As Table 16 shows, variations between European countries are striking, with Britain consistently displaying the lowest turnouts in all levels of election. One of the few attempts at cross-national comparison is the study of factors affecting turnout in French and British local elections, conducted by the Elections Centre at the University of Plymouth. This study was an ambitious attempt to identify common factors driving turnout levels in both countries, concluding that "a good proportion of the variation in turnout between local authorities in [both] England and France can be explained by the examination of the same propositions" (Hoffman-Martinot et al, 1996). There remains a difference in the average level of turnout between the two countries, which, the authors suggest, is explained by the more secure place of independent local government in France, where local turnout is higher (although the very different size of local authorities in France and the UK could equally be a factor).

Today, many commentators are sceptical that turnout can be improved anything more than marginally, however many new schemes are adopted, and some accept the secular decline in turnout as an inescapable corollary of modernity. However, such acquiescence overlooks the fact that local turnout in Britain is lower than in all comparable countries.

Table 16: Average turnout in national, European and local elections (%)

	National	European, 1999	Local, latest
Italy (1996)	83	71	85
Germany (1998)	82	45	72
France (1995)	80	47	68
Spain (1996)	77	64	64
Netherlands (1998)	74	30	54
Britain (1997)	71	24	30

Source: Economist, 1 July 2000, p 36

Local turnout trends in Britain

In Britain, local election turnouts in contested elections were historically higher, and have fallen since 1945. For example, the London County Council (LCC) elections attracted more than half the registered voters for many years, but fell steadily to just over a third by 1961, the last LCC election. Prior to the First World War, even metropolitan borough turnouts were around 50%, but these also fell to under a third in the 1950s. County borough council elections declined more steeply, from 52.6% in 1947 and 52.2% in 1949 to 36.7% in 1972. Turnout in county council elections declined from 43.2% in 1952 to 33.4% in 1970 – the last year of elections under the old system (Denver and Hands, 1977b, p 213).

In recent years, turnout levels have generally fluctuated at these lower levels, although national figures disguise both increases and decreases in turnout in different parts of the country and in different types of authority. Just a third of the registered electors in the metropolitan district councils turned out in 1995 – the same proportion as in 1973 – although turnout had risen by more than 10% in the intervening years before falling again. Over the period since 1973, London turnouts have risen gently, county turnouts have declined slightly, and those in the districts have fluctuated at around 40%; only in Scotland have turnouts declined in a linear fashion. The net effect is that nationwide, local turnouts have increased very slightly since 1973 (Rallings and Thrasher, 1997) and it is this feature that is most often quoted, overlooking the extent of the longer-term decline. All these figures relate to contested elections, but it was formerly commonplace in the rural areas of England, Scotland and Wales, and even in parts of inner London, for seats to go uncontested (76% of them in the second county elections of 1892). Turnout figures for such elections can give a misleading impression of the level of actual political activity. Denver and Hands estimate that if uncontested seats were taken into account, the postwar turnout in Lancashire local elections never rose much above 25% (Denver and Hands, 1997b, p 213).

Whatever the exact shape of these longer-term trends, local election turnouts have slumped dramatically since 1997. In the May 1998 local elections the level of turnout on average was lower than for many years. Scarcely more than a third of electors voted in London, compared with a turnout of more than 40% at each of the previous three London borough elections. In other parts of England the turnout reached historic lows – three metropolitan districts had turnouts of below 20% and there were examples across the country of wards with turnouts of around 10%.

In considering the significance of these figures, we need first to inject a note of caution in relation to the basis on which turnout is calculated. The electoral registers are known to contain a considerable margin of dead wood, so that 'turnout' is often expressed as a proportion of an unreal total of eligible voters. The proportion reported voting is therefore lower than the real proportion of those who would have been eligible to vote, had they been registered. Moreover, this factor is constant neither over time nor from place to place. Interpretation of trends over time are complicated by changing standards of electoral registration, that is, today's registers are more complete than those of the 1970s, when registers were maintained manually and a higher margin of deceased, departed and unregistered voters was tolerated.

The quality of the electoral registers was itself deteriorating prior to recent improvements: the first official estimates made in 1951 found between 3% and 4% of eligible population to have been omitted and a similar number to have moved home or died. A follow-up study in 1966 found a similar level of error but the quality of the register slumped alarmingly in the 1980s. In the following year, the margin of under-registration was estimated at around 10% in Britain as a whole, but around twice this figure in inner London, and very much higher among some minority communities (Todd and Butcher, 1981). Today's computerised registers have made updating easier, and it is national policy to achieve a high standard of accuracy in local registers. However, linking Poll Tax liability to electoral register, together with greater alienation in inner-city areas, may have triggered continuing under-registration in some parts of the country – especially in some London boroughs.

It is also notable that young people – those under 24 – are the least likely to be registered. A recent survey put the figure of 18 to 24 year olds registering to vote in their constituency as no more than 55% (MORI, 1999, p 11). An Afro-Caribbean 18 year old in a deprived area had only a 50% chance of being on the register, compared with the 99% chance of a long established resident of a country town (Butler, 1989, p 56). It is not an easy matter to say how 'real' a particular turnout figure is, but what can be said is that the number of people voting is far fewer than a healthy democracy requires. Even this is contested by those who remain unconvinced that turnout matters.

Does low turnout matter?

Turnout figures, and turnout trends, need to be treated with caution. There remains a considerable uncertainty as to what lessons are to be drawn from low turnout: some have tended to interpret non-voting and the absence of public participation as indicative not of alienation, but of *satisfaction* with local government. In his contribution to *A century of municipal progress*, Lord Snell, chairman of LCC and veteran Labour councillor, offered the classic statement of this view:

> Local authorities in England usually function so quietly and smoothly that little is heard of them outside the council chambers. Their work is taken for granted by the general public, and when the periodical elections take place, only a comparatively small proportion of the electors trouble to record their votes. This widespread apathy is in great part due to the general excellence of local government administration, and to the probity and devotion to the public good of the great and honourable body of men and women whose labours have won for the local government service of their country the admiration of the world. (Snell, 1935, p 78)

This remained a popular view even in the 1970s:

> The picture of indifference is not surprising. Life is short and the potential range of human endeavour and interest is vast. It is not unreasonable to feel that there are other and better things to do than to concern oneself with the problem of local government. Apathy can be

a measure of contentment. If people are satisfied with social conditions why should they bother to change them? (Richards, 1975, p 168)

Despite this acceptance of electoral passivity, the more generally accepted view is that a large turnout at the polls is considered a matter of rejoicing, a small poll something about which one should be ashamed. Low voting figures in local elections might be seen to imply "a grave weakness, if not indeed the effective absence of democracy" (Morris-Jones, 1954, p 26).

The roots of this assumption – in Britain at least – have been traced to three sources. The first is the collective memory of the struggle for universal franchise, in which a failure to exercise a hard-won right "becomes in some way a betrayal of those pioneers ... who fought for it". The second is the trickling down from the aristocracy of the sense of obligation to contribute to local affairs – a type of democratised *noblesse oblige*. The third is a radical tradition which celebrates political activism as a route to achieving social change. These requirements are presumably met by a level of electoral support that is deemed reasonable or sufficient. In particular – the most potent of all arguments – that low turnout threatens the continued existence of the institutions of local democracy, would be satisfied when, say, more than half of the eligible electors go to the polls. But this is not to say that a positive duty to vote falls on each and every individual in those areas where turnout is already adequate to sustain the democratic process. Some would go much further than this, arguing that a "Duty to Vote" [sic] is at the root a totalitarian notion and that:

> The presence of an apathetic part of the electorate is even more than a sign of understanding and tolerance of human variety; it may also have a beneficial effect on the tone of political life itself. For this group is a more or less vivid reminder of the proper limitations of politics, a more or less effective counter-force to the fanatics who constitute the real danger to liberal democracy. A State which has 'cured' apathy is likely to be a State in which too many people have fallen into the error of believing in the efficiency of political solutions for the problems of ordinary lives. (Morris-Jones, 1954, p 37)

Today, few would follow where Morris-Jones' argument sought to lead. This tolerance of non-voting is the antithesis of 'democratic renewal', which views alienated voters as:

the idle (or non-participatory) rather than the active citizens. As such they represent the heathen that the New Labour seeks to convert since, in the world of modernisation, idleness, if not a sin, does not elevate one to a state of grace. (Gray and Jenkins, 1999, p 34)

The moral loading apart, the question of whether non-voting 'really matters' can only be answered by reference to the reasons why people choose whether to vote or abstain. The factors influencing that choice are various, and are thought to include social conformity with peer groups, symbolic identification with a party stemming from early socialisation, habitual voting and issue-based or 'responsive' voting.

The act of voting

The ways in which the act of voting has been interpreted have changed over the years. Early studies showed that voters sought to match their own preferences with the policies of a party; they were also influenced by their own past decisions and by the example of significant reference groups – parents, partners, friends or neighbours (Berelson et al, 1954). However, in the 1950s, a path-breaking analysis by the University of Michigan cast doubt on this approach (Campbell et al, 1960). They found the electorate to be less interested in politics, more ignorant about political issues than expected, and more ready to vote for parties whose policies did *not* reflect their preferences. The majority simply identified with one or the other party, and such an identification in itself was a crucial factor in determining how an individual chose to vote.

Subsequent studies have shown how this identification with a political party develops early in adolescence through imitating parental preferences (Butler and Stokes, 1974; Jennings and Niemi, 1974). Having once voted for a party, the individual begins to label himself as 'belonging' to that party and is then more likely than not to vote for it (Himmelweit et al, 1981, p 7). Campbell and colleagues' model of vote choice postulated that a predisposition or habit, once established, is not easy to dislodge:

The party that wins favour [with an individual] appears to depend predominantly upon social transmission from the family or early reference groups. The critical initial decision appears to be taken most frequently under strong social influence early in life, when involvement in politics is at a low ebb, and presumably political information is most scanty as well ... the self-reinforcing aspects of psychological identification progressively reduce the probability of change in party allegiance. (Campbell et al, 1960, p 212)

This explanation, based on party identification, became hard to sustain in the 1970s in the face of sharp increases in floating voters – those who lack a stable identification. This was the decade which gave rise to *issue voting*:

> The character of this voter, and the influence upon his choices, are not permanent, but change with the circumstances of the times and with political events. Issues are often important to the responsive voter. In the proper environment, public questions and the candidates' issue positions become critical to the electoral decision. Variety in electoral behaviour is most evident, not determinism. (Pomper, 1975, p 8)

This explanation centred on what came to be termed the *responsive voter*. Studies once again began to focus on the importance of electoral attitudes and electors' comprehension of political issues. As apparently non-political animals, floating voters did not appeal to many commentators, some of whom dismissed them as apathetic or dilettante, deviating through lack of involvement rather than disillusionment with one party or greater attraction to another (Blondel, 1969). This scepticism was in turn challenged by studies which found a substantial proportion of floating voters to be, on the contrary, "well informed and interested in politics" (Benewick et al, 1969; Pederson, 1978).

This raises the prospect of considering non-voting, not as an abstention from choice, but as itself *an act of choice*. Just as those who transfer their support from one party to another may be making well considered judgements about the merits of the competing parties' programmes, so too may a non-voter be expressing a considered choice to reject the alternatives on offer, or be at the mid-point of a transition from one party to another. The normative aspect of abstention is by no means as clear cut as is often assumed. It can be argued that providing the level of turnout is sufficient to sustain the existence of local democracy, there is little to be concerned about those individuals who choose not to vote.

Given this, it is regrettable that so little attention has been given to abstention. There are, however, some pointers. Analysis of British Election Study data by Crewe and his colleagues found relatively few 'serial abstainers', that is, those who consistently opt out of elections (Crewe et al, 1977, p 47). The lower average level of turnout in local elections might caution against transposing this finding. However, the most thorough research into local electoral behaviour, that undertaken by Miller, similarly concluded that low turnout was produced by intermittent participation, rather than by an electorate stratified into consistent voters and consistent abstainers (Miller, 1988). The individual elector and the act of voting – or not – will be returned to later in this chapter.

Variations in turnout

Despite the paucity of comparative evidence, it seems reasonable to expect levels of local election turnout to reflect national turnout levels. There is, however, no wholly satisfactory account of those national variations. Lane and Ersson suggest that the explanations of low turnout in the US, Switzerland, Japan and Ireland are to be found in the particular legal or cultural conditions of those countries, which need to be better understood (Lane and Ersson, 1990). At the individual level, it is not clear that non-voters share common characteristics across countries, while the problem remains of distinguishing transient non-voter status from longer-term or permanent opting out of the democratic process (Pettersen, 1989). That said, there are some points of convergence in the identifiable influences on turnout. These include the electoral system itself, as well as the competitiveness of elections, and the social composition of electoral areas.

Electoral systems and arrangements

There is clear evidence that the type of electoral arrangements in place – including factors such as the ease of voter registration, the proportionality of the electoral system used and the normative pressures to cast a vote – have a bearing on voter turnout. Among established democracies, Australia, Belgium, Greece, Italy and Luxembourg all have some form of compulsory voting, as do many southern American states. Not surprisingly, while the extent and enforcement of these laws varies greatly between these countries, compulsory voting produces higher turnouts than in non-compulsory systems. However, the margin is much less than might be supposed, with the average turnout of the *voting-age population* in voluntary systems being only approximately 10% greater under compulsion (IDEA, 1998, p 32). The turnout difference among those *registered to vote* is greater, as "compulsory voting ... places a greater premium on the State ensuring that the register of electors is accurate" (Rose, 1997, p 27).

Different electoral systems also have an effect on turnout. Overall, plurality (as in the UK) or majority systems of voting, taken together with semi-proportional systems, average around 60% turnout, while the various forms of 'straight' proportional representation (PR) systems average 68%. The highest turnouts in national elections are under the 'single transferable vote', with an average of 83% (IDEA, 1998). Interpreting these results is problematic, given that a whole complexity of factors affects turnout in any one country. Nevertheless, a searching analysis by Blais and Carty concluded that "everything else being equal ... turnout is over eight per cent higher in a PR election than in a plurality one" (Blais and Carty, 1990). Moreover, this difference cannot be explained away by factors such as competitiveness or disproportionality, for voting systems appear to have an *independent* and *direct* effect on turnout. PR systems encourage voters to turn out (it is claimed) because they perceive the procedure to be one which brings about a proportional relationship between votes and seats, thus adding value to their vote. This has been termed the 'symbolic' effect of the electoral system.

Political competitiveness

There is international evidence that competitiveness – the extent to which parties are evenly matched in electoral contests – is a factor in driving higher turnout levels. Internationally, a comparison of 542 elections in which the largest party won less than half of the votes, showed turnout to be a full 10% higher than the 263 elections where a single party won over 50% of the popular vote (IDEA, 1998, p 33).

In England, the closeness of the contest between the political parties has been identified as the most important feature of the local political system, for "people are more likely to vote the more they think their vote might effect the outcome" (Rallings and Thrasher, 1997, p 2). In 1964, the first round of GLC elections in which the parties appeared evenly matched, showed huge increases in turnout in suburban London, relative to the levels previously obtained under the 'safe' county councils, only to fall back again as the political spheres of influence became more settled (Young and Rhodes, 1972).

These *competitiveness effects* may be of at least three types. First, political marginality: increased voter turnout in closely fought elections may be due to either the more uncertain outcome attracting more people to the polls, or there being a greater incentive for parties to campaign in all electoral areas, or both (Pimlott, 1973). Second, political intensity: the fact of even one party campaigning vigorously and canvassing frequently

– either to defend its position or in order to unseat the incumbents – can have a positive effect on turnout by raising the salience of the election in voters' minds, irrespective of the likely result. Third, competitiveness may lie in the number or range of parties or candidates contesting an election, for there is some evidence that multi-party (or multi-candidate) competition provides electors with a wider choice and makes casting a vote more attractive. Most of these effects are relatively slight, although marginality (in the sense of the size of the incumbent's majority) appears to exercise the most powerful influence, directly or indirectly.

Class and social status

A recent study of mid-term US congressional elections in the period 1958-94 showed social class to have a strong effect on voter turnout, and to have remained constant even through the period of secular decline in turnout (Shields and Goidel, 1997). The better-off, higher status electorate are more likely to vote, in part, because they have more at stake in elections and are therefore more likely to accept the 'cost' of voting (Jones and Cullis, 1986). Thus, voting is associated with individual social status and stakeholding. While such a finding is commonplace in the US, it has not always been supported in the European context. Indeed, it has been shown that political participation and mobilisation is higher in cities where the blue-collar working class make up a large proportion of the electorate, while in the past, traditional mining communities in Great Britain were reported as having high turnout levels (Eagles and Erfle, 1989). This factor suggests that people living in stable communities are more likely to vote, irrespective of class and, indeed, there is evidence that the newcomers to an area are less likely to vote than long-established residents (in the case of very recent newcomers, the cost of arranging a postal vote or returning to the former place of residence exceeds the perceived benefits of voting). Generally, people take time to develop the local ties that encourage them to conform to the expectation to vote. That expectation may be high in well-defined communities of interest, where people live in close proximity and are subject to strong peer pressures.

Although such evidence is inconclusive, electoral studies have consistently found socioeconomic factors at the area level to provide the most powerful explanations of variations in turnout for every type of authority in England. A rigorous analysis at the local level in Great Britain and France showed strong correlation between the proportion of self-employed and owner-occupier electorate and high levels of turnout (Hoffman-Martinot et al, 1996). Communities with clear financial interests also show high levels of participation:

> [L]ocal business people, in particular, are seen to be affected by the policies pursued by local authorities and would thus want to take full part in the process of the selection of that authority. Indeed the mayor of Grenoble seems to have been voted out of office in 1983 as the result of the mobilisation of shopkeepers in that city. (Hoffman-Martinot et al,1996, p 247)

Such findings are not confined to the US and UK (Jaarsma et al, 1986). There is also US evidence of the turnout gap widening, with clear distinctions appearing between those who have and those who do not have a college education (or, in other studies, have finished high school). One study found that "young whites who had never been to college manifested steep declines in voting turnout between 1964 and 1988" (Bennett, 1991). Some analysts have gone so far as to identify the sharp drops in participation rates among the less educated as the driving force in the US national decline in turnout (Reiter, 1979). However, while literacy is clearly an advantage, it is important not to equate issues concerning the ability to read and write with a voter's *political literacy* – the capacity to make coherent choices and decisions when voting – which is clearly not dependent on formal education levels.

While voting is associated with the possession of social resources, it is also influenced by levels of knowledge of, attitudes to and interest in, politics and local affairs. Related to this is community or civic-mindedness: people are more likely to vote when they are prepared to conform to the social expectation that they should do so (Knack, 1992; Knack and Kropf, 1998). While there is ample evidence that older people are more likely to vote than younger people, it is not clear whether this is because they have accumulated more resources and thus have more to defend, or because they belong to a generation with a stronger civic predisposition (Jirovec and Erich, 1992). For example, of the young non-voters, only a proportion are likely to remain abstainers, their later behaviour depending on whether or not they eventually fall under the influence of strong peer expectations to vote.

Other factors

A range of other factors operating either on the individual or at the local authority level have been suggested. Several studies have pointed to higher political participation in isolated, traditional communities compared with densely populated urban centres (Verba and Nie, 1972; Wolfinger and Rosenstone, 1980). One multivariate analysis tested the hypothesis that high population density and urban location reduce the likelihood of voting, and found strong evidence that this was indeed the case, although it is not clear whether density as such, or size of place were the key factors here (Preuss, 1981). Higher turnout levels are also associated with more autonomous and less mobile areas: cities with high electoral participation are often found to be those with clear well-established spatial and demographic borders – either isolated *communes* or core centres of urban areas whose population is relatively immobile (Hoffman-Martinot et al, 1996, pp 244-5).

In a large federal system such as the US, the possible influence of 'cultural' differences on the variation between states has directed attention to the political styles and social expectations which prevail in different parts of the country. Comparative work and that undertaken in Britain suggests that such local–cultural factors, although sometimes difficult to pin down, do indeed work to produce differential turnouts (Hoffman-Martinot et al, 1996; Rallings and Thrasher, 1997). Rallings and Thrasher concluded that, in Britain, local electoral arrangements – size of council and electoral cycle – have a limited effect on turnout, although councils electing by thirds appear to have higher turnouts, as do contests in single member wards. Finally, it seems reasonable to postulate that the extent of local press coverage of council affairs will have an effect on the salience of electoral contests, although no systematic study has attempted to take this factor into account.

At the individual level, a study of Dutch electoral behaviour in national elections concluded that partisanship – that is, an intensity of adherence to a favoured party – was a powerful factor in propelling voters to the polls (Jennings, 1996). The British evidence supports this. But beyond the simple act of voting lie deeper attitudes to local democracy. The 1994 BSA study asked a series of questions about belief in local politics, some of which had been first asked in the course of the Maud inquiry in 1964, and some in the Widdicombe Committee survey in 1985 (Young and Rao, 1995); comparison of those responses enables us to assess whether there are any trends. Table 17 shows that while the proportion finding

Table 17: Belief in electoral politics (1964-98) (%)

Agree/strongly agree	1964	1985	1994	1998
So many other people vote in local elections that it doesn't matter whether I vote or not	10	16	–	7
The way that people decide to vote in local elections is the main thing that decides how things are run in this area	77	60	54	51
There is no point in voting because in the end it makes no difference who gets in	–	–	26	18
Local council elections are sometimes so complicated I don't know who to vote for	29	34	30	32
Base	2,184	1,144	1,945	1,654

Source: Maud (1967c); Widdicombe (1986c); British Social Attitudes Survey 1994 and 1998

local elections 'too complicated' has remained remarkably stable, as has the small proportion thinking it not worth voting 'because so many other people do so', there has been a considerable long-term decline in the belief that local elections determine local affairs. In 1964, more than three quarters of the respondents agreed with this proposition; in 1985, 60%; during the 1990s, this proportion had stabilised at a little over half.

One might expect that the general decline in people's belief that local elections matter, feeds directly into voting behaviour. Table 18 indicates that this is indeed the case. Those with positive attitudes to local democracy are more likely – by fairly substantial margins – to claim to have voted in local elections. Those who did not vote were more likely to agree that it does not matter whether they vote or not, that voting makes no difference and that local elections are complicated. Non-voters are less likely to agree that local elections decide how things are run locally, and that there should be less central control of local government. Party identification also has a strong connection to voting – with only 19% of those who do not identify with any political party claiming to vote in the last local election – so, too, has membership of local organisations – 34% of voters are members of at least one local community organisation, compared with just 19% of the non-voters. Similarly, there is a strong relationship between interest in local politics and the propensity to vote, with more than four in five of the more interested people claiming to vote, compared with just a third of the least interested.

Past studies have shown a persistent gap between the numbers claiming to have voted and actual turnout figures. Apart from problems with the electoral register, two factors appear to account for this gap. The first is

Table 18: Voting in local elections, by attitudes to local democracy (%)

Agree/strongly agree	Voted in local election	Did not vote
So many other people vote in local elections that it doesn't matter whether I vote or not	3	13
The way that people decide to vote in local elections is the main thing that decides how things are run in this area	59	41
There is no point in voting because in the end it makes no difference who gets in	11	29
Local council elections are sometimes so complicated I don't know who to vote for	25	42
Local councils should be controlled less by central government	32	21

Source: British Social Attitudes Survey (1994)

non-response bias: those who refuse to take part in the survey are more likely to have abstained from voting. The second is response bias: social norms of participation encourage people to report that they voted when in reality they might not have done so.

We have seen that the nature of the local area and its political circumstances have been shown to be important, with the more marginal or politically competitive localities tending to attract higher levels of electoral participation. The characteristics of the individual also have a bearing, with age, gender, education, income, employment status and length of residence having important effects. Also important is the level of interest an individual takes in local affairs and the extent to which they believe local elections matter, or 'make a difference', to local affairs. These factors are especially powerful at the local level, where turnout levels – being generally far lower – are more volatile. First, though, who actually casts a vote?

According to the data, women and men are equally likely to vote, but there are marked differences between them in the various age groups, as Table 19 shows. The youngest women are the *least* likely to report voting, but between the ages of 25 and 44, women are very much *more* inclined than men to vote in local elections. After that, the gap narrows until the oldest age group (65 and over), in which men are slightly more likely than women to vote. Of course, we cannot tell whether *actual* voting varies in this way, only that *reported* voting does so. On this basis, as many as 55% of the survey respondents claimed to have voted – a fairly substantial over-report. Respondents in Scotland and Wales are far more likely to

Table 19: Voting in the last local election: men and women (%)

	Men	Women	Difference, men – women
18-24 years	25	18	+7
25-34	24	41	−17
35-44	50	58	−8
45-54	65	63	+2
55-59	67	69	−2
60-64	74	77	−3
65 and over	78	74	+4
All	55	55	0

Source: British Social Attitudes Survey (1998)

report having voted (72% and 71%, as compared with 54% in England), although this does not correspond with differences in the actual turnout figures in these parts of Britain.

Table 19 also shows a further common feature – the association between age and the likelihood of voting. Older people are three times as likely as younger people to vote in local elections, or at least to claim to have done so. The strength of the association with age directs attention to the types of social attitude that might underlie it. Civility – attitudes to citizenship and social duties – may well propel people to the voting booth. Although this question was not asked in respect of local election voting, respondents *were* asked whether they considered it a duty to vote at general elections, or whether they felt it right that people should vote only when they cared who won the election. Two thirds of all respondents believe that they have a duty to vote in general elections, with just a quarter taking the more instrumental view. Those who believe voting is a duty are also themselves more likely to vote in local elections.

If reported local voting must be treated with caution, reported general election voting may provide a useful check on any inferred relationships. Table 20 shows that a very different relationship between age and voting pertains in local and general elections. We may infer from this that the problem of local election turnout is predominantly related to the younger voter. The very youngest are the least likely to vote in any election (although a small proportion of these were too young to vote in 1997). The likelihood of voting in both general and local elections increases with age, and the difference narrows markedly after 60 years. The most probable explanation is that voting in local elections is a stakeholder activity, indulged in by those who have put down roots in their localities

Table 20: Voting in the last local and general election by age group (%)

Age	Voted in general election	Voted in local election	Difference, general–local election voting
18-24 years	43	21	22
25-34	64	34	30
35-44	79	55	24
45-54	82	64	18
55-59	89	68	21
60-64	86	76	10
65 and over	87	76	11
All	76	55	21

Source: British Social Attitudes Survey (1998)

(which young people have not yet had the chance to do). In any event, it is paradoxical that the political parties should see themselves as competing for young voters, when the returns on their efforts are likely to be very much less than if the focus was on older people whose propensity to vote is very much higher (Pirie and Worcester, 2000).

The question remains as to how non-voters account for their choosing to stay away from the polls. The fact that people are far more inclined to vote in general elections than in local elections has been much commented on in the press. Can a comparison of the reasons for not voting throw any light on this difference? The most important single reason given by those in the 1998 BSA study for not voting was that they were not interested in the election; 39% of the responses record alienation from local electoral politics and 10% from national politics. Clearly, local elections do not hold the same interest for electors.

Who votes? Some new evidence

Given this wide range of evidence, is it possible to say anything about who votes in British local elections? Fortunately so. In order to distinguish the effects of the range of factors touched on above, a series of analyses were carried out on the 1998 BSA dataset. Technical details are to be found in Appendix A, but a basic discussion of the methods employed may still be of value to the non-technical reader.

The starting point is that many of the studies discussed so far are based on more simple analyses, which look for the relationship between one variable and another (bivariate analysis): where the value of one changes, the other is affected. To take an example from an earlier chapter, we might be interested in whether the age of a respondent (the independent variable) has any bearing on their views on women working (the dependent variable). The results may be illuminating – but only to a point. The problem is that in 'the real world of too many variables', matters are never that simple. We cannot expect to find one single cause, but rather a complex of factors which exercise varying influence. In this example, other factors intrude (such as social class, perhaps, or region) and exert an influence on the dependent variable – attitudes to women's work – which cannot be said to be 'caused' by age alone (although it may exercise a dominant influence). Moreover, it may be difficult to distinguish between these independent effects, still less quantify their magnitude. Fortunately, 'multivariate' techniques are available to do just that. In this case, a technique called logistic regression was carried out in order to identify the most powerful influences on people's voting.

Dependent variables

The first step is to specify the dependent variable. The 1998 BSA survey included a number of questions about voting in local elections, of which one – whether or not the respondent voted in the local election held in May 1998 – is the most suitable for this purpose. Only a subset of the whole sample had the chance to vote, and only these respondents were asked: 'A lot of people don't manage to vote in local elections. How about you? Did you manage to vote in this year's local elections in your area?' Slightly different questions were asked of those respondents who lived in areas where elections were held in 1995 or 1997, and a single variable was constructed to express whether they had voted in their most recent local elections. However, the 1997 local elections coincided with the general election of that year, creating an artificial situation and a correspondingly higher turnout, while the Scottish and Welsh elections of 1995 were too far distant to enable this type of analysis intended to be meaningful.

There are trade-offs to be made in selecting this single variable, which captures only 870 of the more than 3,000 individuals surveyed. However, despite the small number of respondents, it is possible to have more confidence in the analysis, which critically requires the dependent variable to relate to a single point in time. Another variable in the dataset related to voting at the last local elections. However, although this variable had the advantage of a greater sample size (nearly 1,300 respondents), the

Table 21: Reasons for not voting in the last general and local election (%)

Did not vote because:	General election	Local election
There was no one I wanted to vote for	3	10
I was too busy	2	14
I/someone in my family was unwell	2	4
I was away from home on election day	3	10
I was not interested in the election	4	19
I was not registered to vote	3	7
I deliberately decided not to vote	3	10
The polling station was too difficult to get to	1	2
None of these/don't know/not answered	3	24

Source: British Social Attitudes Survey (1998)

different *dates* of these elections prevents accurate analysis with regard to, for example, the age of the respondent, or their opinions on issues which might have been affected by current events. This larger subset was used for the basic descriptive analysis, with the exception that those who had a chance to vote in the 1997 local elections were excluded.

A second, and closely related, dependent variable was constructed from responses to a question asking non-voters (those who had not voted in 1998) why they did not do so. The eight possible reasons are set out in Table 21. These responses are particularly valuable in that they indicate whether or not the respondent may be considered a potential voter – that is, someone who might have voted had circumstances not intruded – or is a respondent who actually chooses not to vote through lack of interest or some other, deeper, disaffection. This new dependent variable with its three categories – voter, non-voter and potential voter – was used in the analysis.

Independent variables

A large number of independent variables – those that might be expected to drive voting behaviour – were used in the analyses. The first category related to socioeconomic and demographic factors, which include gender, age, education, tenure and household income. A second category included the region variable. The third category covered a range of attitudes to local government and included people's trust in politicians and faith in local democracy, as well as a composite score derived from respondents' positions on a range of the attitude questions. The fourth classification covered voting in general elections, and the fifth a range of local authority issues, including respondents' knowledge of their local councils, and their views of the council's performance in informing people about service provision.

The simplest form of results are the descriptive statistics for all the variables used in the multiple regression models shown in Table A1 in Appendix A. These results enable us to describe the survey respondents as a group in the following terms: they are on average (slightly) more likely to be female, and to be aged around 49 years old. They are educated to below A level standard and live in areas of high owner-occupation, in households with incomes above the lowest quintile. On average, they are likely to identify fairly strongly with a political party, but not to be particularly trustful of MPs; they are unlikely to know the name of the leader of their local council, and are likely to find politics and government difficult to understand. Nonetheless, they feel fairly well informed about local service provision and about the things that affect them as residents. They are likely to have voted at the last general election, and are indifferent about which day local elections are held on.

The analysis

For the first dependent variable – *voted/did not vote* – a logistic regression was carried out – a form of statistical procedure that is well suited to modelling categorical data. The variable is a categorical variable and, in effect, enables the probability or likelihood of an event (in this case, voting) to be calculated. A further feature of this technique is that it enables the 'odds ratio' of each explanatory variable to be calculated. For example, if the gender variable – coded '0' for male, '1' for female – has an odds ratio of 1.5 in the regression (0 for did not vote, 1 for voted), this means that women are 1.5 times more likely to vote than men. If the odds ratio turned out to be 0.5, this would mean that women were only half as likely to vote as men.

Variables are entered into the regression one at a time and in different combinations, to allow the effects of each upon the others to be observed. Those which are not significant, or which have a high level of multi-collinearity (that is, they interact closely with one another), are dropped from the equation in the interests of 'parsimony' – keeping the model as simple as possible while explaining as much as possible. On these grounds party membership, employment status, respondent's income, interest in politics, television viewing and newspaper readership were among a large number of variables dropped.

Other variables excluded in the interests of improving the model ranged from marital status to age bands (the continuous variable fitted better), views on the duty to vote and on whether government has too much power or confidence in Parliament (missing values limited their utility), and trust in politicians or in government (trust in MPs proved a better measure). The ACORN measure of types of residential area is commonly used to enable a fine-grained categorisation of types of place and was included in this dataset. However, it was found to have far too many categories to be useful and, in any event, proportion of owner-occupancy proved a better measure. Membership of a political party was not useful, as the great majority of respondents were not members. The exclusion of variables with a large number of missing values reduced the sample size from 870 to 551, although this reduction made little difference to the results when the main variable – the composite measure of opinions on local democracy – was dropped.

The second analysis performed was a multinomial logistic regression – a change of modelling technique made to accommodate the move from a dichotomous dependent variable (voted/did not vote) to the three-fold category of *voter, non-voter* and *potential voter*.

Results: the first model

Turning to the logistic regression shown in Table A2 (Appendix A), focusing only on those variables significant at the 5% level and controlling for all other factors, the results show that:

- Age has a strong influence on voting, and for each additional year of their age respondents are 1.02 times more likely to vote.
- Those with fairly and very strong party identification are 2.6 and 2.7 times more likely to vote than those who do not have a very strong identification.
- Those who know the leader of the largest party or group on their local council are almost twice as likely to vote (odds ratio = 1.8004).
- Those who agree that government and politics is complicated, to the extent that they do not know what is happening, are less likely to vote. However, those who neither agree nor disagree with the statement are the least likely to vote (with an odds ratio of 5.6), indicating that this response is probably a more powerful indicator of lack of interest than agreement with the statement.

- Those who reported that they would be more likely to vote if elections were held over the weekend were almost seven times less likely to have voted in the local elections than those who reported that their voting behaviour would not be affected.
- Those who scored high on the composite measure of attitudes to local democracy were more likely to vote, with an odds ratio of 1.19 for each additional point on the score.
- Those who voted at the previous general election were 4.8 times more likely to vote in the local election than those who did not. The concept of the potential voter (introduced in the next model) gains some support from the fact that potential voters at the general election – those who cited circumstances prevented them from voting – were also 4.6 times more likely to vote in the local elections than non-voters (those who did not vote and those who did not give a valid reason).
- Factors that were not statistically significant in the model and, therefore not good predictors of voting behaviour, included gender, education, tenure composition of the locality, household income, trust in MPs and the extent to which local authorities were thought to inform residents on local services and other matters.

Results: the second model

Table A3 (Appendix A) presents the estimates from the multinomial logistic regression focusing on the comparison between voters, potential voters and non-voters. First, taking the comparison between voters and non-voters, focusing only on those variables significant at the 5% level and controlling for all other factors, the results show that:
- Age remains a significant predictor of voting, with the odds ratio increasing from 1.02 to 1.026 for each additional year.
- The tenure composition of the locality becomes statistically significant and positive, with a 1% increase in owner-occupancy increasing the likelihood of voting at local elections by a factor of 1.018.
- Strength of party identification remains a significant predictor of voting behaviour, with those reporting a fairly strong party identification being 2.9 times more likely to vote than those without.
- Those who identify with no party are 2.79 times less likely to vote when compared with those who have a positive but 'not very strong' party identification.

- Overall, the results suggest that 'potential voters' are more likely to have a level of party identification, providing some justification to their classification status.
- Level of understanding of government and politics remains a good predictor of voting behaviour.
- People who reported that they were more likely to vote if polls were held at the weekend are now more likely not to vote.
- Those with higher composite scores of the selected opinions variable are now more strongly associated with the likelihood of voting – the odds ratio rising from 1.1902 to 1.239.
- People who voted at the last election were still more likely to vote at local elections, with a similar odds ratio.

Comparing potential voters with the new category of non-voters, again focusing only on those variables that are significant at the 5% level and controlling for all other variables, we find that:
- Those respondents whose household income is above the bottom quintile are more likely to be a potential voter than non-voter by a factor of 2.418.
- Having no party identification, rather than having a 'not very strong' party identification, reduces the likelihood of a respondent being a potential voter by a factor of almost three.
- Those with a higher composite score on attitudes to local democracy are more likely to be potential voters than non-voters by a factor of 1.12 for every one point increase in the score.

The remaining variables in this part of the multinomial logistic equation were not significant at the 5% level. These included whether or not a respondent was classified as a potential voter at the last general election; that is to say, being a potential general election voter is not a good predictor of being a potential voter at local elections. This result increases confidence in the concept that potential voters are those who report purely circumstantial reasons for not voting.

General conclusions from the analyses

A number of general conclusions may be drawn from these analyses. First, in the logistic regression, three types of variables are of interest: personal characteristics, political behaviour and political attitudes. It was found that socioeconomic and demographic factors are poor predictors of voting behaviour, with the exception of age, which is positively related to voting. In respect of political behaviour, the logistic regression showed the most powerful predictor of local election turnout to be voting at the last general election – general election voters were almost four times more likely to vote in a local election than were non-voters. Political attitudes were also found to be important – those with a high score on a composite measure of attitudes to local democracy were considerably more likely to vote, so too were those who identified with a political party, had some knowledge of their local MP and felt that they could understand politics and government. Attitudes to weekend voting were also important in that those with a preference for it were very much less likely to vote. Of all the predictors of local election voting explored in this model, voting in the last general election was by far the most powerful indicator.

The second model, which took account of potential voting – those who had circumstantial reasons for not voting – largely confirmed these results. The characteristics and reported behaviour of this derived category of potential voter justify creating such a variable. The potential local voters had stronger party identification, and potential general election voters were six times as likely to vote in a local election than were general election non-voters. Overall, the analysis showed that the odds ratios increased when potential voters were separately identified, that is to say, most of the factors identified in the first model had even stronger effects. Generally, the analysis confirms much of the earlier work of Miller (1988) who also found factors such as age, psychological involvement in politics and general election voting were good predictors of local voting. However, the novelty of this new analysis is exploring the importance of this hitherto ignored group of conditional non-voters. Some past studies have postulated an electorate divided mainly into those who vote in local elections and those who do not, what Miller termed 'an electorate of intermittent participants'. It appears that we should instead see the division as basically tripartite: the assiduous voter, those who never take part and those who vote when they can. This last group might be a target for any initiative to increase turnout.

SIX

The third way and democratic reform

In contesting the 1997 general election, the Labour manifesto, *New Labour: Because Britain deserves better* (Labour Party, 1997), offered the electorate "a new politics". This new politics was intended to renew public faith, as the Labour government would govern in the interest of the many and "set British political life on a new course for the future". For each area of policy set out in the manifesto, a new and distinctive approach was mapped out, and presented as "one that differs both from the solutions of the old Left and those of the Conservative Right". This was to be no middle way: it was the 'third way'.

The idea of a third way politics – neither socialist nor free market, but a revitalised social democracy – was fully elaborated by Anthony Giddens (Giddens, 1998). In a later apologia Giddens argued:

> Third Way politics is not, as it is so often portrayed, a capitulation to neo-liberalism. On the contrary, it emphasises the core importance of active government and the public sphere.... The public sphere does not coincide with the domain of the State. State institutions can diminish or discredit the realm of the public when they become oversized, bureaucratic or otherwise unresponsive to citizens' needs. The neo-liberals were right to criticise the State in these respects, but wrong to suppose that the public good can be better supplied by markets. (Giddens, 2000, pp 163-4)

Institutional reform occupied a central place in Giddens' view of the new politics; far from neglecting the public realm, the third way politics "offers the means of reconstructing and renewing public institutions" (Giddens, 2000, p 29). This reconstruction, which aims to restore confidence in government and its performance, is a first priority: government and state institutions need to be made "as effective and quick on their feet as many sectors of business have now become" (Giddens, 2000, p 58). But something more than reform in the interests of efficiency lies at the heart of this project: the most important objective is to make political institutions more responsive and more open. As Giddens puts it, what is needed is a second wave of democratisation – or what he calls the 'democratising of democracy'.

This thinking was elaborated in Tony Blair's Fabian pamphlet which explained:

> The Third Way is not an attempt to split the difference between Right and Left. It is about traditional values in a changed world. And it draws vitality from uniting the two great streams of Left-of-centre thought – democratic socialism and liberalism – whose divorce this century did so much to weaken progressive politics across the West. Liberals asserted the primacy of individual liberty in the market economy; social democrats promoted social justice with the state as its main agent. There is no necessary conflict between the two, accepting as we now do that state power is one means to achieve our goals, but not the only one and emphatically not an end in itself.
>
> In this respect the Third Way also marks a third way *within* the Left.... The Third Way is a serious reappraisal of social democracy, reaching deep into the values of the Left to develop radically new approaches. (Blair, 1998a, p 1)

Because the third way is, above all else, a different way of doing things, it was argued to have immediate relevance to the relationship between local authorities and the people they serve. The contrast between representative and direct democracy was to be seen as "a false antithesis". New democratic experiments "from elected mayors to citizens' juries" were hailed as important pointers to the future. Making government more responsive would enable local government to be open and vibrant, for "diverse democratic debate is a laboratory for ideas about how we should meet social needs" (Blair, 1998a, pp 15-17).

New Labour's modernisation of local government owes its paternity to this thinking: proposals for education, regeneration and other local public services reflect the concepts of partnership, local involvement and decentralisation. Innovation was supposed to follow on from rewarding merit and quality, with 'beacon councils' showing the way for others to follow. The rigidities of Compulsory Competitive Tendering (CCT) were rejected in favour of seeking best value in delivering services through public–private cooperation.

Looking beyond Britain

While the government was setting new directions for Britain, the search for greater public accountability had long gone international (Bartle, 1994). All OECD countries have experienced increasing demand for public services, a slowing of economic growth and restrictions on public spending, creating a crisis of confidence in the governmental process. Governments at all levels – central and local – face demands for accountability, transparency and responsiveness. In Spain, France, Germany, Denmark, Norway, Sweden and the Netherlands, moves to open up local government are directly linked to notions of personal responsibility and civic duty, with a view to creating strong, self-governing communities (Owens, 1991; Owens and Panella, 1991; Pola et al, 1996).

While initiatives to promote participation in local affairs are now common in most advanced countries, some have a longer history of such involvement: governmental initiatives to promote participation in local affairs are not merely a fashion of the 1990s. In the early 1970s, arrangements to promote participation through referenda, or through non-political representative bodies, in countries such as the Netherlands, Switzerland, Norway, Sweden and Finland, were attracting international attention. In Sweden, the efficacy of the system depended on the ability of the parties to formulate and execute a policy that was in agreement with the citizens' wishes. The unique Yugoslav system of local self-government, which had long attracted interest from the British Left, emphasised participation as one of the fundamental principles of its entire philosophy. Not that the presumption that people should participate was necessarily a liberal one – the most systematic provision for integrating citizen views was to be found in the corporatist political regime of Franco's Spain, where individuals were expected to participate in party activities as well as in, for example, trades unions, tenants' associations and other bodies.

The Scandinavian experiments in public service reform have been widely cited as an example of the localisation of decisions, although interest has been most notable in Britain, where the comparison is invoked largely to contrast Scandinavian decentralisation with British centralism. Judged independently, however, the experiments can be seen as attempts to redress highly specific national problems arising from administrative law traditions.

These may be understood as reactions "against the often detailed form of some special enactments which lay duties upon local authorities" (Gustafsson, 1991), which have in turn promoted an over-compliant climate of citizen self-restraint. The particular interest in the Swedish experience is the conscious identification of the problem of reform as one which links together the otherwise separate strands: the localisation of decisions, the co-option of local communities and greater citizen participation (Slunge, 1989).

The Scandinavian interest in reconstructing the relationship between government and the people to whom they provide services is echoed in southern Europe. In Portugal, a national programme of 'de-bureaucratisation' has been introduced, seeking to personalise service delivery under the slogan 'The administration has a face' (Pereira, 1991). Developments in Spain parallel those in her Iberian neighbour, but there is a greater recognition that shifts in approach are inhibited by the distinctiveness of an administrative tradition that has been so deeply coloured by the Franco era and, over a longer term, by the all-pervasive influence of the Catholic Church. The bureaucracy and the courts have proved important sources of resistance to administrative renewal and, despite signs of growing interest in Catalonia (driven by the need to facilitate industrial development), the outcome is at present uncertain. A particular conflict arises between the attempts to make administration more accessible to citizens (as in the 'single window' experiments in Valencia) and the persistence of the *Gestorias* – professionalised intermediaries who deal with individuals' problems on a fee paying basis (Mateo, 1991).

Other countries have concentrated on finding means of enhancing community involvement in public service decisions via local consultative mechanisms. Citizen advisory boards for specific services are well established in the US, while neighbourhood-based advisory committees have been established in Washington DC, Dayton Ohio, New York City and Boston (Hatry, 1983). Another mode of involving clients or consumers in service planning is through survey instruments to measure satisfaction and elicit preferences. This practice is not unknown in the US and, in the summer of 1986, the Italian Confederation of Local Government Public Service Providers polled opinions of service quality in 13 large Italian cities (Rupeni, 1989). In Germany, the representative social survey has been grasped as a counterbalance to group pressure and is used to assess needs and preferences both with respect to specific categories of service recipient and among the wider population. More radically, there have been experiments with the creation of 'planning cells', involving randomly chosen citizens for a limited period to develop services or shape decisions with the support of local officials.

Other modes of involvement seek to empower those who use public services. For example, Britain's health service reorganisation of the 1970s led to the establishment of a network of local consumer representation and watchdog bodies, the Community Health Councils (CHCs). Having survived rather hostile reviews, the CHCs have long been regarded as ineffective. However, their establishment arguably preceded the conditions of citizen activism and consumer claims that would have made them more vocal; and those conditions are now present. The recent health service review provided the opportunity for CHCs to rearticulate their aims at a time when interest in citizen and consumer participation within the healthcare professions was increasing (Leneman et al, 1986). But the degree of professionalisation of healthcare in Britain makes it unusually difficult for consumer bodies to gain an effective voice. Some CHCs have led the way in developing a public service advocacy role; the current debate on the future is lively, and from it emerges a notion of the CHC as citizen counter-bureaucracy, working as a countervailing force to management and the professions (Hogg and Winkler, 1989).

The widening experiment with consumer participation in Britain undoubtedly reflects a rise in public assertiveness and the waning of service recipient passivity. In the case of social welfare, this new assertiveness is consciously supported and fostered by some professionals, who justify it as providing more sharply focused indications of need. However, the debate is moving beyond this one-dimensional version of the consumer of services:

> The relationship between social services departments and people with disabilities has traditionally been one of service providers and service users. That is still the predominant relationship. However, changes are under way in the voice which people with disabilities have in determining the content of services and how they are delivered; in the assumptions which underpin the relationship; in the opportunities for disabled people to have a voice in social service departments other than as service users. (Connelly, 1990)

Moreover, while shifts in professional opinion were taking place – more recognisably in social welfare than in healthcare – it was the voluntary sector which was setting a new agenda for the relationship between social providers and the provided for.

New Labour and local government

By 1997, the climate of the relationship between government and the governed was changing across Europe. A variety of mechanisms designed to ensure that local governments inform people about issues and decisions, provide opportunities for the public to influence decision making, and promote public knowledge and awareness, were to be found in many countries outside Britain. This was bound to affect the ways in which critics and supporters alike regarded the future of local democracy in Britain; it was becoming widely recognised that effective participation rests on well-informed citizens. It was against the background of these wider experiences that New Labour framed its approach: promoting communication and openness, and enhancing accountability through wider participation. These would provide the common context in which developments in areas such as education, regeneration and community development would be taken forward.

Education

New Labour's agenda for education focused on improving standards and targeting resources to the areas of greatest deprivation, establishing education action zones (EAZs). The overall approach, with its emphasis on standards, built on Conservative policy, although its origins are traceable to the previous Labour government and to Prime Minister James Callaghan's Ruskin College speech of 1978. New Labour's education White Paper, *Excellence in schools*, set out their core objectives and in October 1997 a Qualifications and Curriculum Authority (QCA) combined responsibilities for vocational and school curricula and qualifications. The QCA establishes standards and oversees the national curriculum and the publication of school league tables of examination results.

The 1998 School Standards and Framework Act placed some new duties on local education authorities (LEAs) and abolished grant-maintained status, with all school funding being routed through the LEA. The LEA's new duties include raising standards and producing education development plans to show how improvements will be achieved. Parents are given a stronger role, with increased representation on governing bodies and education committees, and all schools are to produce home–school agreements. The Act tilts the balance against Labour's *bête noire* – selection – by prohibiting admission to schools on the basis of ability and permitting local ballots on the future of selective grammar schools. Subsequent regulations provided a trigger for local ballots which had to be held where 20% of parents signed a petition requesting one. However, specialist schools, including the former city technology colleges, retain the ability to select up to 10% of their pupils on grounds of aptitude. In a continuation of the Conservative's local management of schools scheme, LEAs are required to pass on 90% of their education budget to schools.

Like the Conservatives before them, New Labour balanced the further empowerment of schools and parents with the strengthening of central functions of inspection. Ofsted (Office of Standards in Education) – established under the 1992 Education (Schools) Act – was reinforced in 1997, giving powers to the Chief Inspector of Schools to inspect LEAs and placing LEAs under Audit Commission scrutiny. Labour's 1998 School Standards and Framework Act granted the Secretary of State power to intervene directly in a LEA's affairs if satisfied that it is failing in its duties. In extreme cases, the Secretary of State can appoint a third party – a private or non-profit organisation – to take over a school. Thinking the administratively unthinkable was a hallmark of New Labour's approach and this could be seen in the London Borough of Islington's acceptance late in 1999 of the possibility of handing over the management of all local schools to an education consultancy.

The EAZ represented another strand of continuity between Conservative and Labour thinking in that they sought the active involvement of business in revitalising education in 25 poorly performing areas. Each EAZ is run by an Education Action Forum (EAF) which channels the funding from the Department for Education and Employment to the schools, and produces an action plan for the three- to five-year period of the initiative. Most radically, the EAF became – albeit for a limited period – the education authority for its area. Some fear that these new mini-authorities, with their right to opt out of the national curriculum and pay awards, and their prominent business involvement could be the harbingers of a broader privatisation of public education (Hill, 2000). The working of the EAF with an increasing emphasis on business involvement and no clear requirement to return the schools to LEA control at the end of the EAZ's life, reflects the Conservative's earlier Housing Action Trusts experiments. In sum, New Labour has brought about a new partnership in education – one in which the tripartite relationship between LEAs, schools and the Secretary of State is shifted substantially towards the latter; the LEA role becomes one of enabler, relating to schools through a code of practice, setting benchmarks and advising on good practice.

Regeneration

Although New Labour's electoral base is much broader than that of the old Labour party, its social policy initiatives remain firmly targeted on areas of urban deprivation. It is in regeneration that local authorities have maintained their status as major players in rebuilding communities. Local authorities are encouraged to develop anti-poverty strategies within a broad approach to improving employment prospects and skills, promoting sustainable regeneration and quality of urban life, and empowering people to participate in regeneration activities. One novelty introduced by New Labour to address these issues is the Social Exclusion Unit (SEU), established within the Cabinet Office, reporting to 10 Downing Street and working with a network of ministers and officials across Whitehall.

The SEU's 1998 report, *Bringing Britain together: A national strategy for neighbourhood renewal* (SEU, 1998), was critical of both central and local government for its past failures in relation to urban policy. Its analysis of this 'costly policy failure' pulled no punches, especially with regard to the fragmentation and lacunae of past policy initiatives. Established, in part, to demonstrate New Labour's concern with 'joined up' government, the SEU recommended a series of action teams headed by a minister, with the membership drawn from across Whitehall and beyond to work with local people, firms and the local authorities (SEU, 1998). Local authorities, not spared from the SEU's criticisms, find their role changing. Within the broad framework of the New Deal for Communities programme, pathfinder authorities focus on their most deprived neighbourhoods, but the local initiative is taken by community and voluntary groups within an overall local authority plan.

This notion of partnership lies at the heart of New Labour's approach to regeneration: it is a concept which, in practice, calls on public, private and voluntary bodies to overcome their boundaries and learn to work together. In deprived areas a combined approach is seen as the only possible means of success. In healthcare, the local partnerships between councils and the National Health Service aim to tackle the social and economic causes of poor health and improve the delivery of healthcare.

Local authorities are also expected to work with the new Regional Development Agencies in addressing the economic deficit in the English regions.

It is within this context of partnership that local authorities are to discharge their new duty: to promote economic, social and environmental well-being in their areas. In taking decisions affecting their area or its people, local authorities are to assess the likely effects of a decision against their economic, social and environmental objectives. This new duty is underpinned with a general discretionary power to promote the well-being of their area and those who live, work and visit there. This may not be used in ways that prejudice other council functions, or the functions of other statutory bodies, while a reserve power to exclude particular activities or to set a financial limit is retained by the Secretary of State.

Best Value

Central to New Labour's approach is an emphasis on joint working to maximise results: collaboration in matters of health, education, crime reduction and tackling social exclusion would, in the government's view, tackle some of the weaknesses of the existing system and improve the quality of service delivery. Implementing Labour's manifesto commitment to introduce a duty on local authorities to obtain 'best value' in partnership with other bodies was to be the principal means by which improvements could be achieved: councils will not be forced to put their services out to tender but will be required to obtain best value. The key argument was that CCT – introduced under the Conservatives – had proved inflexible in practice and incurred significant costs for employees, while little had been achieved in terms of the efficiency and quality of service provision.

The 1999 Local Government Act laid down that a new regime of Best Value would be applied to a wide range of services in place of CCT, and would require councils to secure continuous improvements. The duty of Best Value is one that local authorities will owe to local people, both as taxpayers and the customers of local authority services (DETR, 1998b, Chapter 7). Competition will continue, but as an important management tool rather than a requirement, while setting performance targets and publication of local performance plans will be fundamental in demonstrating that Best Value is being achieved. Local authorities were required to publish their first performance plans by 31 March 2000 and annually thereafter. As in the past, it will be the task of central government to set the basic framework for service provision and ensure that local targets adhere to national standards. Independent auditors will have the responsibility to report publicly on whether Best Value has been achieved and to agree to measurable targets for improvement. Inspection reports are intended to enable the public to assess their local authority's performance, and the government to see whether its policies are working on the ground. Where services are seen to be failing, ministers will intervene with remedial action. More generally, the government will be able to identify and disseminate good practice for other authorities to follow.

Section 5 of the 1999 Local Government Act requires authorities to conduct Best Value reviews of their functions in accordance with the provisions. In carrying out their reviews, authorities are obliged to meet four requirements. First, to *challenge* how and why a service is being provided. Second, to secure *comparison* with the performance of others across a range of relevant indicators, taking into account the views of both service users and potential suppliers. Third, to *consult* local taxpayers, service users, partners and the wider business community in the setting of new performance targets. Fourth, to use fair and open *competition* wherever possible as a means of securing efficient and effective services.

The government acknowledges that rising demands from the public for high quality services, together with advances in methods of service delivery, would make it unlikely that any one provider can guarantee Best Value by itself. Diversity is seen as essential to the way in which services are to be delivered and in the choice of providers. To this end, authorities are required to draw from the best providers, whether they lie in the public, private or voluntary sectors. A council-wide approach to partnership under Best Value is strongly urged, so that local authorities can ensure the development of corporate objectives, together with clear strategies for community consultation, procurement and staff development.

'Beacon' councils – the very best performing authorities – will set the pace of change and encourage the rest to innovate and to modernise. The government has established a scheme to identify and select these beacon councils as recognised centres of expertise and excellence to which others should look. Ministers decide on applications to be awarded beacon status, and are assisted by an independent advisory panel with an appropriate mix of academics, business people, local government figures, practitioners and service users. The panel advises ministers both on selection criteria, and on individual applications.

Authorities are able to apply for beacon status in relation to particular service areas, or for the council as a whole: it is possible to be awarded the status of beacon housing council, beacon education council or beacon social service council. A council with beacon status for a particular service will be given wider discretion in how that service is managed and delivered. For example, a council could be given more freedom to make capital investment in its beacon service, subject to the council making a proper analysis of the budgetary implications, or controls in secondary legislation on service delivery could be eased for a council's beacon service. An authority that obtains beacon status in several service areas is well placed to apply for overall beacon council status.

The criteria for overall beacon designation include responsiveness to the local community, modern management structures, a successful Best Value regime demonstrated by high standards of efficiency and effectiveness, and a high level of support from local people and the business community. Ministers will also take account of performance in service delivery against national and local performance targets and indicators, inspectorate reports, and auditors' statements on financial management. Beacon status is awarded for a fixed period, after which a council needs to reapply and be reassessed. It will be possible to lose beacon status if, for example, a serious service failure arose.

Integral to the Best Value/beacon council regime is a requirement for effective participation and public consultation. Public forums have been identified as key arenas where issues of particular local concern or interest could be addressed and considered. Such forums would not only provide opportunities for councils to explain to the public their policies and actions, but could serve as platforms for democratic debate. Although there is no one way in which these forums are expected to operate, it has been suggested that there is scope for them to work on a similar basis to Parliamentary Select Committees. This would enable backbench councillors with a particular interest to form a committee, take evidence in public and report on their findings, and make recommendations where appropriate for the council or others. No changes to the formal lines of accountability of other public bodies are envisaged and the government cautions against any changes that would hinder a council's relationships with other local players. In the government's view, no system is to be encouraged which would "run contrary to the spirit of partnership and voluntary cooperation on which all effective relationships must be founded".

So great is the emphasis on partnership working that the government has given councils clear discretionary powers to engage in partnership arrangements with other bodies in support of the core function of promoting the economic, social and environmental well-being of the area. The powers provide greater opportunities for pooling or sharing resources, accommodation, IT or staff. It is hoped that these powers will enable councils to plan with greater certainty on a whole range of matters, and tackle difficult cross-cutting issues. Many authorities have already developed links with some of the bodies operating in their area, and a clear trend in this direction has been discernible for some years, but there is often a lack of cohesion between the various interest groups, and confusion over the powers of councils to participate with other stakeholders in partnership activities.

Joint collaboration and working across boundaries can be best achieved in a climate of flexibility, openness and freedom from bureaucratic constraints. Recognising the dangers of the current statutory framework, which could potentially limit the scope for joint working and inhibit local innovation and diversity, the government has set itself the longer-term objective to allow beacon councils greater scope to meet local needs and priorities. The government argues that such a framework would open greater opportunities for innovation and the testing of new ideas for the benefit of the local area and local people. A system of rewards and incentives will ensure that councils which perform consistently well will be able to acquire additional powers and freedoms that, over time, will be significantly wider than those available to councils which are performing less effectively. These arrangements will provide an incentive for councils to modernise the ways in which they work. In the long term, such a scheme would also enable the government and councils to test alternative means of service delivery and to pilot new ideas, such as those emerging from departments in respect of action zones or from the Better Government project.

Modernisation and new political structures

The overall strategy for local authorities, with its new duty to promote local well-being under a Best Value regime, amounts to a fundamental change of ethos and approach. To ensure that they are equipped to function in this new era, political structures are also required to modernise and the standards of conduct within councils need to improve – a package implied in the title of the then 1999 Local Government (Organisation and Standards) Bill. A new ethical framework has been established, building on the recommendations of the Nolan Committee's third report on *Standards of conduct in local government*. The new framework provides clear guidelines for councillors and officers, and safeguards against misconduct through the establishment of standards committees in each local authority. Councils are also required to adopt a code of conduct to regulate the behaviour of councillors, parts of which will be mandatory, and parts tailored to local circumstances. An independent body – the Standards Board – will investigate allegations of infringements. A separate Adjudication Panel will be able to impose penalties ranging up to disqualification from office. As part of these reforms, the statutory provisions for surcharge for wilful misconduct – long found irksome, and condemned by Redcliffe-Maud in 1969 – are repealed.

Alongside a better framework for regulating conduct, appropriate management structures are seen as crucial if councils are to become more responsive to their local communities and excite the interest and enthusiasm of local people. The 'community leadership' concept, which developed during Labour's years of opposition, came into its own after May 1997, and informs the entire gamut of New Labour's programme for local government:

> Community leadership is at the heart of the role of modern local government. Councils are the organisations best placed to take a comprehensive overview of the needs and priorities of their local areas and communities and lead the work to meet those needs and priorities in the round. (DETR, 1998b, p 79)

This notion of the local authority playing the central local role implies new decision-making structures to create "a clear and well known focus for local leadership" (DETR, 1998b, p 24). Decision makers have to become visible, and their processes transparent. Local people should know who takes decisions, who to hold to account and who to complain to when things go wrong. They should be encouraged to become involved with their council, perhaps to consider themselves as potential councillors.

The zeal with which this overall package of reforms is put forward has not been seen for more than a century, nor has local democracy been so celebrated since then. Clearly, New Labour has given local government a central place in its agenda to modernise British institutions, but the key question is whether or not the package is likely to work. It is not hard to see that Best Value offers greater flexibility and brings in wider considerations of service than CCT and the beacon council scheme makes sense as a model for diffusing and encouraging innovation. It is also hard to disagree with the proposition that the new ethical framework has a

SEVEN

The modernising agenda: enhancing participation

The origins of the Labour government's revitalisation programme can be traced back to the party's third successive election defeat in 1987. A policy review process was set in motion in an attempt to break with past commitments and images that were thought to have contributed to Labour's unelectability. Two years later, *Meet the challenge, make the change* (Labour Party, 1989) was published – a precursor of the wave of modernisation documents that would follow within a few years. The intensification of central government control over local councils during Mrs Thatcher's third term leant an air of desperation to Labour thinking. Time, it seemed, was running out and the 1992 general election manifesto committed the party to "radical constitutional reform".

Despite the pain of the unexpected defeat at that election, the constitutional reform bandwagon continued to roll and, under John Smith's leadership, took a revivalist approach to democratic politics. A working group under Tony Blair produced a comprehensive programme, entitled *A new agenda for democracy* and, when in 1994 Blair took over the leadership after Smith's untimely death, the future Labour government's commitment to reform could no longer be in doubt. Nor could the implications of democratic renewal for local government itself. As the 1995 publication *Renewing democracy, rebuilding communities* had put it:

> Local councils exist to serve and speak up for local people. They can only do that properly if they keep in touch with local people and local organisations. Democratic elections are the bedrock on which the whole system is built.... But the ballot box is only part of the story. It is therefore imperative that councils keep in touch with local views between elections. (Labour Party, 1995, p 13)

This was not something that could be left to chance. Control or influence over many local services had passed from locally elected representatives to appointed bodies. As the influence of locally elected representatives diminished, "more resources have been wasted and many of these services have got worse, more expensive and less in touch with local needs" (Labour Party, 1995, p 3). The reforms envisaged are "intended to restore civic pride and renew the very idea of public service. They will contribute to the much-needed renewal of the democratic fabric of our society" (Labour Party, 1995, p 5).

The Labour manifesto for the 1997 election, while less specific and offering fewer rhetorical hostages to fortune, promised more independence for local government. Decisions would be taken "as near to local communities as possible", local authorities would become "less constrained by central government and also more accountable to local people" (Labour Party, 1997, p 32). The only specific commitments, however, were to more frequent elections and "democratic innovations, including elected executive mayors in cities" (Labour Party, 1997, p 34).

Early in 1998 the new government published its proposals for modernising local government in a series of six consultation papers. These papers ranged widely, from community leadership, improved financial accountability and capital finance, to a new ethical framework for the conduct of people in local government. Subsequently, in July 1998, the government published the White Paper *Modern local government: In touch with the people* (DETR, 1998), which set out its overall strategy for the reform of local government. The White Paper was a revivalist charter – the proposals were comprehensive and ambitious. If achieved, they would amount to nothing less than a thoroughgoing renewal of local democracy.

The distinctiveness of Labour's approach to revitalising local government lay in their programme of 'democratic renewal' through involving communities, fostering electoral turnout and enhancing public participation in key decisions affecting local authority service provision. The underlying assumptions were that people were insufficiently interested in their local authorities, knew little about how they were run, and were poorly informed by them. A 'better deal' was called for, and "a bigger say for local people" (DETR, 1998b, p 19). This would be achieved by new political structures to "create a clear and well-known focus for local leadership" and provide for clear accountability (DETR, 1998b, p 24). Most radically, the government proposed to bridge the gulf between the people and local government by increasing the visibility of political leaders through the creation of directly elected mayors (see Chapter Eight). It also promised the reform of electoral systems and procedures to provide for greater public participation, ease of access and enhanced electoral turnout. Local authorities were encouraged to involve people directly in consultative processes through new forms of public involvement, including citizens' juries, panels and referenda.

New Labour's critique

The justification of Labour's far-reaching call for renewal lay in the comprehensive defects of the current system. The 1998 White Paper pulled few punches in its criticisms of local authorities but, in themselves, the criticisms were not new; the difference was one of tone rather than one of substance. As we have seen, successive governments struggled to bring about change in Britain's local authorities through structural reform, alterations to internal management, or a combination of both. For example, claims that "the current framework in which local government operates has not kept pace with the way people live their lives today" (DETR, 1998b, p 13), that local government law "is straight out of the 19th century" (DETR, 1998b, p 15), or that the failings of local government could be attributed to councils' lack of attempts at tackling public apathy and ignorance could have been made by any government since the mid-1960s.

Work carried out for the Maud Committee in 1965 reported that:

> ... very little indication was found that members play a significant role in supplying information about the council and its policies to the public in their locality. (Maud, 1967a, p 27)

In 1969, the Royal Commission on Local Government in England found the relationship between local authorities and the public to be unsatisfactory, and concluded that it was "not uncommon to find contempt expressed" (Redcliffe-Maud, 1969, vol 1, p 28). A subsequent survey published in *The Times* on 6 August 1973 revealed a "widespread lack of public confidence', and warned that unless the central government took action "they will be condemning local government to an era of public distrust'.

Even New Labour's declarations that people have the right to expect decent quality services wherever they live and that differences in service quality cannot be explained solely by local diversity, had a familiar ring, echoing as they did the debates over 'territorial justice' of the 1970s. At the same time, the White Paper went further, focusing its criticisms on specific targets. The tone was hard-hitting, with few concessions to the fact that the Labour Party controlled the great majority of local authorities. The local government framework was accused of allowing inefficiencies to persist and reinforcing an inward-looking culture which failed to put the interests of the people first. Some councils "failed badly in key local services" (DETR, 1998b, p 13) in ways that were "very damaging for local people, their families, and the local community" (DETR, 1998b, p 13). Such failures were "not acceptable and must be tackled" (DETR, 1998b, p 13).

Moreover,

> Too often within a council the members and officers take the paternalistic view that it is for them to decide what services are to be provided, on the basis of what suits the council as a service provider. The interests of the public come a poor second best. The culture is still one where more spending and more taxes are seen as the simple solution rather than exploring how to get more out of the available resources. (DETR, 1998b, p 14)

Despite the attempts of its predecessors to require local authorities to build partnerships with other service providers, some councils stood aloof, and remained insulated from the public gaze in ways which could "open the door to corruption and wrongdoing" (DETR, 1998b, p 14). The inward-looking character of local government prevented councils from building strong and effective relationships with local businesses, detracting from councils' capacity to involve business as a key stakeholder in the local community.

Drafting a political document, the authors of the White Paper could not resist laying the blame at the door of the previous government. They argued that the reforms of the Thatcher/Major years, far from revitalising local democracy, had eroded public attachment to local government. The Conservatives had "weakened public interest and confidence in local government, and reduced councils' capacity to serve their communities".

These trenchant criticisms were tempered by the acknowledgement that some councils are exemplary. The aim would be to level up and make excellence universal rather than sporadic:

> ... change is needed to drive up standards overall, make best practice more widespread, and address those occasional failures. The aim is not to strangle diversity or create dull uniformity, but to make success universal throughout English local government. This is what the Government wishes to see – strong and effective councils everywhere

playing their part in giving people greater opportunities and building a fairer country. (DETR, 1998b, p 13)

The slogan that captured this aim was 'putting local people and communities first'. To achieve this end, a mix of compulsion, opportunity and incentive would be offered to encourage innovation without stifling diversity. The underlying principles of the new framework would be:

> ... to give councils all the opportunities they need to modernise, to promote the well-being of their communities, and to guarantee quality local services; and to provide effective incentives for councils to embrace the modernisation agenda. (DETR, 1998b, p 20)

In that respect the government could be said to be going with the grain of public feeling, for there was growing evidence that the British public were demanding a deeper and more regular involvement in decisions affecting local services and the local environment (Phillips, 1994; Rallings et al, 1994).

What did the modernisation programme imply for the relationship between a council and its community? The principles were simple: first, listening to and involving people; second, redressing the problem of non-voting. Carrying the principles into practice would require a combination of national and local actions.

Listening to and involving people

The White Paper announced the government's wish to see "consultation and participation embedded into the culture of all councils" (DETR, 1998b, p 39) and made central to the production of local authorities' community plans. Although there would be a new statutory duty on councils to consult and engage with their local communities on these issues, they would be able to adopt whatever methods they considered best suited their own particular circumstances. However, the effectiveness of that consultation would be taken into account in the government's assessment of how far an authority is meeting its duty of Best Value. These new requirements went far beyond the existing statutory framework. The 1995 Local Government (Access to Information) Act placed duty on local authorities to ensure public access to information about their decision making and performance. However, the requirements are not exacting and the great majority (81%) of those surveyed in that year found no difficulty in comfortably exceeding the statutory minimum requirements (Steele, 1995, pp 32-3).

The central aim of the new requirements was to increase councils' capacity for two-way communication with local people and thereby influence how decisions are made. In order to reap the benefits of this more open style, local authorities were urged to develop clear strategies for consultation: "[They] need to react openly to feedback or campaigns from those they serve ... and develop a clear view on how to encourage involvement..." (DETR, 1998a, para 4.5). In addressing that task, they would have some prior experience on which to build.

The range of past initiatives

Attempts to reconnect local authorities with the public are not new. During the 1980s, many of those in multiracial areas devised extensive structures of consultation and involvement with minority communities, using forums, specialist committees and widespread cooption to service committees. Thereafter, interest in community consultation expanded and, since the early 1990s, a number of authorities experimented with novel initiatives to increase community input. The techniques currently favoured range from opinion surveys, referendums, citizens' ballots and consensus conferencing, to deliberative opinion polls, standing citizens' panels, citizens' juries and focus groups. A wide range of participatory devices can be found today, almost all seeking to obtain a closer involvement in local issues of small numbers of local people. Some of these amount to entirely new departures in consultative politics, for example, consensus conferencing has been used to seek the informed views of ordinary citizens on scientific or technological matters (Stewart, 1995a). First developed in Denmark for technology assessment in respect of childlessness, food irradiation, electronic identity cards and air pollution, the technique has been imported to Britain and used for the assessment of plant biotechnology and nuclear waste disposal. Its use is spreading rapidly.

Local referendums, on the other hand, are no novelty, but have a long history in Britain. The 1850 Public Libraries Act enabled referendums to be held on the question of whether free public libraries should be established instead of, or in addition to, local museums. Some aspects of the regulation of public houses in Wales and Scotland were similarly decided, while between 1932 and 1972 the Sunday Entertainments Act provided for referendums to be held on whether cinemas should be allowed to open on Sundays. A number of local authorities have also held referendums on a range of topics from comprehensive education to the sale of municipal undertakings (Alderman, 1978, p 196). Referendums have, however, been little used in recent years, although proposals to use them more widely were made by Michael Heseltine in an early draft of the 1980 Local Government Finance Bill. There is some evidence that voters favour such devices and survey research has shown strong support for their employment as an alternative to governmental decisions as far back as 1969 (Jessop, 1974, p 103). Referendums are commonly used in Switzerland, Germany, New Zealand, Italy, Denmark and the US. Referendums might be instituted by the local authority or at the request of the citizens. They could precede decisions, be taken in between decisions to ratify or to endorse, or be taken at any time. Questions to be raised at the referendum could be determined by those instituting the process, moderated by higher level government or settled by an independent agency.

Another, rather similar approach, but one which has attracted considerable attention, is the citizens' jury. This method involves the careful selection of a representative group of local residents to deliberate on a specific issue. Citizens' juries were first introduced in Germany and the US to address a wide range of welfare policy issues, and were promoted in Britain by the Institute of Public Policy Research (Stewart et al, 1994). They give people the opportunity to become involved through a process of selection to obtain a representative group in terms of age, gender, ethnicity, housing tenure and other characteristics. By this means, local authorities can access a range of views from a cross-section of society, and perhaps improve the quality of the eventual decision. One-off focus groups are a less elaborate mechanism for sounding out people's views on specific issues.

Unlike ordinary opinion polls, deliberative opinion polls model what the public would think if they had a more adequate chance to consider the issues. Developed originally in the US to inform presidential candidate selection, Fishkin (1991) advocated the use of deliberative opinion polls in Britain in relation to law and order issues, and his work has been built on in Norwegian experiments (Aars and Offerdal, 2000). In Sweden, study circles have been developed around existing organisations – trades unions, churches, neighbourhood groups and so on – to enable groups of participants to discuss issues. This approach has been adopted in the US in order to set goals for city governments – a device emulated more recently in Britain (Stewart, 1995a). Standing citizens' panels and research panels are among other initiatives in Britain which have been proposed for local authorities to provide local community input to decision making and foster the habit of citizenship.

These are some of the pioneering initiatives being explored by local authorities in the UK. Councils have developed their own mix of strategies to reflect the diversity of local needs and political preferences. Developments in communications technology may extend these experiments to enable larger numbers of people to comment on matters of common concern. Telephone phone-ins have become popular for the media, the publication of email addresses is now more common, video conferencing possibilities have been explored, while interactive television provides radical possibilities for the future (Cooper et al, 1995).

The uptake of initiatives

Local authorities labour under certain basic requirements as to openness and transparency, although these requirements are not particularly exacting. Complaints procedures and consultation forums are the most widespread in practice, while the latest initiatives such as juries and panels are apparent in only a handful of authorities. In a survey of more than 300 local authorities, designed to explore the extent of their adoption, and carried out for the Local Government Management Board (LGMB) in 1996, all but 2% had complaints procedures in place, and all but 21% consultation forums (see Table 22). The use of satisfaction surveys was also comparatively widespread, with 85% reporting their use. In contrast, only 7% of authorities had established citizens' juries.

A study focusing specifically on community consultation carried out for the Department of the Environment, Transport and the Regions (DETR) in 1998 showed a broadly similar pattern. This later survey showed that most councils use a number of forms of consultation and that their use is growing. The trends are clear. Local authorities have in the past acted as closed political and professional communities, often concerned to defend their decision-making processes against public intrusion. Today, they are moving steadily towards more extensive and intensive forms of community consultation (Lowndes et al, 1998, pp 15-18). Although the use of traditional methods, such as consultation papers and public meetings, is much more widespread than more innovative approaches to participation, the uptake of these is increasing.

The government's exhortation to 'listen to and involve' local people has fallen on fertile ground as far as local authorities are concerned. If

Table 22: The adoption of new initiatives in 1996 (%)

Public consultation forums	79
Area-based working	54
Decentralisation	39
Complaints procedures	98
Consumer satisfaction surveys	85
Consumer panels	29
Citizens' juries	7
Base	*307*

Source: LGMB (1997)

the hidebound local authorities of the postwar years are seen as analogous to the 'close' corporations of the 1830s, then the steps being taken today by councils throughout Britain do indeed amount to a second age of reform. To that extent, New Labour is going with the flow, riding the tide of change while encouraging it onward. The end result – if such a term can be applied to the kaleidoscopic patterns of change in a diverse, if small, country – will depend on the interaction of local people desiring (or declining) to take part in local affairs, and local institutions offering (or withholding) the opportunities to do so.

Do people want to be involved?

"Listening to and learning from the public" lies at the heart of Labour's modernising government project (Cunningham, 1999). However, its success depends on how far people actually want to become involved. A number of recent surveys have asked people how well they thought their local councils communicated with them, both about local services and about their own willingness to engage with local issues through consultative processes. Of course, however laudable in itself, providing information, whether read or not, falls a long way short of genuine consultation. Even so, responses were mixed.

Satisfaction with information on local services runs at about the same level as satisfaction with the provision of information on other local matters, and in both cases about as many people are satisfied as dissatisfied (see Table 23). However, it would be a mistake to imagine that such figures reflect variations in actual local authority initiatives. A later survey showed – perhaps surprisingly – that there was no relationship between the amount of consultation a council carries out and the extent to which

Table 23: Council communication with residents (%)

	Council informs about local services	Council informs about other local matters
Very well	8	7
Fairly well	44	42
Not very well	35	37
Not at all well	11	12

Source: British Social Attitudes Survey (1998)

local people feel themselves to be well-informed about its activities (Bromley et al, 1999). Yet survey evidence suggests that many people would welcome opportunities to become more involved, while the 1998 BSA found that more than eight out of 10 of the respondents agreed that 'Local councils would make better decisions if they made more effort to find out what local people want'.

Although there appears to be a broad ground swell of opinion in favour of greater involvement, people's responses are very much conditioned by their own personal characteristics and circumstances, and by the issue under consideration. A recent study carried out for the DETR explored public attitudes to involvement in financial and other decision making. The proportion saying that they would like to take part in important budgetary decisions was as high as 54% among the 25- to 44-year-olds, but only 28% among the over 60s. Only a small minority (15%) took the traditional view that it was the job of councillors and staff to run the council. Men were much keener than women to take part in decisions (52% as against 38%); graduates much keener (62%) than non-graduates, and those with no qualifications the least keen at 27%. Overall, more than half said they would like to be involved and, for a further 16%, their willingness to become involved depended on the issue at stake. One in five wanted no involvement at all (Bromley et al, 1999).

Of the issues people wanted to get involved in, tackling crime rated first (41%) followed by education (33%), traffic and transport. However, the forms of consultation preferred by people emphasised the more passive forms of 'involvement'. Nearly half expressed an interest in contributing via the completion of a postal questionnaire and 30% by telephone survey. However, less than one in four would be prepared to go to the traditional public meeting, fewer still were interested in meeting a councillor. Very few were interested in taking part in citizens' juries, panels, or even having contact with officials.

Of course, few respondents will have had actual experience of taking part in juries, which have received little publicity and cannot be expected to be well known. Nevertheless, the pilot citizens' juries in the UK have shown that the majority of participants found it a rewarding exercise, enhancing their interest in, and awareness of, local government. Reported levels of satisfaction among jury participants are high. For the local authority, participation offers a fresh acquaintance with the views of ordinary people, provides greater visibility for local developments and guides strategic planning (Tsouros, 1990).

Although few would wish to take part in a citizens' jury themselves, people seem well disposed towards them, placing a high degree of trust in their ability to find the right solution to problems. Crucially, that is a trust that seems often denied to councillors themselves. The 1998 BSA survey presented respondents with a hypothetical proposal inviting them to imagine a scheme for 'a major new building development in this neighbourhood'. They were asked first, how much they would trust their local councillors 'to come to the best view about the proposal' and, how far they would trust 'a "jury" of 12/15 ordinary local people chosen at random' to do so. Table 24 below shows that respondents make a sharp distinction between the ability of councillors and ordinary people to 'come to the best view'. While well over half were prepared to place their trust in juries most of the time, many fewer would trust councillors with local development issues. The study undertaken for the DETR on perceptions of local finance found comparable results, with 35% trusting councillors always or most of the time on building development, and 54% trusting the citizens' jury. This distrust of councillors appears to extend beyond the handling of ad hoc proposals, for two thirds of the BSA respondents agreed that 'A council that wants to increase the council tax by more than inflation should have to get a majority vote in favour through a local referendum'.

Table 24: Who to trust on local development? (%)

	Trust councillors	Trust 'jury'
Just about always	2	8
Most of the time	33	55
Only some of the time	45	27
Almost never	15	6

Source: British Social Attitudes Survey (1998)

Limitations

Just as the experience of widening participation suggests ways forward for local authorities, so too does it expose the limits of such initiatives, and temper the claims made for them. Is participation effective? What bias might it introduce to local decision making? And do people know enough about their councils and the issues they face to participate meaningfully?

First, how effective are these various initiatives? Table 25 shows that few authorities in 1996 claimed any of these initiatives to have had a major effect on their decision making. Irrespective of the type of initiative, only between a quarter and a third of those adopting them cited major change following their adoption. The 1998 study for the DETR produced a comparable pattern for initiatives in general, but went further by demonstrating a range of claimed benefits. These, however, related mainly to specific ad hoc decisions (the siting of traffic calming measures, for example) rather than strategic priorities. More than one fifth of the responding authorities had reported 'very little impact'; a similar proportion reported a 'strong' influence. Another fifth found their decisions confirmed by consultation, while 16% thought their decisions 'better informed' (Lowndes et al, 1998, p 49). Valuable though these gains might be, they are modest, and hardly amount to a revitalisation of local democracy.

Despite a cautiously favourable reception by local authorities, the difficulties encountered in implementing community participation should not be underestimated. Citizen participation in decision making can slow up the process, opening up the potential for more conflict. Lack of official or political support and the difficulty in determining *who* should participate may undermine the aims of participation as a means of securing

Table 25: The effect of new initiatives (%)

	Major effect	Minor/no effect	Not adopted
Public consultation forums	27	52	21
Area-based working	18	36	46
Decentralisation	12	27	61
Complaints procedures	20	78	2
Consumer satisfaction surveys	30	55	15
Consumer panels	8	21	71
Citizens' juries	2	5	93

Source: LGMB (1997)

informed lay views in the decision process; the right to participate may be contested between groups and their representatives. Furthermore, participation provides an opportunity for protest against, and criticism of, local policies that may encourage members and officers to discount community input and sideline or terminate participatory programmes.

Nor are participatory initiatives free from the risk of bias. Where standing arrangements have been made for citizen participation in health decision making, evidence suggests that, in the past, participants tended to be drawn from local elites, at the expense of minority and excluded groups (Klein and Lewis, 1976; Piette, 1990; Jeffrey, 1997). Arrangements of this type thus suffer from a tendency to bias in favour of the more resourceful elements; since,

> The political preferences of these segments usually do not mirror those of the total population, there is every reason to believe that without sufficient institutionalisation of new forms of participation, [equality of outcome] would be impaired, which would result in social conflict and de-legitimisation. (Kaase, 1984, p 314)

Even where a more representative community group has been involved, real influence may not follow: a major international report on citizen involvement observed a widespread tendency to leave actual decisions in the hands of professionals, with too little attention given to facilitating lay input (Euro Reports, 1983). The current initiatives may be seen as attempts to overcome these characteristic problems.

The third problem concerns lack of knowledge. It is commonly agreed that a vital local democracy rests on people possessing a good understanding of local politics and taking sufficient interest in local affairs. It is equally recognised that understanding is limited. A number of surveys undertaken since 1985 have explored the extent to which people understand and are aware of their local authority and what it does (Widdicombe 1986b; Bloch and John, 1991; Lynn, 1992; Young and Rao, 1995, 1997a; Bromley et al, 1999; Rao and Young, 1999). A composite measure of overall knowledge, applied consistently across several surveys, rated half the respondents as uninformed (Young and Rao, 1997a, pp 120-7). Levels of knowledge vary with educational background, occupation, age, gender and household status, with older and better educated male heads of household – the paradigmatic local citizen – the most knowledgeable (Emmerson et al, 1998).

Knowledge and understanding are partly a matter of exposure to

information. A study of people's levels of exposure to council publications
– Council Tax booklets, leaflets and council newspapers – categorised
almost half of the respondents as having a low level of exposure, defined
as having glanced (at most) at a circulated publication, or having picked
up a leaflet about the council's finances as shown in Table 26 (Bromley et
al, 1999). Only 12% were rated as having a high level of exposure, defined
as having received and read the main forms of council communication.
Not surprisingly, levels of exposure were strongly related to length of
residence and age, with the large majority of younger and more transient
residents reporting either no, or scarcely any, exposure to council
communications.

Local authorities seek to make headway in the face of these problems
of limited effectiveness, risks of conflict and lack of public knowledge of
their operations. However, many have acted in the past on an unquestioned
assumption that they themselves are best placed to promote public
involvement. This may not be so. Because of their responsibilities in
executing public policy, and the limits on their actual powers, local
authorities are necessarily constrained in their relations with the wider
public. To invite public participation is to imply a commitment to act,
even on issues where political priorities and professional judgement run
counter to public preferences. Nor is it clear where accountability lies
when public choices do prevail. It can be argued that rather than promote

Table 26: Exposure to council information (%)

	Low	Medium	High	Base
Age				
18-24	76	23	1	147
25-44	55	35	10	791
45-59	40	46	14	518
60+	35	46	19	612
Length of residence				
Less than 2 years	68	28	4	268
2-5 years	55	36	9	322
5-10 years	42	46	12	293
10-15 years	47	42	11	284
15+ years	42	41	16	894
Total	48	39	12	2,074

Source: Bromley et al (1999, pp 34-7)

and encourage participation, public authorities should stand back and allow other, non-statutory bodies – political parties and pressure groups – to run campaigns. This would enable local authorities to determine the strength of public feeling before they act, for a further problem underlying all sponsored participation is that British people are characteristically unwilling to involve themselves in community affairs.

Levels of involvement

Community participation implies that local people have both the opportunity and the capacity to make a contribution to local decision making. Despite councils' attempts to disseminate information, and consult and involve communities, the British public's spontaneous willingness to involve themselves in local affairs itself is known not to be high. Rather, there is an active minority of 'joiners' who are the most likely to get caught up in participation initiatives. Membership of organisations is associated with both political self-confidence and activism or quality of the few rather than the many. Even those who not consider their involvement in organisations to have political relevance, and from whom little active participation is expected, are nonetheless likely to have higher levels of political confidence or efficacy than non-members. And studies undertaken during the 1960s found that such people were also more likely to actually participate in political life than the public at large (Almond and Verba, 1963, pp 307-22; Berry, 1969, pp 196-207).

Surveys conducted since the 1980s (see for example Table 27) showed only a minority of the British public to have ever been involved in local political party organisations. While levels of political awareness may be high, and some may even profess an interest in politics, few are prepared to spend time participating in local affairs. In this respect, Britain is not dissimilar to other European countries, but falls far behind the US where conventional forms of political participation are found to be substantially higher. For example, whereas only 11% of British electors reported having the experience of working through organised groups, a similar measure in the US found that as many as 34% had done so. Whereas fewer than one in 10 Britons had contacted their MP, more than twice that proportion of Americans reported having contacted their Congressman. Many more Americans claim to have actively worked for a party or candidate during an election than is the case in Britain (Parry et al, 1992, pp 44-5). However, there is some evidence that the willingness of Britons to contact their elected representatives is increasing.

Table 27: Reported political activity (%)

Have done at least once:	
Party campaigning	
fund-raising	5
canvassing	4
clerical work	4
attended election rally	9
Group activity	
informal group	14
organised group	11
raised issue in group	5
Contacted	
MP	10
civil servant	7
councillor	21
town hall	17
media	4

Source: Parry et al (1992)

Another regularly used measure of community activism is attendance at council meetings. A 1992 DoE study asked whether respondents had ever attended a meeting of a county, borough, district, city or parish council or a committee meeting, and asked for the reason why, in those cases where a respondent had done so. Overall, 8% of respondents had attended a local meeting over the last 12 months (excluding meetings in relation to the Community Charge). Respondents were also asked if they had ever attended a public meeting on a local issue; 9% had done so, with a higher proportion of non-manual workers, the middle-aged and better qualified and owner-occupiers attending (Lynn, 1992). A comparable question in the 1994 BSA produced similar responses.

In Britain, the search for the 'community-conscious elector' has centred on those with a strong sense of community responsibility, as measured both by their attitudes and by their involvement in local organisations. The Maud Committee survey explored the characteristics and predispositions of those most likely to participate in local affairs (Maud, 1967c). These were – unsurprisingly, in the light of the US studies – middle-aged men of longstanding residence. The likelihood that an individual will be a member of a local organisation is similarly associated with length of residence. Today, as Table 28 shows, few Britons are actually members of local community groups.

Individuals vary quite considerably in their propensities to become involved and in the participatory styles they manifest. Only a minority of members are actually active in the organisations to which they belong. Active members of any of these organisations are more likely to be middle-aged, better qualified, non-manual workers, and owner-occupiers. Further analysis shows that women are slightly more likely to be members of local organisations, despite their under-representation in local elective politics and, as we have seen, they are slightly more likely to vote in local elections.

The 1994 BSA survey elicited responses to such statements as 'People like me can have a real influence on politics if they are prepared to get involved'; and 'I feel I could do as good a job as councillor as most other people'. Both statements received positive responses from around a third of those interviewed, showing that more people feel confident in their ability to influence political decision making than actually exert themselves to do so. Not surprisingly, there are striking differences between groups, with older people and women notably less confident than middle-aged people and men in respect of both their sense of potential influence and their ability to be a good councillor.

Generally, women are less involved in political life than men, despite their higher rate of membership of local organisations. However, the

Table 28: Membership of local organisations (%)

Respondent is member of:	
Local environmental group	8
Other local community group	7
Local conservation group	2
Neighbourhood council	1
Neighbourhood watch scheme	13
Parish/town council	1
Political party	3
Parent/teacher association	3
Tenants'/residents' association	5
School governing body	1
Base	*2,302*

Source: British Social Attitudes Survey (1998)

pattern becomes far more complex when different age groups are taken into account, for while younger women are very much more active than older women, age makes less difference to participation rates among men. Taking men and women together, both life cycle and generational effects bear on political action, suggesting that the future of political participation in Britain will be very different from the past. In the words of Parry and his colleagues:

> The strong commitment to voting and party campaigning, so discernible amongst older citizens ... may be eroded and slowly replaced by commitments to ... more directly issue-based participation.... Whether this is so will only be fully revealed after the tide of events has moved on. It may be that the sense of youthful disaffection from conventional politics was only a passing feature of the 1980s, or it may be a more lasting and therefore consequential change. (Parry et al, 1992, pp 170-1)

Attachment to the community

In the US, a prerequisite for local political involvement appears to be community identification, or sense of attachment to the local community. Putnam found that longer standing residents or those who have 'settled down to stay' identify most strongly with the locality and are the most sensitive to local issues (Putnam, 1966). Similarly, Schwartz's analysis of the background characteristics of aspirants to political office found that they tended to come primarily from those closely tied to their community by residence of more than 20 years' standing (Schwartz, 1969, pp 561-8). Actual or intended length of residence drives participation in local affairs more powerfully than any other factor.

Despite these differences, so few people actually report being involved in local political life that it is difficult to explore how their characteristics differ from those of the non-involved. But what can be said is that, if, as in the US, community involvement is driven by a sense of attachment or rootedness, then the reason for low levels of participation in Britain might be sought in the low levels of community attachment. Contrary to what might be expected, most British people are not particularly attached to where they live. Redcliffe-Maud's study, carried out in 1967 by the Government Social Survey, found electors to have varying degrees of attachment to their local areas. Around 80% of the respondents could identify a 'home' area – an ability that increased with length of residence within it. But these areas they generally saw as being substantially smaller than their local authorities, most (about two thirds) of the respondents being oriented to an area the size of their ward or parish.

Reanalysis of studies of more than 48,000 electors in non-metropolitan England, carried out for the Local Government Commission and published in 1996, supported this finding. Despite more than quarter of a century of urban and social change, many people expressed attachment only to the smallest level of social organisation – that of the neighbourhood. This attachment was strongest in rural areas and in the more affluent suburbs. Within these areas, it was the longest standing residents who were the most strongly attached to the imagined local community. Yet these 'villagers' were not the largest group within this large sample, for they accounted for just a quarter of all the respondents. The largest group – almost a third in all – were dubbed 'the unattached': those with no sense of affinity with the place where they lived, at any spatial scale from neighbourhood to county.

Although such a finding is startling in itself, the actual structure of this group held few surprises. The most powerful factor shaping non-identification was length of residence – there being a strong linear relationship between the length of time lived in the locality and the ability to identify at any level. Those who have lived in the locality for a year or less were the most likely to be unattached, with a gradual tailing off to the resident of long standing (20 years or more) who is the least likely to be found in this group. For the longer standing residents among the unattached, those in rural areas were the least likely to be found, and those in urban areas the most likely. So it would appear that type of area and personal circumstance combine to drive attachment to the community. Longstanding residents in rural or semi-rural areas are at one end of a continuum, and recent movers in the most urban – especially older urban – areas at the other (Young et al, 1996).

The questions of who participates and who does not, and what conditions promote or constrain participation are clearly important. The extent to which an individual possesses the characteristics that are associated with political participation tells us how likely they are to be active in their community's politics. More interesting by far is the question of *why* people behave, politically, as they do. There is another factor to be considered: the extent to which people believe their own participation in local political life to be worthwhile, in that it would make a difference to the state of affairs in their area. And as it happens, low levels of participation are matched by modest levels of confidence which people express in their own efficacy – the belief that, if they wished, they could achieve something in the world of politics. This is something which the Maud Committee's researchers defined as "a reflection of the individual's standing in the community and his or her power to influence local events" (Maud, 1967c, p 76), a critical factor in the prospects for revitalising local democracy.

Redressing the problem of non-voting

The low turnout typical of British local elections, explored in Chapter Five, has prompted the search for ways of motivating electors and improving turnout. The importance of voting is, first, that the right to vote is *universal*, whether or not it is exercised, and second, that there is some presumption that citizens have a *duty* to vote, a presumption that is not extended to other forms of political participation.

The White Paper *Modern local government: In touch with the people* (DETR, 1998b) acknowledged that the process of voting is an integral part of the wider discussion of political participation, with issues of electoral reform needing to be set in a broad context of ways to achieve democratic renewal. The government's analysis of the state of local democracy seems broadly accurate: low levels of interest and engagement in local politics, and only faltering support for local democracy. Many people have little information about what role local government performs and lack stable opinions on the subject. Miller (1988) has shown that some opinions on local government issues may, to some extent, be no more than 'pseudo-opinions': more or less random responses to questions that are not seen as particularly meaningful. Although our own analysis shows that a composite score on a set of attitude questions has some predictive value for voting behaviour, the overall conclusion is inescapable – that local democracy has a painfully low salience.

The government is committed to changing this situation and bringing about democratic renewal through stimulating interest in both local politics and electoral reform to make it easier and more convenient for people to cast a vote. This second commitment, already filtering through into legislation, addresses just one side of an equation, the resolution of which is the sum of individual acts of voting. It must be conceded that electoral arrangements bear on the cost of voting, in the sense of the inconvenience that must be undergone if a vote is to be cast – voting is not cost free. But can the cost be significantly lowered? Probably, however low the cost of voting can be forced – telephone voting from home would be the device of lowest conceivable cost – there will still be a substantial number of non-voters. These are people who are simply not interested enough to vote, however low the cost. Other factors are less directly amenable to government influence: people's interest in, and commitment to, local democracy, their attachment to the political community, or the importance they vest in their locality's future.

In the government's view, new methods must be found to remove the disincentives to vote, to promote greater electoral participation by making voting easier and streamlining the processes both of casting votes and of counting them. While recognising the strengths of British electoral practice – in particular the "enviable record of electoral probity" – the White Paper argued that the current arrangements have failed to keep pace with change (DETR, 1998b). Accepting that, in the main, British elections are free and fairly conducted and that, in principle, every citizen has the right to vote, the government argues that there are barriers and obstacles that have to be overcome before the public can fully exercise the right to vote. Their proposals for reform date back to the Labour party's internal review of electoral systems, undertaken some years earlier. That report concluded that:

> There is a growing unease that the conduct of elections is inadequate and inefficient. Modern forms of electioneering are governed by outdated rules, without proper regulation, as are many constitutional and electoral matters.... (Labour Party, 1993, p 40)

The complexity of the local electoral system was criticised by the Maud Committee and the Redcliffe-Maud Commission in the 1960s, while the later Widdicombe Committee acknowledged that "... a system which is as complex and inconsistent as the present one is hardly calculated to encourage electoral participation" (Widdicombe, 1986a, para 7.15). Widdicombe went on to argue that:

> ... citizens have a reasonable expectation that the electoral arrangements should be simple, and that when they move from one area to another the arrangements should be the same unless there is a clear case to the contrary. We cannot see such a case. The current differences seem to be almost entirely a matter of historical accident, relating to the electoral fashion at the time the antecedents of the current authorities were created. (Widdicombe, 1986a, para 7.15)

These points apply with particular force to the complex situation whereby different types of local authorities operate different types of electoral arrangements.

Local authorities' responses to the government's proposals for annual elections were mixed, with some concerned about 'voter fatigue' setting in. Despite this hesitation, the government decided to build on this system of elections held in three years out of four for one third of the councillors. Already the system exists in the metropolitan districts, and it may be extended to the unitary district councils and the London boroughs. In the 'fallow' year, in which there would be no election for councillors, other elections – for example for directly-elected mayors – would be held. It was deemed important, in two-tier areas, to avoid having annual elections for both counties and districts. In these areas, districts and counties will elect by halves in alternate years, with half of the district council elected in one year, half of the county council elected in the next and so on, with all councillors thus serving a four-year term. Changing the local electoral system in this way, the government argues, will enhance accountability, be simpler, and more readily understood by electors.

The contrary argument – which the government dismisses – is that authorities need continuity in order to press ahead with their policies without the costs and uncertainties that come from continuously attending to electoral prospects. These were matters which particularly exercised the Widdicombe Committee in the mid-1980s. The merits of the system of annual elections were seen to be primarily on grounds of sustaining political continuity and sharpening accountability. Equally, while allowing for opportunities to resolve problems in hung councils without having to wait for a long time, the Committee argued that a system of annual elections would produce councils that are more representative of the political complexion of an area. It would therefore be possible to avoid the whole council being elected in an untypical electoral year, when one party may be particularly popular or unpopular because of mid-term national factors.

At the end of the day, however, Widdicombe was persuaded by the argument that too frequent elections would put policy continuity and consistency at risk and discourage forward planning. Importantly, a move to annual elections was seen as having a negative effect on public interest and the Committee concluded that "public interest is likely to be heightened if the whole council is being elected and there is thereby a greater chance of changing the political control of the council". Annual elections were also not considered cost-effective and on balance it would be advantageous to have whole council elections throughout England and Wales (Widdicombe, 1986a, para 7.26).

Similar arguments are to be found in the current proposals for changing electoral procedures. It is claimed that the procedures for voter registration and for the casting of votes do not recognise the higher levels of mobility today. Where people live, and therefore vote, is often not where they work. People move home more frequently and compiling electoral registers annually cannot accommodate this. Ignorance is a major barrier and the government urges local authorities to carry out their statutory duty to make every effort to ensure maximum registration through effective local publicity.

The government has already moved to reform electoral practices and maximise voter registration by maintaining rolling registers to encourage participation in elections and improving access for people with disabilities under the 2000 Representation of the People Act. Local authorities are permitted to experiment in electoral practice, including electronic voting, mobile polling stations, voting in different hours, on different days, or over a number of days holding elections entirely by postal vote.

Public responses to electoral reform

The 1998 BSA survey was part-funded by the DETR and included a question module which largely corresponded to the government's proposals for the renewal of local democracy. This survey enables us to consider how far the changes put forward are likely to win public support and from whom. Not all the 3,400 respondents were asked for their views on these issues. For the most part, the local democracy questions were put to a third of the respondents. These are sufficient for us to assess, first, the extent of support for change and, second, whether the changes are likely to bring about increases in electoral turnout.

Support for change

Taking first attitudes to annual elections and whole council elections, opinion was evenly divided, with 45% supporting the proposition that 'Local elections should be held every year so that we can soon make it clear if we think our local council is doing a bad job'. Almost the same proportion (42%) supported the contrary proposition that 'Local elections should be held every three or four years or else local councils will never get anything done'. Although 11% could not decide, the figures here are comparable with those obtained when the question was last asked, in the Widdicombe survey of 1985, with rather more non-voters than voters favouring a four-yearly cycle.

Another proposal is to move local elections from the traditional Thursday ballot to the weekend, to give the greatest opportunity to vote at times when people are likely to be available. Respondents were asked to state their preference between Thursday and weekend elections – a choice that was presented in terms of the supposed advantages of each. Almost half expressed no particular preference for either, the remainder being more or less equally divided (see Table 29).

Table 29: Voting at weekends and on Thursdays (%)

Local elections should be held over a weekend because more people would be able to go and vote	30
Local elections should still be held on a Thursday because people have better things to do with their time at the weekend	20
I don't mind either way	48

Source: British Social Attitudes Survey (1998)

The government has set out to target young voters, and it is indeed younger people – those under 34 – who have the strongest preference for weekend over Thursday voting. The difference narrows with rising age, with those over 60 showing a distinct preference for the existing system. A survey carried out by MORI revealed similar findings in that younger people were found to be more receptive to changes than older age groups (1998). Clearly, this relationship reflects people's availability to vote, with those over 60 finding it easier to vote during the week. However, as noted in Chapter Five, it is confirmed non-voters – those who chose not to vote in the 1998 local elections – who most strongly favour change of polling day to the weekend.

The next proposal considered is the option to vote by post, rather than by travelling to the polling station (see Table 30), in recognition of the more mobile patterns of modern life, wherein increasing numbers of people may live outside the electoral district in which they are registered, or even in another authority.

The BSA survey found strong majority support for continuing the present arrangements for voting at the polling station (Table 30). In exploring these patterns we are looking for broad differences between subgroups rather than precise measurement of those differences. Accordingly, we can use the wider definition of non-voting to mean

Table 30: Voting by post and at polling stations (%)

Everyone should be allowed to vote by post in local elections because more people would use their vote	38
People should normally have to go to a polling station to vote because that is the only way we can be sure that elections are run fairly	59

Source: British Social Attitudes Survey (1998)

those who actually did not vote, for whatever reason, in the last local election in which they had the opportunity to do so. The more restricted measure used in the first model reported in Chapter Five is less appropriate here. That said, there were marked differences in the responses of those who actually voted, and those who did not. Two thirds of the 'voters' thought it proper for votes to be cast at the polling station, and just one third favoured postal voting. Among the 'non-voters', opinion was evenly divided on this issue. Again, younger people were more likely to support innovation, but it should be remembered that they are the least interested in local politics and very much the least likely to vote.

Respondents were also asked which of two ways of voting they would prefer to use, filling in a ballot paper, as at present, or 'pressing a computer button' in some unspecified location. The majority of people had no preference on this issue. However, three quarters of those who stated a preference would choose to mark their ballot paper. However, as with the other aspects of proposed reforms to local elections, it is the 'voters' who show the strongest preference for the traditional ballot paper – 38% – compared with just 23% of the non-voters. Also, older people are more committed to the traditional system than are the young and, as we have seen, they are themselves more likely to vote.

At this point, it is possible to pull together the findings on the various proposed changes to electoral arrangements and consider their reception among those who do, and those who do not, vote. The case for change, however, depends, in the first instance, on non-voters registering stronger support for a departure from the present practice, for it is their behaviour that government seeks to influence. Table 31 shows that these four changes are supported to a greater extent by non-voters than voters, although in the case of annual elections the margin is very small. It is also important to note that the proportion of either group expressing support for change is, in the case of voting by computer, quite low. This is because large proportions in both groups are indifferent as between a reformed system and the *status quo*. The sterner test of reform proposals is, of course, whether people think they would act differently under changed conditions.

Reviving local democracy

Table 31: Reaction to proposed reforms among voters and non-voters (%)

	Preferred by voters	Preferred by non-voters
Annual elections to local councils	44	47
Weekend voting	25	36
Postal voting	32	46
Voting by computer	7	17

Source: British Social Attitudes Survey (1998)

The likely effects of change

The important issue is whether support for reform is likely to translate into actual changes in behaviour. In other words, would the government's proposals, if implemented, succeed in bringing about change by enhancing participation and strengthening local democracy? Enhancing electoral participation is central to the modernisation programme. The programme stands or falls on its likely effect on those who do not at present vote. In the third section of this chapter we examine the likely effect of the reforms on actual behaviour.

To begin, it is useful to return to the several propositions discussed above, to discover how people respond to electoral arrangements being changed in the ways suggested. The respondents were asked, 'Do you think you would be *more likely* to vote if local elections were held over a weekend rather than a Thursday, *less likely*, or would it *not make any difference?*' Table 32 below shows that for a large majority none of these changes would make a difference to the likelihood of their voting.

Table 32: Likelihood of voting under new arrangements (%)

	Weekend voting	Postal voting	Voting in shop/ Post Office
More likely to vote	16	20	22
Makes no difference	75	71	68
Less likely	7	8	9

Source: British Social Attitudes Survey (1998)

The comparison of the likely reactions of those who reported that they voted in the last local election and those who reported that they did not is crucial, and is shown in Table 33. The figures must be handled with

158

Table 33: Likelihood of voting, by reported voting (%)

	More likely to vote	No difference	Less likely to vote	Net difference
Weekend elections				
voters	7	85	9	−2
non-voters	29	65	6	+23
Postal voting				
voters	9	81	9	−
non-voters	34	60	6	+28
Voting in shops				
voters	13	76	11	+2
non-voters	35	59	6	+29

Source: British Social Attitudes Survey (1998)

great circumspection as there is considerable overreporting of voting. Whether they would behave differently under electoral reform can only be judged from their statement that they would be more, or less likely to vote. The broad conclusion to be drawn is that the three changes in the voting system investigated here produce a much more positive response from non-voters than from voters. This suggests that turnout might well be increased by holding elections on weekends, by introducing postal voting and voting at shops and Post Offices.

The BSA survey did not explore the further possibility of voting by telephone using a secure PIN number, although this has also been considered by the government and is likely to feature in the next phase of the debate on renewing local democracy. However, this item *was* included in the 1998 survey by MORI and proved to be the most likely of all the changes to encourage people to vote. The survey revealed similar findings to those of the BSA Survey, but on a more refined range of options for reform. Overall, people were more likely to vote through the introduction of postal voting by a margin of 14%; voting at shops, 35% more likely; and at supermarkets, 32% more likely.

Making polling stations more convenient would, however, be the easiest reform to implement, and the MORI study concluded that:

> Polling stations open for a limited period on one weekday does not suit many people's lifestyles. In particular, it affects commuters and people who work shifts. Extending the voting period to accommodate different work patterns is necessary to help ensure everyone has the best opportunity to exercise their right to vote. (MORI, 1998, p 24)

Furthermore,

> Having a polling station in more convenient, more prominent locations
> would certainly be beneficial. For those who are either too busy to
> vote or simply not aware of the election, combining voting with either
> shopping or commuting would fit better to modern lifestyles. The
> added advantage of the local supermarket or shopping centre is that
> most people in the area know where it is. (MORI, 1998, pp 25)

The general supposition is simple and intuitively right: if the cost of
voting is lowered, people are more likely to vote. A reading of Table 34
shows that changes to electoral arrangements can be expected to have
quite marked effects on actual voting behaviour. On each of these issues,
non-voters report that they are far more likely to vote. In terms of
overall electoral turnout, the net benefits appear to be strongly positive.
The MORI survey findings extended to identifying the group most likely
to be affected by change. Younger people were much more in favour of
making voting easier, including improving access to the locations they
visit, extending opening times and greater use of technology.

However, it must be remembered that the measures used are notoriously
imperfect: use of reported voting has limited validity given the extent of

Table 34: Response to voting reform initiatives by age group (%)

More likely to vote if...	all	18-24	25-34	35-44	45-54	55-64	65+
Voting from home using the telephone	40	49	50	45	39	33	26
Polling stations at shopping centres	38	46	40	44	38	38	27
Polling stations at supermarkets	37	45	42	42	36	34	24
Extending voting for more than a day	32	53	41	35	25	22	22
Voting by post	26	29	35	30	18	20	21
Voting on the internet	26	35	37	31	27	17	8
Polling stations open 24 hours	24	37	38	25	20	15	9
Voting on Saturday rather than Thursday	22	28	29	25	20	16	14
Voting on Sunday rather than Thursday	16	21	20	18	17	9	11
To have polling stations at train stations	14	12	18	14	14	14	11

Source: MORI (1998)

over-reporting. At the same time, changes to the local electoral system may have so low a salience as to evoke only indifference and near random responses which lack reliability. The overall conclusion must be no more than that the effects of these reforms on actual turnout are likely to be positive but probably rather weak.

Will reform bring renewal?

New Labour's modernisation agenda covers both the enhancement of participation and the establishment of new forms of political leadership. The two are not unconnected, for it is assumed that focusing authority on a single personality – a directly elected mayor – will bring the voters to the polls. Responses to the new political leadership proposals are a matter for the next chapter; suffice at this point to consider the likely effects of the participation proposals.

The first thing to be said is that when local authorities are castigated for their reluctance to open up their processes to popular participation and, at the same time, praised for doing just that, it becomes difficult to disentangle truth from the web of claims and counterclaims. The evidence from large-scale studies of local authority practice carried out toward the end of the 1990s suggests that authorities are indeed picking up on this aspect of the modernisation agenda, that modest changes have become widespread and indeed were doing so well before May 1997. It is less clear, however, that the 'innovative' forms of participation commended by New Labour have been particularly widely adopted, or that they are seen as having major effects on local decision making.

Against this modest record can be set the persuasive evidence that the public wish to see a far wider participation, with many more opportunities to contribute to local deliberations, on both services and financial policies. Although never more than a minority, it is the most active minority – the well-endowed middle class – who press most strongly for a seat at the table. This is the social group most likely to participate in community affairs, and it is plausible to expect opportunities to participate to be eagerly taken up. However, drawing in the more peripheral or excluded social groups will take effort and ingenuity. Everything known about public participation suggests that the effort needs to be made if the familiar result of the middle-class 'capture' of participation initiatives is to be avoided.

Meanwhile, most people display rather low levels of trust in their elected representatives, with majorities favouring referenda and placing greater trust in the ability of a lay 'jury' to take development decisions than in a committee of elected councillors. None of this augurs well for local representative democracy. Nevertheless, the representative process remains, supplemented, rather than replaced, by the growth of participatory or consultative mechanisms.

New Labour came to office with a commitment to democratic renewal. Many of its criticisms about how local elections work have been aired before and command wide assent. Some of the newer ideas – particularly the exploitation of technology for electoral purposes – remain to be tested. The evidence reviewed in this chapter suggests variable enthusiasm for aspects of electoral reform, with proposals tolerated rather than warmly supported by those who have the habit of voting. This is not surprising: those who vote are less likely to see the need for radical change. Those who do not vote support change, often by large margins, and, most importantly, it is they who claim that they would be more likely to vote were reforms to be introduced.

Whether this happens remains to be seen. The factors which bear on the decision to vote are complex. Certainly, the cost and convenience of doing so must be taken into account, and lowering the cost of voting can be expected to increase turnout to some extent. On the other side of the equation are the civic inclinations that, when present, make people feel that they should vote, or even that they positively want to do so. Democratic renewal must operate on that side of the equation too, and for that we must look to the government's proposals to renew local democracy by modernising local leadership.

EIGHT

The modernising agenda: new forms of political leadership

The British system of local government, rooted in its 19th-century tradition, is essentially 'government by committee'. Councils make decisions through their committees, to whom they may delegate their powers. All decisions originate as committee decisions and all councillors – including those from the minority parties – are, in theory, able to participate in decision making. The particular strengths of the committee system relate to its historic role in political development, which Harold Laski, writing in 1935, judged this to be of great significance:

> on the whole, anyone who compares the quality of local government today with what it was one hundred years ago, cannot avoid the conclusion that ... the committee system has proved itself. It stands, with the Cabinet and the modern Civil Service, as one of the fundamental English contributions to the difficult art of self-government.... It has not only been a nursery of local statesmanship, some of it of remarkable quality; it has served also as a means of fertilising Westminster with the results of local experience. Its success has been a safeguard against that easy tendency to centralisation which is the paralysis of effective self-government ... the techniques of the committee will certainly be found to be the pivot which makes possible the democratic operation of local government. (Laski, 1935, pp 107-8)

This essential quality of local government remains, albeit in a state of continuous change and development. True, the wide diffusion of power typical of the past is today rarely found in practice, for most authorities are run on party lines, with key decisions *made* behind closed doors by the majority group before being presented to committee and council to be formally *taken*. Similarly, the overall direction of council business is no longer left to the vagaries of collective decision, for most councils recognise the position of leader – usually the strongest person among the majority party members. Nevertheless, the committee system remains a procedural, if not a political, reality for all local authorities.

Laski's applause notwithstanding, this defining characteristic has also been local government's most criticised feature. For more than 30 years the traditional shape and operation of local government has been subject to near-continuous examination and proposals for reform. It was recognised as early as the 1930s that "the great fault of committees, which seems to be widespread, is the tendency to do detailed administration themselves instead of leaving it to the officials" (Redcliffe-Maud, 1969, p 352; Bains, 1972, pp 4, 16). Increasing complexity of local authority business made it more difficult to achieve quick and efficient decision making through the traditional committee system; the committee system functioned as a brake on sensible delegation, as councillors were reluctant to let go of any powers. The Maud Committee considered the participation of the members in so much detail "to be the root cause of local government's administrative troubles" (Maud, 1967a, p 10). This involvement in time-consuming detail took away energy from "a crisp and substantial involvement in matters of policy" (Dearlove, 1979, p 187).

So the criticism was three-fold. First, a slow, cumbersome and indecisive means of getting business processed; second, an institutionalised disincentive to delegate decisions to officials; third, a propensity to attend to detail at the expense of policy. For many years, local authorities have been taking steps to remedy these admitted shortcomings, streamlining their decision-taking structures in the interests of greater efficiency and effectiveness. This has typically involved reducing the number of committees, their size and the frequency of their meetings. Until now, the alternatives contemplated have been based on the traditional premise: that the system of decision making should continue to be one in which the authority remains a corporate body with decisions taken openly by the whole council, or on its behalf in committee. The Blair government's 2000 Local Government Act is intended to bring about a radical departure from that assumption and usher in a new era of local authority decision making.

New Labour's critique

Attacking the committee system of decision making for its alleged inefficiency, New Labour added further criticisms of opaqueness and lack of accountability. Few local people, it was said, know who runs their council. Most are unsure who to hold to account, or who to complain to when things go wrong.

> Significant decisions are, in many councils, taken behind closed doors by political groups or even a small group of key people within the majority group. Consequently, many councillors, even those in the majority group, have little influence over council decisions. (DETR, 1998b, p 25)

Accordingly, local people often do not know who is really taking the decisions: "People identify most readily with an individual, yet there is rarely any identifiable figure leading the local community" (DETR, 1998b, p 25). This shortcoming is attributed, not to the failings of local politicians themselves, but to the system within which they are forced to work. New executive arrangements are required.

Another key aim of the government's proposals is to make councils more representative and attract new people into local government. This is no new concern. Chapter Three showed how a desire to make local government more attractive to a wide range of people was behind the establishment of the Maud Committee in the early 1960s and coloured all its considerations. The preoccupation remained for the governments that followed, with ministers regularly lamenting the quality of councillors. But while the aim then was to attract people of greater 'calibre' in the interests of improved management, today, achieving representativeness is seen as valuable for its own sake. Minister for Local Government Hilary Armstrong declared:

> We need people from all groups in our communities to come forward and offer their services as councillors. We need to break free from the pattern so often found today where many councillors are relatively old, few are women, and even fewer are drawn from ethnic minorities. (Armstrong, 1999, p 21)

Towards greater representativeness

There are, of course, no direct means by which a government can achieve greater representativeness. Changes in the characteristics of councillors depend on the net flows of people entering and leaving council service; these, in turn, result from decisions made by potential candidates, party selectors, the voters themselves and serving councillors. The assumption is that changes to internal management – concentrating power in an executive, and developing a scrutiny role for the remaining councillors – will encourage different types of people to enter and exit council service:

> The Government believes that the combination of the new rewarding roles envisaged for councillors and ... steps to address some potential financial and other disincentives to serve will encourage a wider cross section of the community – more employed people, more women, more people from ethnic minorities, more young people and people with young families – to serve their communities in future. (DETR, 1998b, p 36)

It is hoped that, in future, more councillors will be drawn from these under-represented groups and, in particular, "for more talented, vigorous young people in local government able and willing to make a difference to the world around them" (DETR, 1998b, p 36).

> Notwithstanding the powerlessness of governments to bring about change of this type, spontaneous change has been occurring over these three decades, albeit less rapidly than critics would wish. The once-familiar phenomenon of the long-serving councillor is indeed disappearing, for only 15 per cent have served 20 years or more, and 57 per cent of all councillors have served less than 10 years. Nevertheless, councillors are still predominantly late middle-aged or elderly. It remains the case that many councillors enter council service in their middle years even if, unlike the past, they do not remain long. (Rao, 2000a)

One of the more striking changes – and one probably facilitated by the increased turnover of councillors – is the emergence of the woman councillor. Today, there are far more women councillors than in the past, having increased from 12% in 1964 to 25% in 1999, as Table 35 shows. As relatively recent arrivals, the average length of service of women councillors

Table 35: Proportion of women councillors (1964-99) (%)

	1964	1976	1985	1993	1999
Men	88	83	81	75	75
Women	12	17	19	25	25
Base	3,497	4,731	1,552	1,665	2,860

Source: RAO (2000a)

Table 36: The gender balance among office holders (%)

	Men	Women
Leaders	3	1
Deputy leaders	4	2
Council chairs/mayors	6	7
Committee chairs	32	27
Sub-committee chairs	34	31
Base	2,176	684

Source: Rao (2000a)

is eight years, compared with 10.7 years for male councillors; and as many as 53% of them are under the age of 55, compared with just 43% of male councillors.

At the time of the Maud Committee, there was little expectation that women would be found among councillors – especially among office holders. Indeed, a multivariate study undertaken for the Redcliffe-Maud Commission at that time actually used the proportion of women in a committee's membership as a *negative* indicator of its status (and, in contrast, the proportion of aldermen taken as a positive indicator). The evidence today is that women are well represented among office holders, although, as Table 36 shows, they have yet to attain parity with men.

Women's continuing under-representation among councillors may be attributed, in part, to discrimination against them in the local power structures and, in part, to a lesser willingness to take part in political life and offer themselves for political office. In one sense women have traditionally been regarded as disproportionately having a particularly important prerequisite – the time to give to community and political affairs, however, social change has eroded this advantage. Today women are more likely to be working than in the past, while continuing to carry out the greater part of domestic duties. Council service is not incompatible with employment, and it is the rare councillor who runs foul of a restrictive and unsympathetic employer (Courtenay et al, 1998). Nevertheless, time is a finite resource, and employment inevitably competes with a political career. If discrimination against women in political life is receding, the ground gained by politically ambitious women may be offset by the difficulties of combining work, home and public service.

The competition between work and council service was always bound to favour the retired councillor. Indeed, the proportion of councillors who are retired from work has risen steadily to peak at 35%, and retired people now make up the largest single occupational group. The average age of councillors has fallen, and the growth of councillors in 'retirement' is misleading in this respect, as more than a third of former working councillors have left work, voluntarily or involuntarily, at well below the statutory retiring age. The average age of the retired councillor is just 66 for men and 65 for women.

At the same time, councillors continue to be far better educated, with this gap widening over time – more than half of all councillors now have a degree or a professional qualification. In this sense, at least, councillors have become markedly less representative of the general population although this has not become a matter of concern. The old arguments about 'calibre' have been tacitly accepted, with a general supposition that better-educated councillors will be more effective decision makers. There is a reluctance to revisit the dilemmas discussed in Chapter Three, for greater social representativeness would have to be traded off against effectiveness; the better-educated councillor of today is likely to be younger. Councillors are also more middle class than ever before, and thus less representative in this sense also. Although the proportion of the general population in 'blue-collar' employment has declined, it has declined faster still among councillors, with only one in five councillors coming from a manual background and the great majority of these are skilled workers (see Table 37).

It must be recognised that these considerable social changes in the councillor population are the result of long-term social trends working their way through, and owe nothing to any specific action on the part of government. What does lie within the scope of government is to identify and remove the barriers that impede particular social groups from entering council service. Foremost among these are the time demands of council

Table 37: Social class background of councillors (%)

	1985		1999	
	Councillors	GB population	Councillors	GB population
I Professional and so on	9	3	11	5
II Intermediate	50	20	56	26
III Skilled (non-manual)	10	18	12	20
III Skilled (manual)	16	23	15	18
IV Partly skilled	4	18	4	15
V Unskilled	1	6	1	5

service, which have been thought to operate as a powerful deterrent to the working councillor. The government urges councils "to take all opportunities, particularly in the context of streamlining their structures, to consider how their meetings can be scheduled to accommodate those with jobs or other commitments" (DETR, 1998b, p 36). In reality, however, there is little evidence that reconciling the demands of working life and council responsibilities presents difficulties to the extent that someone in employment would be unable to serve. The fall in the proportion of working councillors is attributable more to the changing structure of employment than to the pressures of local government (Courtenay et al, 1998).

Part of the government's plan is to attract new talent and a wider range of people into local government as councillors by removing financial and other barriers. Steps will be taken to ensure that the financial arrangements for councillors support the now well-established expectation that there should be no disincentives to people serving in local politics, and that council service should be cost-neutral. At the same time, it is recognised that:

> ... executive mayors, and some others in political executive positions or the scrutiny function in councils, may spend much if not all of their time on council business with a possible subsequent loss of earnings and pension rights. (DETR, 1998b, p 35)

In such cases, the payment of pensionable salaries will be made possible.

Since 1995, the level of allowances for councillors has been a matter for local decision. The government has promised to encourage councils "to take a radical look at the way in which their remuneration and allowances structures can reinforce the new approach to local government"; this will involve breaking "the attendance culture" (DETR, 1998b, pp 35-6). As councils reframe their allowances and remuneration schemes, they will be required to place them before a local independent panel. It is considered vital that there should be "an external public source of advice on what seems an appropriate payment for each of the different roles being performed by members of the council" (DETR, 1998b, p 36). As part of a general review of member support, the government will enable councils to subsidise the childcare or other care costs which councillors incur when they attend council meetings, and review current rules on travel and subsistence for councillors. By removing financial and practical burdens in these ways, the government calculates that younger people might be drawn into council service.

A new political executive

Greater representativeness is valued, but there are no direct means proposed for achieving it. The government can do no more than pin its faith on changes in council composition flowing from a major reconstruction of councillors' roles, with some marginal changes to allowances and entitlements. It has taken the view that the roles played by a councillor at present are insufficiently rewarding and attractive. Councillors are not putting their time to good use, due to the conflation of the executive and representative roles that flow from the tradition of 'government by committee'.

Restructuring councillors' roles is the primary means by which the aims of the modernisation agenda will be achieved. A small executive body of councillors will provide for community leadership, while the majority will play only a representative role. The government maintains that "each role can only be fully effective when it is separated from the other".

> The executive role would be to propose the policy framework and implement policies within the agreed framework. The role of backbench councillors would be to represent their constituents, share in the policy and budget decisions of the full council, suggest policy improvements, and scrutinise the executive's policy proposals and their implementation. (DETR, 1998b, p 26)

In the government's view, a small executive will speed up decision making, enhance responsiveness and enable local authorities to meet community needs. Increased transparency will enable people to measure the executive's actions against the policies on which it was elected, and thus sharpen local political debate and increase interest in local elections.

As was seen in Chapter Three, the idea of a separate executive has been argued before, but to little effect. It was strongly advocated by the Maud Committee more than 30 years ago, and overwhelmingly rejected in the debate that followed; 20 years later the Widdicombe Committee reopened these issues, and considered the desirability of introducing a Maud-style management board. Widdicombe conceded the advantages of this model in terms of sharpening accountability and speedier and more effective decision taking, but found against the scheme on grounds of the split loyalties that it would require from officers. Traditionally the servants of the council as a whole, officers would be required to work to the management board, thus isolating the 'backbench' councillors. Significantly, Widdicombe also argued that such a concentration of power would be undemocratic; the need was to disperse power between parties and within the majority group.

Widdicombe also considered separating the executive from the council, with no overlap of membership. It was thought at the time that this separation might take two forms: one in which the executive is chosen by the electorate (as in the present directly-elected mayoral proposal), and one in which an executive officer is appointed by the council and ultimately held to account by them. The first of these was rejected on grounds of the potential conflict between two sources of elected authority – the mayor and the council. The second was dismissed as unhealthy, representing a fundamental shift in the character of local democracy, with too much power being ceded from the elected members to an administrator. Widdicombe concluded that the traditional council and committee system was the most appropriate as it gave a meaningful role to every councillor.

This was not the last to be heard of these options. Within five years of the Widdicombe Committee's report, Michael Heseltine – reinstated as Secretary of State for the Environment – issued a series of consultation papers. One of these – on internal management of local authorities – reviewed a wider range of options, including streamlining the existing committee system; introducing a 'cabinet' system; and – a more radical option – directly electing an executive mayor. The Major government's approach was permissive, and relied on local authorities to take up reform proposals if they chose to do so: the Conservatives held back from legislating to make radical change a real option, still less from enforcing it. Councillor opposition to change was widespread and, despite continuing encouragement from the government, scarcely anything changed.

New Labour embraced these same ideas with fervour. Minister for Local Government Hilary Armstrong was caustic:

> We have to re-ignite the enthusiasm of local people in local politics by ending the outdated, arcane committee system. It is easier to trace the medieval origins of the current committee system than to state its relevance for the twenty-first century. With its cumbersome and

corrosive impact on the interest and involvement of local people, the council committee system should be consigned to the history books. (Armstrong, 1999, p 21)

The distinctive feature of the Blair government's approach to these recurrent debates was its determination to transform local government decision making by legislating for change. It was the first time any government acted to change the internal management of local government since the system was established in the 19th century. The House of Lords blocked the option of imposing change, leaving change to choice. The government saw the cutting edge of its modernisation programme fatally blunted, and reversed the Lord's decision in the Commons (see Appendix B for details).

The executive and scrutiny roles

Where earlier advocates of change made their case solely in terms of management processes, the novelty of the Blair government's proposals lay in their conception of 'community leadership'. The executive is intended to exercise political leadership in the local community, representing the locality to other bodies and negotiating with government, with national and international public bodies, as well as with companies to attract inward investment. In this broader representative role the executive will promote the growth and well-being of the community and oversee the delivery of services within the area.

Such separation of roles is expected, not only to provide a sharper focus for executive responsibility, but also to enable the majority of non-leading members to be freed from the pressures of council business, and so devote more time to representing their constituents. At the same time, the non-executive role will also provide for greater scrutiny of executive action. While the government acknowledges that the formation of a small separate executive will confirm their exclusion, non-executive councillors will, they claim, gain the compensatory power to challenge or scrutinise decisions. To this end, councils will be required to establish scrutiny committees composed of non-leading councillors, whose duty would be to review and question the decisions of the executive. These committees will also review broad policy and submit alternative proposals to the executive. The principle of proportionality – introduced in the the wake of Widdicombe Committee by the 1989 Local Government

Act – will apply to scrutiny committees, which must reflect the political balance on the council.

Under the new arrangements, non-executive (or 'backbench') councillors will be expected to spend less time in council meetings and more time in the local community, representing their constituents' aspirations, concerns and grievances to the council, and bringing to its decision-making processes "a full knowledge of what their local communities need and want" (Armstrong, 1999, p 21). More specifically, they will play an advisory role on local issues, reviewing decisions of the executive, approving the budget and taking quasi-judicial decisions. Aware of the extent of the opposition to the earlier Heseltine proposals, the Blair government aims to persuade councillors that the benefits of the separation of roles will outweigh the losses:

> This enhanced role will provide new opportunities to backbench councillors. The role could be less time-consuming but it will be high profile, involving real and direct responsibilities for the well-being of their community and will be more challenging and rewarding. (DETR, 1998b, p 34)

Not everyone was so persuaded. The county councils, in particular, voiced reservations, arguing that the government's proposals were "disappointingly light in identifying meaningful roles for non-executive councillors" (CCN, 1999, p 2).

The essence of the scheme is for councillors to work together in new ways. The government's plan, seeking as it does to bring about radical change, is crucially dependent on councillors developing their new roles. Clear and close relationships will be required between both executive and backbench councillors and between both types of councillor and their communities. Adaptation will also be required of the relationship between members and officers because:

> A modern council, based on the proposed separation of roles, will rely on the ability of all of its members, whether in the executive or backbench role, to adapt to different ways of working. All councils should give those serving as councillors or as co-opted members the officer support, facilities and training necessary for them to fulfil their role, be it executive or otherwise, as effectively as possible. (DETR, 1998b, p 35)

This idea of a clear separation of roles underlies all three of the basic models put forward in the White Paper and subsequent Bill.

The three models

The purpose of the new legislation is to enable and encourage councils to adopt new political management structures, based on this separation of roles. The options are three-fold: a directly-elected mayor with a cabinet; a directly-elected mayor and council manager; a cabinet with a leader.

A directly-elected mayor with a cabinet

Chosen by the local electorate, a directly-elected mayor would serve as the political leader for that community, supported by a cabinet drawn from among the council members. Depending on local political circumstance, the cabinet may be single-party or a coalition. Cabinet members would have portfolios (much like present-day chairpersons) but, unlike today, would themselves be empowered to take executive decisions. Widdicombe's objection – that council officers would face split loyalties – is to be met by defining their duties to correspond with the division of councillor roles. Specifically,

> The chief executive would have particular responsibility for ensuring that both executive and backbench councillors received all the facilities and officer support necessary to fulfil their respective roles. (DETR, 1998b, p 27)

A directly-elected mayor and council manager

A directly-elected mayor's role would primarily be one of influence, guidance and leadership. The mayor would delegate strategic policy and day-to-day decision making to the council manager. Of all the models, this is the one most obviously an import from the political experience of the US and Germany. A fundamental change of process, it cannot be said to evolve out of the traditional manner of conducting business, as could be said of the third model, which represents a type of logical progression.

A cabinet with a leader

Under this model, a leader would be elected by the council and the cabinet would be made up of councillors, either appointed by the leader or elected by the council. As with a directly-elected mayor model, the cabinet could be drawn from a single party or a coalition. This model is very similar to the first, except that the leader (sometimes known as an indirectly-elected mayor) relies on the support of members of the council rather than the electorate for his or her authority and can be replaced by the council. While the leader could have similar executive powers to a directly-elected mayor, in practice they are likely to be constrained by the absence of a direct mandate from the electorate. As at present, a leader would be as powerful as his or her colleagues allowed them to be.

The key difference between the third and the first model is this: a directly-elected mayor is intended to be seen as the political leader for the entire community, putting forward policy for approval by the council and steering implementation by council officers. The mayor depends for his authority on the electorate at large, and thus has a mandate separate from that of the council. Under the cabinet system the leader (who might conceivably function as an indirectly-elected mayor) draws his authority from the members of his council.

The advantages of having strong executive have been disputed on the grounds that, while such a system focuses public attention, it could lead to undue personalisation and a dangerous concentration of power. Contrasting the different systems in Germany, Bullmann and Page concluded that, while the presidential system of the south offered clearer lines of accountability, other systems offered citizens clearer choices at elections. They argued that the advantages to be gained through clearer choice could be outweighed by current moves to 'personalise' local politics through direct elections for key officials. Such moves, they concluded, "reflect a desire to stifle the lively political debate about basic issues of economic, social and environment policy taking place at the local level rather than any real commitment to improve the quality of local self-government" (Bullmann and Page, 1994, p 52).

Even the advocates of change recognise the dangers of so great a concentration of power leading to 'elective dictatorship'. Strong leadership at the centre needs to be counterbalanced by the creation of other centres of local power. Stewart (1995a) cites the case of Oslo, which introduced a city cabinet elected by the council with the authority to control the administration, with full-time members paid on a salary basis. However, at the same time, the council strengthened neighbourhood committees with responsibility for the day-to-day running of certain services in the area. Scrutiny committees were set up, not only to appraise performance, but also to consider proposals put forward by the cabinet to the council. In these ways, a centralisation of political control was coupled with a capacity for responsiveness to neighbourhood concerns.

Local government's own criticisms of New Labour's proposals reflect much of the same spirit. Responses to the 1999 Local Government (Organisation and Standards) Bill called for councils to be given a right to delegate a decision-making role to area bodies – something that was conceded during the passage of the Local Government Bill (as it became). Other objections, made by opposition peers, sought to make the new executive structures optional rather than mandatory, to set a minimum threshold below which a referendum vote would not be binding and, more importantly, to restrict the powers of the Secretary of State to impose a referendum. These issues were brought into sharp focus during the passage of the Local Government Bill, introduced into the Lords, which made detailed provision to ensure that change would happen (see Appendix B).

Making it happen

The government's proposal was that all councils (except parishes) would be required to prepare proposals for their own decision-taking arrangements, based on these models, together with a timetable for their implementation. Government guidance is provided on the issues they need to address – in particular the rights of the public and councillors to receive information, and the implications for councils' standing orders.

Local authorities will be able to choose which of these models they prefer and the details of how they wish to operate within the broad definition of the model; however, the scope of executive decision making and the role of scrutiny committees is prescribed by regulation. The political formation of a council is expected to affect both decisions. The several models will have different appeal to those councils whose ruling groups are coalitions, or where frequent changes of control are likely, or to those whose political make-up are more predictable. Nevertheless, the government's view soon hardened to make consideration of the adoption of one or another model compulsory.

Traditionally, the political management of local authorities displayed a great deal of diversity – the council and the committee system permitted the utmost flexibility in which everything from a strong single party regime to a council of non-aligned independence shared a common statutory framework. A major issue is how far this diversity will survive the imposition of referendums on approved questions, to determine whether a new model should be adopted locally. Will local authorities be truly able to maintain arrangements that reflect their local circumstances? The government insists that they will:

> The scope for diversity, innovation and local choice will be even greater under the Government's proposed new framework than it is under the single model, which exists today.... Not only will local government be more effective and more accountable, but councils everywhere will have greater scope to design a system of governance which is best suited to local circumstances. The Government's proposals will open up a much richer variety of local democratic structures. (DETR, 1998b, p 31)

Originally conceding that councils "will need to move at their own pace, setting their own timetable for adopting one of the three models" (DETR, 1998b, p 32), the government eventually determined that all authorities should have their new structures in place by May/June 2002. Local people will be given the right to call for a referendum on whether there should be a directly-elected mayor. Such a referendum would be triggered by a petition, signed by 10% (a figure later reduced to 5%) of the council's electorate, must be held not less than two months and not more than four months after a valid petition, and the result would be binding. Where a council has developed proposals with a timetable but has not carried them forward, or has not yet developed any proposals at all, the Secretary of State would have the power to require the council to hold a referendum on one of the approved models. The government would set the proposition, again with binding effect. Referendums would normally be combined with an election for the council. In the event of a negative vote, the council could continue with their existing arrangements or bring forward alternative proposals. And in any five-year period, only one referendum on the political management structure for a council would be allowed, triggered by the government, council or by public petition.

Referendums were not to be the only route to change, nor necessarily the initial trigger. All authorities were to consult on and finalise proposals to be sent to the Secretary of State not later than six to nine months after the 2000 Local Government Act and its regulations came into force.

Consultation would have to be comprehensive and inclusive, and should cover all the options, not simply the one favoured by the council. The Secretary of State would have the power to direct that a referendum be held in any instance that he or she considered the local consultative process to have not been fair, or not in compliance with his or her guidance.

Streamlining and delegation

Implementing the new arrangements is more than simply a matter of organising consultation or responding to a referendum. Considerable changes in the councils' decision-making structures, and the distribution of power and responsibility are implied by the adoption of any of the new models. For example, some further degree of delegation to council officers will be required if local authorities are to meet the expectations of the new political management regime. Streamlining political management is seen as freeing council officers to "devote more of their time to the effective management of the council and successful policy implementation, with clear direction from the political leadership". The government accordingly pressed the case for more extensive delegation, foreseeing that "backbench members will scrutinise the actions of the executive – both those of the executive's political leadership and those of officers implementing that leadership's policies" (DETR, 1998b, p 37). At the same time,

> the extent of delegation to officers will depend on the precise arrangements a council adopts ... the mayor and council manager model would require considerably more delegation to officers than is currently the norm or would be expected under other models. (DETR, 1998b, p 37)

The advocacy of greater delegation to officers is no new thing; nor is the reluctance of many councillors to accept it. But just what is implied by delegation under these new circumstances is far from clear; for new arrangements mean new roles for both councillors and officers. On the one hand, officers will continue to serve the whole council and support all councillors in their new roles, providing councillors with the information and facilities they need, whether as members of the executive or as backbench councillors engaged in scrutinising executive actions. On the other hand, some officers will have the specific role of supporting backbench councillors, others that of supporting the mayor, or the leader and cabinet. Therefore, there will be a division of function – arguably of interest – within the officer body. Meanwhile, the chief executive will continue as the head of the paid service, and to him or her will fall much of the burden of ensuring officer–member relations, and those relations between officers, operate in the council's interest. These are the provisions of a new legislative framework for local democracy, but how have they been received?

The impact of New Labour's agenda

New Labour has introduced the most radical reconstruction of local government decision making since the establishment of the framework of local democracy in the 19th century. Yet, despite the government having taken statutory powers to enforce change, the commitment to (limited) 'local choice' means it has little chance of determining the *actual* choices made. How radical the shifts are in practice will depend on a complex interplay of local authority preference, public opinion and governmental influence. We can map the alignments at the initial stage of the programme; experience will show how they shift over time as political decisions come to be made.

The initial reception

To some extent, local authorities were already moving in the direction of the new government's proposals, as both Labour policy and 'best practice' had been converging for some time. The new single representative body, the Local Government Association (LGA), was emphatic in its support:

> Modern councils need effective decision-making. The traditional committee system, although it has many strengths, was not designed to support the new community leadership role that we are arguing for in local government. (LGA, 1998, p 11)

At the same time, the LGA argued for the provisions to be permissive rather than mandatory. Councils should be able to experiment with innovations on the condition that sufficient safeguards to protect the rights of minority parties and groups were provided (LGA, 1998, p 11).

Even among the county councils, by 1999 there was considerable interest in experimenting with new executive arrangements, and a number were prepared to accept reorganisation around a separate executive. However, some counties persisted in affirming the need for local distinctiveness to be maintained, with decision-making structures more closely reflecting the patterns of county politics. While the introduction of a separate executive might offer the potential for improving existing systems of decision making,

> it may not suit the wide variety of different local authority types and circumstances that exist, and that a fourth model, based on an 'improved committee system' may better secure the objectives of change in some cases. We hope the legislation can provide accordingly where this can be demonstrated to better meet the objectives of change than the three models set out in the consultation paper. Such openness should also extend to other possible models which may be developed, such as, for example, one based on a radically decentralised approach to political decision-taking. (CCN, 1999, p 5)

One of the reforms of parliamentary procedure which came about under New Labour has been the appointment of joint select committees to consider the implementation and workability of legislative proposals. The Joint Select Committee on the Local Government (Organisation and Standards) Bill expressed considerable doubts about the separation between executive and scrutiny roles. It remarked that the government's stress on the sanctity of this principle was 'unrealistic' and was based on a misreading of overseas experience. It was inevitable that "there would be far more interaction" between executive and backbench members "than the government seems to suppose" (House of Lords and Commons, 1999). The Joint Select Committee highlighted the extent of ministers' powers to determine these matters by regulation, and expressed concern at the lack of criteria for their application. These were not matters that should be settled nationally; the interaction between the executive and the council was something to be worked out locally. In that context, the committee called attention to the diversity within local government and, in particular, the fact that some councils enjoyed an independent tradition – one in which the traditional committee system worked well and could still meet the fundamental principles of transparency, accountability and efficiency.

The government's proposals were by no means uncritically welcomed, but of the three sets of players involved – government, the public and councils – it is the last of these that will take the formal decisions on reshaping local political structures. So how receptive are councillors to the proposed changes? How strong is their attachment to the present system? How do they see changes affecting their involvement in policy making and representation? In particular, what do they see as the advantages and disadvantages of streamlined decision making or directly-elected mayors? Comparable questions can be asked of the public to assess the extent of their support for change, as the elected mayor proposals have had sufficient airing to gauge public interest. How do they rate the elected mayor proposals, and do they trust councillors to determine the future governance of their localities?

Councillors' responses

Fortunately it is possible to measure directly, not only the strength of councillors' support for the new decision-making structures, but also the extent to which attitudes today have moved – if at all – since the time of Michael Heseltine's identical proposals in the early 1990s. A 1993 national survey of councillors focused on how councillors saw their roles. It covered the extent to which their aspirations were satisfied by the traditional committee-based system of local government, and the implications for them of adopting a greater concentration of executive power in either the cabinet or directly-elected mayor form (Young and Rao, 1994). These questions were repeated in a follow-up survey in the summer of 1999 (Rao, 2000b).

First, we look at councillor satisfaction with the existing system and their experience of any more limited changes that their authorities might have made in recent years. In both 1993 and 1999, the great majority of councillors abjured reform and expressed satisfaction with the traditional committee system. In the 1999 survey, those who rejected the traditional committee system had generally experienced streamlining within their own authority, which they had found to make their role more effective, although not all councillors had this benign view of streamlining. A similar proportion of councillors in authorities that had already streamlined reported that change had made little or no difference, or had affected them adversely.

The views on the proposed alternatives are more striking. Although the majority of councillors still prefer the present decision-making structures, since 1993 there has been a considerable shift – of some 20 percentage points – in favour of a 'cabinet' system with responsibility vested in a small group of councillors. Only a third of all councillors, however, favour this option. As in 1993, there is negligible support – just 3% – for radical change to vest power in an executive mayor. These figures are consistent with a survey by the LGA which revealed scarcely any support for directly-elected mayors, while showing that 80% of authorities favoured changing to a cabinet and leader system. Three quarters of councils had, by the end of 1999, already considered proposals for some form of new executive system (LGC, 1999). Table 38 summarises responses to the two councillor surveys carried out by the author.

The figures in Table 38 suggest that the government's proposals on new political leadership structure have rather fewer supporters than might be assumed among existing councillors. The reasons are to be found not in the executive role itself, but in its implications for those councillors who find themselves relegated to the margins of decision making to positions of little influence. The government argues that a more streamlined system will enable the majority of councillors (who will take up non-executive roles) to devote more time to representing their constituents. On this point councillor opinion has shifted since 1993. The proportion of councillors who accept that a cabinet system would enable backbench councillors to devote more time to their constituents has doubled from 22% to 43%; those who feel that more time would be devoted to performance review and monitoring by such councillors has trebled from an inconsequential 15% in 1993 to a substantial 42% today. Yet the argument is only half won, for there remains the separate issue of whether scrutiny and representation of constituents' interests combine to create a meaningful role for the 'backbench' councillor.

It is perfectly consistent for councillors to acknowledge the greater space that reform will give them to devote to non-executive tasks, while

Table 38: Councillors' views on proposed new management structures (%)

	1993	1999
Preference for:		
The present system – formal responsibility resides with the whole council	84	63
A more streamlined system – responsibility passes to a small group of councillors	13	34
A radical change – responsibility is given to an executive mayor or equivalent	3	3
Base	1,640	1,220

Source: Young and Rao (1994); Rao (2000b)

at the same time deploring the loss of that more significant decision-making role. Thus, a large majority of the councillors surveyed – some 65% – feel that the government's changes would 'Deprive ordinary members of influence over strategic policy making', although this figure represents a marked shift from the 80% agreeing with this statement in 1993 (see Table 39). Moreover, a majority of councillors (57%) still agree that 'Ordinary members would be deprived of the incentive to remain on the council', although here too there has been a softening of opposition since the 76% level recorded in 1993 (see Table 39). It is clear that opinion is changing quite rapidly in the direction of accepting the new system. Whether it will move far enough and swiftly enough to make the government's programme workable remains to be seen, for acceptance of the new structures is a matter of choice and not, as was intended, of compulsion. To some extent, the swing towards acceptance of the cabinet system reflects the predominance of Labour councillors in the 1999 survey, for they are markedly warmer towards the new executive structures than councillors from other parties. Even so, there are few party differences on the perceived effects of change and on their implications for member roles.

The political management arrangements emphasise the need for greater delegation to officers to support these new, streamlined structures. Councillors are often opposed to delegating any of their powers to officers, and securing greater delegation is often frustrated by this resistance and by the lurking suspicion that officers are not to be trusted to take the decisions that councillors themselves would have taken. In the author's 1993 survey, 87% of councillors did not want to see further delegation to officers and, in the follow-up survey conducted in 1999, just 5% had

Table 39: Views on effects of concentrating responsibility in the hands of leading members (%)

	1993	1999
Agree that concentrating responsibility would...		
Enable ordinary members to devote more time to performance review and monitoring	15	42
Enable ordinary members to devote more time to the problems of their constituents	22	43
Deprive ordinary members of influence over strategic policy making	80	65
Deprive ordinary members of the incentive to remain on the council	76	57
Base	1,636	1,226

Source: Young and Rao (1994); Rao (2000b)

moved towards accepting greater delegation. The climate appears to remain hostile to any further transfer of power from the councillors themselves to the council's officers.

For and against the mayor

Elected mayors are seen as the cornerstone of New Labour's plans for the reform of local government – a directly-elected mayor is seen as providing a clear 'voice' for the local area. Such a focus of authority would establish clearer lines of accountability locally, by making it explicit who should be held responsible when things go wrong. At the same time, through bypassing the traditional committee cycle, mayoral power would expedite decision making and make it easier to get things done. However, objections have been levelled against elected mayors – most significantly, that too much power would reside with one person, leaving ordinary councillors with too little influence. In Scotland, the McIntosh Commission considered whether mayors and provosts should be directly elected and found little support for this innovation during the course of their consultations. They nevertheless concluded that it remains an option for Scotland, and proposed to keep developments in England and Wales closely in view.

A report by the Commission for Local Democracy (CLD) set out some advantages of having a directly-elected executive:

> The post would be highly visible and thus highly accountable. Local decisions would be more readily identified with one person than with the more abstract notion of a party group. We accept that this might increase the role of 'personality' in British local government. We see this as no bad thing in boosting public interest and turnout at elections. Local elections might be dragged back from being national opinion polls to show more concern for local issues.... A network of elected Leaders/Mayors would provide a more powerful voice for local government in Whitehall and Westminster. Their visibility and elected status would give them the opportunity and the authority to speak, negotiate and make demands on behalf of their communities. The innovation offers a means of bridging together the fragments of central–local government relations and attracting media attention to local government. In particular it would help restore the political self-confidence of the big cities and re-identify local leadership with local democratic institutions. (CLD, 1995, p 22)

A survey carried out by MORI supported the CLD's claim that the introduction of a directly-elected mayor would make a significant impact on local electoral turnout: while 62% said it would make no difference, the net result was that some 10% of the electorate would be more likely to vote. For those living in London this figure rose to 22%.

However, we have seen that very few *councillors* supported the proposals for a directly-elected mayor. In the author's 1999 survey, councillors were asked for their views on the advantages and disadvantages of establishing a system of directly-elected executive mayors to provide a focus for community leadership. As Table 40 shows, few councillors concede the advantages of a mayoral system, with the great majority agreeing that it would give too much power to one person, leaving local councillors with little say.

However, the public opinion about directly-elected mayors is much more positive: in the 1998 BSA study, respondents saw clearly the positive features in terms of a clearer focus for community leadership. More than a third of the public believes that having an elected mayor would 'make it easier to get things done'. Three in five agree that an elected mayor would provide 'someone who could speak up for the whole area'. Nearly half of those members of the public questioned agreed that having an elected mayor would mean 'it was always clear who was responsible when things go wrong'. It is notable that only one of the claimed strengths of the plan – the provision of a single clear 'voice' for the area – is recognised by as many as three out of five respondents. In considering the options

Table 40: Councillors' views on the effects of a directly-elected mayor (%)

	Agree strongly/ agree	Neither agree nor disagree	Disagree/ disagree strongly	*Base*
A directly-elected mayor would...				
Make it easier to get things done	20	20	61	*1,055*
Give too much power to one person	86	4	11	*1,063*
Mean there was someone who could speak up for the whole area	29	23	49	*1,045*
Mean local councillors would have too little say	80	8	11	*1,064*
Mean that it was always clear who was responsible when things go wrong	33	21	46	*1,056*

Source: Rao (2000b)

for the future governance of local authorities, their currently low political visibility must be borne in mind: only 100 of the 2,400 people questioned could correctly name their local council leader.

Despite this almost universal lack of knowledge, nearly 40% of the respondents believed that they were in a better position than the councillors themselves to judge who was best fitted to lead the local council. Responses to the question 'Councillors know better than voters who is the best person to lead the local council' were divided, with (not surprisingly, perhaps) 30% of those questioned having no view, although only 28% agreed. This might suggest that popular opinion favours placing the choice of a local leader in the hands of the electorate – something that only the directly-elected mayor model offers. However, at the same time the survey respondents were not oblivious to the negative aspects of an elected mayor system insofar as it risks an undue concentration of power. Almost half agreed that having an elected mayor 'would give too much power to one person' although, as Table 41 shows, people are generally indifferent to the corresponding diminution in the role of the ordinary councillor.

The comparison is sharp: the government's proposals have set councillors and the public against each other, and the use of identical questions provides an accurate measure of the gulf between them. At another time this would be a source of concern. However, the government has made it clear that people – not their councillors – should have the determining voice in shaping the future governance of their communities. The government's measures have a fair wind behind them in terms of public

Table 41: Advantages and disadvantages of a directly-elected mayoral system: public and councillor views compared (%)

	Public agreement	Councillor agreement
Having an elected mayor would...		
Make it easier to get things done	37	20
Mean there was someone who could speak up for the whole area	59	29
Mean that it was always clear who was responsible when things go wrong	46	33
Give too much power to one person	45	86
Mean that local councillors would have too little say	26	80
Base	2,071	1,063

Source: British Social Attitudes Survey (1998); Rao (2000b)

opinion, and the use of imposed referendums as a mechanism for bringing about change makes it more than likely that councillor resistance will be overcome, and change brought about.

New leadership for London

In just one area – Greater London – the new community leadership programme promises to be exempt from the clash of mandates which bedevils the elected mayor proposals elsewhere. Since the Thatcher government abolished the Greater London Council (GLC) in 1986, Labour has promised the restoration of metropolitan government in one form or another. Since then, the government of London has operated at three levels. At the local level, the 32 london boroughs and the City Corporation enjoyed freedom from GLC 'interference'. Governance at the regional level lay in the hands of a complex array of joint arrangements and ad hoc organisations set up to provide some area-wide continuity of function. In truth, metropolitan power was exercised by Department of the Environment, through (after 1994) the Government Office for London and other agencies of the national government. The metropolitan level had been the subject of prolonged and intense criticism since the Conservatives' proposals were first unveiled in their White Paper *Streamlining the cities* (DoE, 1983).

The dissolution of the GLC shifted responsibility onto a complex network of joint bodies (Hebbert and Travers, 1988): strategic planning became the concern of the London Planning Advisory Committee, support to the voluntary sector that of the London Boroughs Grants Committee, and research and intelligence that of the London Research Centre. Other functions were removed altogether from the influence of elected bodies, with transport falling once again under the control of ministers, whose strategies took the place of those formulated by the GLC. In the absence of a strategic authority, the Whitehall departments were forced to 'second guess' the borough councils and often duplicated work undertaken at the borough level. Ministers and their departments found themselves drawn into local matters, and local issues came to be seen as of national importance (Hebbert and Travers, 1988, pp 21-2). Labour's critique commanded general assent; generally, assessments of the working of the post-1986 arrangements were not favourable (Travers, 1991; Travers and Jones, 1997).

The 1997 Labour manifesto set out an approach to the problem that was not just a riposte to abolition, but a great step forward from the unthinking restoration of the GLC. It declared that:

London is the only Western capital without an elected city government. Following a referendum to confirm popular demand, there would be a new deal for London, with the strategic authority and a mayor, each directly elected. Both will speak up for the needs of the city and plan its future. They will not duplicate the works of the boroughs, but take responsibility for London-wide issues – economic regeneration, planning, policing, transport and environmental protection. London-wide responsibility for its own government is urgently required. We will make it happen. (Labour Party, 1997, p 34)

Armed with a manifesto commitment endorsed by the electorate, the government acted swiftly to ensure that the new bodies would assume their powers within three years of it taking office. Following circulation in July 1997 of a consultative document, *New leadership for London* (DETR, 1997), the government published its White Paper, *A mayor and assembly for London* (DETR, 1998c), in March 1998, holding its promised referendum in the spring of 1998. Whereas 12 months usually elapses between the election of a new body and its assumption of power, London's transition would take place in a matter of weeks following the election. Under the 2000 Greater London Authority Act, the elections for the mayor and the Greater London Assembly were scheduled for May 2000. Their assumption of office on 3 July marked the beginning of a new chapter in the government of Greater London.

The Act establishes the office of executive mayor for Greater London for the first time, which, together with a Greater London Assembly, constitutes the new Greater London Authority (GLA). This body covers the same area as the former GLC, but has differently constituted powers. Its establishment marks a new beginning for London government, after a period of 14 years during which there has been no overall strategic authority. Now, four of the former pan-London organisations have been absorbed into the GLA, while a number of other bodies remain outside. Two of these will be executive bodies – Transport for London and the London Development Agency – which will run transport and economic development respectively, and be accountable to the mayor, who will appoint their boards. The new Metropolitan Police Authority will be the first such body in London's history to be locally accountable, and will be funded by the mayor, who will appoint assembly members to its board. The London Fire and Emergency Planning Authority will be similarly structured.

The 1998 referendum produced strong endorsement of the government's plans, with more than 70% of the votes cast in favour. The relationship between the mayor and the Assembly is the crux of the working of the new system of London government, but, starting as they are from scratch with only weeks to settle into place, there will be little opportunity to develop ground rules and procedures before the system 'goes live'. The White Paper refers to the need for "the right balance" between them, and the need to avoid "frivolous or destructive intervention" on the part of members, while allowing the Assembly to scrutinise mayoral proposals and, if they so choose, to amend the budget (DETR, 1998c, para 3.24). In the longer term, this relationship will depend on political harmony between the mayor and assembly.

The most radical change in the governance of London will be in the relationship between the mayor and Whitehall. The mayor's role, in particular, is a strategic one, but the experience of the GLC suggests that, on key strategic issues, ministers will be tempted to overrule any metropolitan body and substitute their own judgement. Some foreshadowing of this can be seen in the exchanges between government spokesmen and potential Labour mayoral candidates over the financing of the London Underground. London's position as capital city places a considerable political price on the decisions of the mayor, who is likely to find him or herself in constant negotiations with ministers. Additionally, the Secretary of State has taken reserve powers with respect to the GLA's duty to promote the social, economic and environmental well-being of Londoners. Since 1986, Whitehall departments have allegedly become accustomed to promoting the interests of their own particular functions in the London region; adapting their approaches to the existence of an authoritative metropolitan body will pose a particular challenge. Small wonder, then, that both major parties found themselves in deep water over the selection of their candidates for the post of Greater London Mayor.

The reception of *New leadership for London* revealed support for "a new style of governance – non-confrontational, inclusive ... building consensus" (DETR, 1998c, para 3.3). In particular, duplication with the boroughs was to be avoided, and a clear delineation of roles established. The system established by the 1963 London Government Act had been marred by turf disputes between the GLC and the boroughs; considerable attention has been given to avoiding such conflicts under the new system, with a much clearer definition of the strategic role and fulsome references to the delivery of "agreed London-wide policies" (DETR, 1998c, para 1.24). Nevertheless, the GLA will have specific powers and duties in relation to

NINE

Prospects for a new politics

'Modernising' local democracy offers a new perspective on old problems. The need to involve people and boost electoral participation has long been recognised. Equally, the desire to improve the decision-making process has been a continuing theme in postwar political debates. The novelty of New Labour's agenda lies not in the particular proposals put forward, but in the comprehensiveness of the overall programme: electoral procedures and arrangements, mechanisms for public involvement and consultation, and new structures for local authority decision making, combine to promise 'modernisation'.

This is an ambitious package, but does it amount to real substantive change? Or is it merely symbolic politics – a gesture designed to enhance the image of a government at the cutting edge of change? Linking local government reform to the third way, as Tony Blair did in his Institute for Public Policy Research pamphlet, *Leading the way: A new vision for local government* (Blair, 1998b), evokes some justified scepticism. For, while the third way can be read as providing a strategy for changed times, it may equally be criticised for lacking substance – as an amorphous political project. The question of whether the new politics of local government should be seen as symbol or substance requires two questions to be answered: Does it address a real problem? And is there a serious intention to deal with it?

The answer to the first question will be apparent from the discussion set out in the first half of this book. There is indeed a real problem, as the foundations of local democracy have eroded over the last 100 years – nowhere has this been more apparent than in the contemporary popular disdain for local government. As Chapters Three to Five show, the loss of trust and faith in governmental institutions has undermined local democracy to the extent that, today, few take an active interest in local politics and scarcely any would consider standing for election to their local council.

There is, to this extent, a curious symmetry between the present situation and that of the late 19th century: now, as then, the idea that there is a crisis of democratisation is gaining currency. There was then, as there is now, a growing recognition of the need to bring the governors and the governed into a closer relationship. The 19th-century solution was to create representative institutions: first in the boroughs, then in the counties, filtering down by the end of the century to district and parish level. The assumption was that those chosen to represent the people would be responsive to their interests, even if they did not share their actual circumstances or characteristics. The framework of local democracy was founded on the assumption that government should be based on representation, and elements of direct democracy were restricted to the smallest parishes.

Since then, representative government has itself undergone significant changes. The political parties developed electoral machines, reached out to the people, and sought to express their views and interests. In this way they transformed the nature of representation, from that of a simple relationship between the representative and the represented to a more complex triad of the parties, representatives and the represented. And, while they complicated the representative process, the entry of parties represented a further advance towards democracy: the parties brought representatives closer to the people by selecting candidates whose social position, way of life and concerns were close to those of the grassroots. A greater degree of identity and resemblance between governors and governed was to follow (Manin, 1997, pp 195-6).

However, over the course of time, several factors came to undermine party democracy. The intensity of electoral competition meant that parties had to appeal beyond their core vote, to those voters who were unaligned, or who could be persuaded to detach themselves from a rival party. In an age of mass communication, this produced a campaign that stressed style and symbol at the expense of issues that matter to people:

> Each party used to propose to the electorate a detailed program of measures which it promised to implement if returned to power. Today, the electoral strategies of candidates and parties are based instead on the construction of vague images, prominently featuring the personality of the leaders ... those moving in political circles today are distinguished from the rest of the population by their occupation, culture and way of life.... Politicians generally attain power because of their media talents, not because they resemble their constituents socially or are close to them. The gap between government and society, between representatives and represented appears to be widening. (Manin, 1997, p 193)

The result has been growing cynicism and disenchantment, reflected in the negative judgements frequently made about parties and government. Only a minority support the party system in local government, while a large majority consider parties to be mere vote seekers which pay little attention to people's views.

This gap has been widened by the very success of the parties in appealing to the marginal voter for, in doing so, they have eroded their own core vote. From the 1970s, a process of dealignment began. Not only did voters begin to 'shop around', but their strength of attachment to *any* party declined, as did party membership itself. For many years, representation had been founded on a powerful and stable relationship of trust between voters and political parties, with the vast majority of voters identifying themselves with, and remaining loyal to, a particular party. Today, however, many people change the way they vote from one election to the next, and surveys show that an increasing proportion refuse to identify with a party – although they may still vote for it. Outside general elections, parties today have scarcely any popular base.

Democratic renewal is about restoring public confidence, trust and attachment; it recognises the failings of existing institutions, and calls for a new politics capable of 'democratising democracy'. To that extent, it is clear that New Labour has identified and arraigned itself against a real problem in the modern polity, but do the substantive policies of the modernisation programme address it?

That there is a serious intention to deal with this problem can be seen in Chapters Six to Eight: for the first time, a government has clearly demonstrated its commitment to tackling the problems in tangible ways. New processes to achieve a more inclusive public involvement and novel initiatives to promote a more open and transparent style of government reflect New Labour's determination to make an impact. Together with changes to service provision and local finance, consultation, political management and electoral participation are aimed at producing a genuine renewal of local democracy and promoting the well-being of communities.

In pushing forward with reform, New Labour has been riding a wave of change, as a growing number of local authorities have shown their willingness to adopt new initiatives to reconnect them with local people: citizens' juries, standing panels, ad hoc surveys and referendums, are now widely used, if not yet commonplace. Within the town hall, a few authorities have been pioneering cabinet or mayoral executives, balancing them with the appropriate scrutiny and review committees. There is acceptance and positive enthusiasm for improving electoral practices to make voting in local elections more convenient. But the government is doing more than simply encouraging change. Its legislation to enable councils to experiment is backed by powers to impose reformed electoral procedures and practices throughout the country. This is not merely symbolic politics.

How well, though, have these initiatives been received? New Labour's analysis of the condition of local democracy is an accurate one, and its diagnosis of the shortcomings of local authorities is broadly reflected in public opinion. People value the service-providing role, but see their councils as closed, unresponsive and inaccessible. Moreover, most people are not interested in local politics, even when they are interested in politics generally – this is particularly true of the youngest electors, of whom only around one in five casts a vote in a local election. Many non-voters explain their abstention in terms of disenchantment with political processes. This lack of faith in local democracy is general, with the public displaying little confidence in the efficacy of the electoral processes and still less in their elected representatives. People place far greater faith in the ability of a 'jury' of ordinary citizens to make the right decision on local issues than they do in their councillors.

The high level of dissatisfaction with local politics is reflected in strong support for the government's proposals for electoral reform – particularly among those who do not, at present, vote. It is not unreasonable to expect such support, given that the proposals are designed to make voting easier and more convenient. Young people are the strongest supporters of changes such as weekend voting, postal voting and electronic voting, while older people are much more committed to traditional methods. At present, young people – the government's key target group – have the lowest turnout in local elections, so it is at least possible that changes to electoral arrangements could lead to higher turnouts in local elections.

If people at large are well-disposed toward the modernisation agenda, councillors are not, and there is only a narrow base of support for the options proposed for the reform of the decision-making process. The most radical alternative – that of a directly-elected mayor – has scant support, while Westminster-style cabinets are unwelcome among many councillors who see themselves losing the very power they sought on election. The House of Lords reflected local opinion in insisting that options remain just that, rather than be subject to centrally-imposed changes. There are differences in the expressed opinions of local councillors and these, not surprisingly, appear, at first, to reflect partisan divisions: Labour councillors appear to be warmer toward the proposed changes.

Yet this partisan division does not run deep and all councillors – whether they belong to a political party or not – share anxieties about the potential concentration of power in executive hands and the marginalisation of the non-executive councillor.

Despite these reservations, the modernisation agenda appears to be taking root in local practice. However, it is too easy to conflate 'modernisation' and 'democratic renewal' in New Labour's rhetoric. At this point, a clear distinction must be drawn between them: modernisation is the means, democratic renewal the end. The means are clear, well-supported and are being substantially achieved, but whether such success can, in itself, bring about a renewal of democracy is another matter. New Labour assumes that people are willing to engage with their local authorities, exercise their right to vote in far greater numbers and become actively involved in local political life, recapturing the forgotten civic virtues of 19th-century municipal life. Such a reversal of cultural change will require a sustained reconstruction of political life. In taking such a long-term view, *democratising democracy* inescapably becomes a distant and an uncertain prospect.

Bibliography

Aars, J. and Offerdal, A. (2000) 'Representativeness and deliberative politics', in N. Rao (ed) *Representation and community in western democracies*, Basingstoke: Macmillan.

Addison, P. (1975) *The road to 1945*, London: Jonathan Cape.

Alderman, G. (1978) *British elections: Myth and reality*, London: Batsford.

Alexander, A. (1982) *The politics of local government in the United Kingdom*, London: Longman.

Almond, G.A. (1989) 'The intellectual history of the civic culture concept', in G.A. Almond and S. Verba (eds) *Civic culture revisited*, London: Sage Publications, pp 1-36.

Almond, G.A. and Powell, G.B. (1984) *Comparative politics today: A world view*, Boston, MA: Little Brown.

Almond, G.A. and Verba, S. (1963) *Civic culture: Political attitudes and democracy in five nations*, Princeton, NJ: Princeton University Press.

Annan, N. (1990) *Our age: Portrait of a generation*, London: Weidenfeld and Nicolson.

Armstrong, H. (1999) 'The key themes of democratic renewal', *Local Government Studies*, vol 25, no 4, pp 19-25.

Ascher, K. (1987) *The politics of privatisation: Contracting out public services*, Basingstoke: Macmillan.

Audit Commission (1989) *Public service management: The revolution in progress*, London: Audit Commission.

Aves, G.M. (1969) *The voluntary worker in the social services*, London: Allen and Unwin.

Bains, M. (1972) *The new local authorities: Management and structure*, London: HMSO.

Bartle, M. (1994) 'Initiatives and experiments', *DEMOS Quarterly*, issue 3, pp 36-7.

Benewick, R.J., Birch, A.H., Blumer, H. and Ewbank, A. (1969) 'The floating voter and the liberal view of representation', *Political Studies*, vol 17, no 2, pp 177-95.

Bennett, S.E. (1991) 'Left behind: exploring declining turnout among non-college young whites, 1964-1988', *Social Science Quarterly*, vol 72, no 2, pp 314-33.

Berelson, B., Lazarsfeld, P.F. and McPhee, W.P. (1954) *Voting: A study of opinion formation in a Presidential campaign*, Chicago, IL: University of Chicago Press.

Berry, D. (1969) 'Party membership and social participation', *Political Studies*, vol 17, no 2, pp 196-207.

Bevan, A. (1952) *In place of fear*, London: Heinemann.

Birch, A.H. (1959) *Small town politics*, London: Oxford University Press.

Blair, T. (1998a) *The third way: New politics for the new century*, London: Fabian Society.

Blair, T. (1998b) *Leading the way: A new vision for local government*, London: Institute for Public Policy Research.

Blais, A. and Carty, R.K. (1990) 'Does proportional representation foster voter turnout?', *European Journal of Political Research*, vol 18, no 2, pp 167-81.

Bloch, A. and John, P. (1991) *Public attitudes to local government*, York: Joseph Rowntree Foundation.

Blondel, J. (1969) *Voters, parties and leaders*, Harmondsworth: Penguin.

Boaden, N., Goldsmith, M., Hampton, W. and Stringer, P. (1982) *Public participation in local services*, Harlow: Longman.

Briggs, A. (1952) *A history of Birmingham: Volume 2: Borough and City, 1865-1938*, London: Oxford University Press.

Bromley, C., Stratford, N. and Rao, N. (2000) *Revisiting public perceptions of local government finance, a decade of change*, London: DETR.

Bruno, L. (1961) *Freedom and the law*, Princeton, NJ: Princton University Press.

Bullmann, U. and Page, E. (1994) 'Executive leadership in German local government', in *Local leadership and decision-making: A study of France, Germany, the United States and Britain*, York: Joseph Rowntree Foundation, pp 32-52.

Butler, D. (1989) *British general elections since 1945*, Oxford: Blackwell.

Butler, D. and Stokes, D. (1974) *Political change in Britain*, 2nd edn, London: Macmillan.

Campbell, D., Converse, P.E., Miller, W.E. and Stokes, D.E. (1960) *The American voter*, New York, NY: Wiley.

Cannadine, D. (ed) (1982) *Patricians, power and politics in nineteenth century towns*, Leicester: Leicester University Press.

CCN (County Councils Network) (1999) *Response to 'Local leadership, local choice' and draft Bill*, London: CCN.

Chester, D.N. (1968) 'Local democracy and the internal organisation of local authorities', *Public Administration*, vol 46, no 2, pp 287-98.

Clark, T.N. and Hoffmann-Martinot, V. (eds) (1998) *The new political culture*, Boulder, CO: Westview Press.

CLD (Commission for Local Democracy) (1995) *Taking charge: The rebirth of local democracy*, Final report of the Commission for Local Democracy, London: Municipal Journal.

Clements, R.V. (1969) *Local notables and the city council*, London: Macmillan.

Clifton, G. (1989) 'Members and Officers of the LCC, 1889-1965', in A. Saint (ed) *Politics and the people of London: The London County Council, 1889-1965*, London: Hambledon Press, pp 1-26.

Connelly, N. (1990) *Raising voices: Social service departments and people with disabilities*, London: Policy Studies Institute.

Cooper, L., Coote, A., Davies, D. and Jackson, C. (1995) *Voices off: Tackling the democratic deficit in health*, London: Institute for Public Policy Research.

Courtenay, J., Finch, S., Rao, N. and Young, K. (1998) *The impact of releasing people for council duties*, London: DETR.

Crewe, I., Alt, J. and Fox, A. (1977) 'Non-voting in British general elections, 1966-October 1974', in C. Crouch (ed) *British political sociology yearbook, Volume 3: Participation in politics*, London: Croom Helm.

Cunningham, J. (1999) 'Do people's panels represent the panel', Lecture to the Public Management and Policy Association, London: CIPFA, 17 March.

Davis, J. (1988) *Reforming London: The London government problem, 1855-1900*, Oxford: Clarendon Press.

Dearlove, J. (1979) *The reorganisation of British local government: Old orthodoxies and a political perspective*, Cambridge: Cambridge University Press.

Denver, D.T. and Hands, H.T.G. (1977a) 'Politics to 1929', in J.D. Marshall (ed) *The history of Lancashire County Council, 1889 to 1974*, London: Martin Robertson, pp 50-75.

Denver, D.T. and Hands, H.T.G. (1977b) 'Politics 1929 to 1974', in J.D. Marshall (ed) *The history of Lancashire County Council, 1889 to 1974*, London: Martin Robertson, pp 194-244.

DES (Department of Education and Science) (1983) *Teaching quality*, London: HMSO.

DES (1984a) *Parental influence at schools*, London: HMSO.

DES (1984b) *Education (Grants and Awards) Act*, London: HMSO.

DES (1985a) *Better schools*, London: HMSO.

DES (1985b) *Good teachers – Education observed*, London: HMSO.

DETR (Department of the Environment, Transport and the Regions) (1997) *New leadership for London – A consultation paper*, London: DETR.

DETR (1998a) *Modernising local government: Local democracy and community leadership*, London: DETR.

DETR (1998b) *Modern local government: In touch with the people*, Cmnd 4014, London: The Stationery Office.

DETR (1998c) *A mayor and assembly for London*, London: DETR.

DETR (1999) *Local leadership, local choice*, London: DETR.

DHSS (Department of Health and Social Security) (1989) *Caring for people: Community care in the neaxt decade and beyond*, Cm 849, London: HMSO.

DLGRP (Department of Local Government and Regional Planning) (1970) *Reform of local government in England*, Cmnd 4276, London: HMSO.

DoE (Department of the Environment) (1971) *Local government in England*, London: DoE.

DoE (1983) *Streamlining the cities*, Cmnd 9063, London: HMSO.

DoE (1987) *Housing: The government's proposals*, Cm 214, London: HMSO.

DoE (1991a) *Local government review: The structure of local government in England: A consultation paper*, London: DoE.

DoE (1991b) *Competing for quality: Competition in the provision of local services*, London: DoE, November.

DoE (1992) *Competing for quality in housing: Competition in the provision of housing management: A consultation paper*, London: DoE.

Eagles, M. and Erfle, S. (1989) 'Community cohesion and voter turnout in general elections in the 1970s', *British Journal of Political Science*, vol 19, no 1, pp 115-25.

Emmerson, C., Hall, J. and Brook, L. (1998) *Attitudes to local tax and spending*, London: Institute of Fiscal Studies.

Euro Reports (1983) *Primary health care in industrialised countries: Report on a WHO meeting*, Bordeaux: Euro Reports.

Finlayson, G. (1963) 'The Municipal Corporation Commission and Report, 1833-35', *Bulletin of the Institute of Historical Research*, vol 36, pp 36-152.

Fishkin, J.S. (1991) *Democracy and deliberation: New directions for democratic reform*, New Haven, CT: Yale University Press.

Flynn, N. (1985) 'Direct Labour Organisations', in S. Ranson, G. Jones and K. Walsh (eds) *Between centre and locality: The politics of public policy*, London: Allen and Unwin, pp 119-34.

Flynn, N., Leach, S. and Vielba, C. (1985) *Abolition or reform? The GLC and the metropolitan county councils*, London: Allen and Unwin, pp 1-18.

Fraser, D. (1979) *Power and authority in the Victorian city*, Oxford: Blackwell.

Game, C. and Leach, S. (1989) 'The county councillor in 1889 and 1989', in K. Young (ed) *New directions for county government*, London: Association of County Councils, pp 22-62.

Giddens, A. (1998) *The third way: The renewal of social democracy*, Cambridge: Polity Press.

Giddens, A. (2000) *The third way and its critics*, Cambridge: Polity Press.

Girvin, B. (1990) 'Change and continuity in liberal democratic political culture', in J.R. Gibbins (ed) *Contemporary political culture: Politics in a postmodern age*, London: Sage Publications, pp 31-51.

Goodin, R. and Dryzek, J. (1980) 'Rational participation: the politics of relative power', *British Journal of Political Science*, vol 10, no 3, pp 273-92.

Gorer, G. (1955) *Exploring English character*, London: Cresset Press.

Gosden, P.H.J.H. (1976) *Education in the Second World War: A study in policy and administration*, London: Methuen.

Grant, W. (1973) 'Non-partisanship in British local politics', *Policy & Politics*, vol 1, no 3, pp 241-54.

Grant, W. (1977) *Independent local politics in England and Wales*, Farnborough: Saxon House.

Gray, A. and Jenkins, B. (1999) 'Democratic renewal in local government: continuity and change', *Local Government Studies*, vol 25, no 4, pp 26-45.

Gustafsson, A. (1991) 'The changing local government and politics of Sweden', in R. Batley and G. Stoker (eds) *Local government in Europe: Trends and developments*, Basingstoke, Macmillan, pp 170-89.

Gyford, J. (1984) *Local politics in Britain*, 2nd edn, London: Croom Helm.

Gyford, J. (1986) 'Diversity, sectionalism and local democracy', in Committee of Inquiry into the Conduct of Local Authority Business, *Research Volume IV, Aspects of local democracy*, Cmnd 9801, London: HMSO.

Halevy, E. (1935) 'Before 1835', in W.I. Jennings, H.J. Laski and W.A. Robson (eds) *A century of municipal progress: The last hundred years*, London: Allen and Unwin, pp 15-36.

Hall, D. and Stewart, J.D. (1996) *Citizen's juries in local government: Report for the LGMB on the pilot projects*, Birmingham: INLOGOV.

Halsey, A.H. (1995) *Change in British society from 1900 to the present day*, 4th edn, Oxford: Oxford University Press.

Hanham, H.J. (1959) *Elections and party management: Politics in the time of Disraeli and Gladstone*, London: Longman.

Hartley, K. and Huby, M. (1986) 'Contracting out policy: theory and evidence', in J. Kay, C. Mayer and D. Thompson (eds) *Contracting out policy: Theory and evidence in privatisation and regulation – the UK experience*, Oxford: Oxford University Press.

Hasluck, E.L. (1936) *Local government in England*, London: Cambridge University Press.

Hatry, H.P. (1983) *A review of private approaches for delivery of public services*, Washington, DC: Urban Institute.

Heath, A. and Topf, R. (1987) 'Political culture', in R. Jowell, S. Witherspoon and L. Brook (eds) *British Social Attitudes: The 1987 report*, Aldershot: Gower, pp 51-67.

Heath, A. and Topf, R. (1992) 'Consensus and dissensus', in R. Jowell, L. Brook and B. Taylor, *British Social Attitudes: The eighth report*, Aldershot: Gower, pp 1-21.

Hebbert, M. and Travers, T. (1988) *The London Government Handbook*, London: Cassell.

Henney, A. (1984) *Inside local government: A case for radical reform*, London: Sinclair Browne.

Hennock, E.P. (1973) *Fit and proper persons: Ideal and reality in nineteenth-century urban government*, London: Edward Arnold.

Herbert, G. (1960) Royal Commission on Local Government in Greater London, 1957-60, *Report of the Commission*, Cmnd 1164, London: HMSO.

Hewison, R. (1995) *Culture and consensus: England, art and politics since 1940*, London: Methuen.

Hill, D.M. (2000) *Urban policy and politics in Britain*, Basingstoke: Macmillan.

Himmelweit, H.T., Humphreys, P., Jaegar, M. and Katz, M. (1981) *How voters decide: A longitudinal study of political attitudes and voting extending over 15 years*, European Monographs in Social Psychology, no 27, London: Academic Press.

Hirst, P. (1995) 'Quangos and democratic government', in F.F. Ridley and D. Wilson (eds) *The quango debate*, Oxford: Oxford University Press in association with The Hansard Society for Parliamentary Government, pp 163-81.

HLG (1963) Draft letter from Dame Evelyn Sharp to Sir Keith Joseph, PRO/HLG/100/1.

HLG (1964a) People in local government: discussion with Local Authority Associations, PRO/HLG/100/1.

HLG (1964b) Sir Francis Hill, Association of Municipal Corporations, PRO/HLG/100/1.

Hoffman-Martinot, V., Rallings, C. and Thrasher, M. (1996) 'Comparing local electoral turnout in Great Britain and France: more similarities than differences?', *European Journal of Political Research*, vol 30, no 2, pp 241-57.

Hogg, C. and Winkler, F. (eds) (1989) *Community/consumer representation in the NHS*, London: Greater London Association of Community Health Councils.

Hogwood, B. (1995) 'The "growth" of quangos: evidence and explanations', in F.F. Ridley and D. Wilson (eds) *The quango debate*, Oxford: Oxford University Press in association with The Hansard Society for Parliamentary Government, pp 29-47.

Horn, P. (1984) *The changing countryside in Victorian and Edwardian England*, London: Athlone Press.

House of Lords (1996) *Rebuilding trust, Select Committee on Relations between Central and Local Government*, vol 1, Report, Session 1995-96, HL 97, London: HMSO.

House of Lords and Commons (1999) Report of the Joint Committee on the Draft Local Government (Organisation and Standards) Bill, HL papers 102-1, HC 542-1, London: The Stationery Office, 27 July.

Inglehart, R. (1990) *Culture shift in advanced industrial societies*, Princeton, NJ: Princeton University Press.

IDEA (1998) *Voter turnout from 1945 to 1997: A global report on political participation*, Stockholm: International IDEA.

IPF (Institute of Public Finance) (1986) *Competitive tendering and efficiency: The case of refuse collection*, London: IPF.

Jaarsma, B., Schram, A., van Winden, F. and Linssen, G. (1986) 'Voter turnout in the Netherlands: an empirical investigation, *Acta Politica*, vol 21, no 1, pp 39–55.

Jeffrey, B. (1997) 'Creating participatory structures in local government', *Local Government Policy Making*, vol 23, no 4, pp 25-31.

Jennings, M.K. (1996) 'Partisan commitment and electoral behaviour in the Netherlands', *Acta Politica*, vol 31, no 4, pp 391-415.

Jennings, M.K. and Niemi, R.G. (1974) *The political character of adolescence*, Princeton, NJ: Princeton University Press.

Jessop, B. (1974) *Traditionalism, conservatism and British political culture*, London: Allen and Unwin.

Jirovec, R.L. and Erich, J.A. (1992) 'The dynamics of political participation among the urban elderly', *Journal of Applied Gerontology*, vol 11, no 2, pp 216-27.

Jones, G.W. (1973) 'The Local Government Act 1972 and the Redcliffe-Maud Commission', *Political Quarterly*, vol 44, no 2, pp 154-66.

Jones, P.R. and Cullis, J.G. (1986) 'Is democracy regressive? A comment on political participation', *Public Choice*, vol 51, no 1, pp 101-7.

JRF (Joseph Rowntree Foundation) (1996) 'Erosion of local government powers must cease says report', Press release, 22 October, York: JRF.

Kaase, M. (1984) 'The challenge of the "participatory revolution" in pluralist democracies', *Internal Political Science Review*, vol 5, no 3, pp 299-318.

Kavanagh, D. (1971) 'The deferential English: a comparative critique', *Government and Opposition*, vol 6, no 3, pp 333-60.

Kavanagh, D. (1985) *British politics: Continuities and change*, Oxford: Oxford University Press.

Kavanagh, D. (1989) 'Political culture in Great Britain: the decline of the civic culture', in G.A. Almond and S. Verba (eds) *Civic culture revisited*, London: Sage Publications, pp 124-76.

Keith-Lucas, B. (1952) *The English local government franchise*, Oxford: Basil Blackwell.

Keith-Lucas, B. (1978) 'Municipal corporations' in *Aspects of government in nineteenth century Britain*, Dublin: Irish University Press, pp 69-96.

Keith-Lucas, B. and Richards, P.G. (1978) *A history of local government in the twentieth century*, London: Allen and Unwin.

Klein, R. and Lewis, J. (1976) *The politics of consumer representation: A study of Community Health Councils*, London: Centre for Studies in Social Policy.

Knack, S. (1992) 'Civic norms, social sanctions, and voter turnout', *Rationality and Society*, vol 4, no 2, pp 133-56.

Knack, S. and Kropf, M.E. (1998) 'For shame: the effect of community co-operative context on the probability of voting', *Political Psychology*, vol 19, no 3, pp 585-99.

Labour Party (1942) *The future of local government: The Labour Party's post-war policy*, London: Labour Party.

Labour Party (1989) *Meet the challenge, make the change*, London: Labour Party.

Labour Party (1993) *Working Party on the Reform of Electoral Systems*, London: Labour Party.

Labour Party (1995) *Renewing democracy, rebuilding communities*, Conference Document, London: Labour Party.

Labour Party (1997) *New Labour: because Britain deserves better*, London: Labour Party.

Lane, J.-E. and Ersson, S. (1990) 'Macro and micro understanding in political science: what explains electoral participation?', *European Journal of Political Research*, vol 18, no 4, pp 457-66.

Laski, H.J. (1935) 'The committee system in local government', in W.I. Jennings, H.J. Laski and W.A. Robson (eds) *A century of municipal progress: The last hundred years*, London: Allen and Unwin, pp 82-108.

Lee, J.M. (1963) *Social leaders and public persons*, Oxford: Oxford University Press.

Leneman, L., Jones, L. and MacLean, U. (1986) *Consumer feedback for the NHS: A literature review*, London: King's Fund.

LGA (Local Government Association) (1998) *Making a difference: A White Paper for local government*, London: LGA.

LGC (1999) 'Reform bids lack genuine scrutiny role', *Local Government Chronicle*, 10 September.

LGMB (1997) *Portrait of change*, London: Local Government Management Board.

Loney, M., Boswell, D. and Clarke, J. (1983) *Social policy and social welfare*, Milton Keynes: Open University Press.

Lowe, R. (1993) *The welfare state in Britain since 1945*, Basingstoke: Macmillan.

Lowndes, V., Stoker, G., Pratchett, L., Wilson, D., Leach, S. and Wingfield, M. (1998) *Enhancing public participation in local government*, London: DETR.

Lynn, P. (1992) *Public perceptions of local government: Its finance and services*, London: HMSO.

Maclure, S. (1988) *Education re-formed: A guide to the Education Reform Act 1988*, London: Hodder and Stoughton.

Malpass, P. (1992) 'Housing policy and the disabling of local authorities', in J. Birchall (ed) *Housing policy in the 1990s*, London: Routledge, pp 10-28.

Mandelson P. and Liddle, R. (1996) *The Blair revolution*, London: Faber and Faber.

Manin, B. (1997) *Principles of representative democracy*, Cambridge: Cambridge University Press.

Marris, P. and Rein, M. (1967) *Dilemmas of social reform: Poverty and community action in the United States*, London: Routledge and Kegan Paul.

Marsh, A. (1977) *Protest and political consciousness*, London: Sage Publications.

Marshall, J.D. (1977) 'The government of Lancashire from 1889: its roots and characteristics', in J.D. Marshall (ed) *The history of Lancashire County Council, 1889 to 1974*, London: Martin Robertson, pp 3-22.

Marwick, A. (1998) *The sixties*, Oxford: Oxford University Press.

Mateo J. F. (1991) 'Improving access to administration in Spain', in R. Batley and G. Stoker (eds) *Local government in Europe: Trends and developments*, Basingstoke: Macmillan, pp 146-54.

Maud, J. (1967a) *Committee on the Management of Local Government, Vol 1, Report of the Committee*, London: HMSO.

Maud, J. (1967b) *Committee on the Management of Local Government, Vol 2, The local government councillor*, London: HMSO.

Maud, J. (1967c) *Committee on the Management of Local Government, Vol 3, The local government elector*, London: HMSO.

Maud, J. (1967d) *Committee on the Management of Local Government, Vol 4, Local government abroad*, London: HMSO.

Mill, J.S. (1861) *Considerations on representative government* (1972 Everyman edition, edited by H.B. Acton), London: J.M. Dent.

Miller, W.L. (1988) *Irrelevant elections? The quality of local democracy in Britain*, Oxford: Clarendon Press.

Minogue, M. (1977) *Documents in contemporary British government, Volume 2*, Cambridge: Cambridge University Press.

MORI (1998) *Encouraging people to vote: A MORI survey on people's attitudes to local elections*, London: Local Government Association.

Morris-Jones, W.H. (1954) 'In defence of apathy: some doubts on the duty to vote', *Political Studies*, vol 2, no 1, pp 25-37.

Moylan, P.A. (1978) *The form and reform of county government: Kent 1889-1914*, Leicester: Leicester University Press.

Municipal Review (1989) 'Local Government Bill: last Major legislation', April, p 9.

Nordlinger, E. (1967) *The working class Tories*, London: MacGibbon and Kee.

Owens, J. and Panella, G. (1991) *Local government: An international perspective*, Amsterdam: North Holland Press.

Owens, J. (1991) 'Local government taxation', Paper to the Conference 'Local Government Taxation: the Challenge of Economic and Monetary Union in Europe', Paris, May.

Parry, G., Moyser, G. and Day, N. (1992) *Political participation and democracy in Britain*, Cambridge: Cambridge University Press.

Pateman, C. (1970) *Participation and democratic theory*, Cambridge: Cambridge University Press.

Pateman, C. (1983) 'Some reflections on participation and democratic theory', in C. Crouch and F.A. Heller (eds) *Organisational democracy and political processes, 1*, New York, NY: John Wiley & Sons.

Pederson, J.T. (1978) 'Political involvement and partisan change in presidential elections', *American Journal of Political Science*, vol 22, no 1, pp 18-30.

Pereira, A. (1991) 'The system of local government in Portugal', in R. Batley and G. Stoker (eds) *Local government in Europe: Trends and developments*, Basingstoke, Macmillan, pp 134-45.

Pettersen, P.A. (1989) 'Comparing non-voters in the USA and Norway: permanence versus transience', *European Journal of Political Research,* vol 17, no 3, pp 351-9.

Phillips, A. (1994) *Local democracy: The terms of the debate*, CLD Report No 2, London: Commission for Local Democracy.

Piette, D. (1990) 'Community participation in formal decision-making mechanisms', *Health Promotion International*, vol 5, no 3, pp 187-97.

Pimlott, B. (1973) 'Local party organisation: turnout and marginality', *British Journal of Political Science*, vol 3, no 2, pp 252-5.

Pirie, M. and Worcester, R. (2000) *The big turn-off*, London: Adam Smith Institute.

Pola, G., France, G. and Levaggi, R. (1996) *Developments in local government finance: Theory and policy*, Cheltenham: Edward Elgar.

Pomper, G.M. (1975) *Voters' choice*, New York, NY: Dodd, Mead and Co.

Prashar, U. and Nicolas, S. (1986) *Routes or road blocks?*, London: Runnymede Trust.

Pratchett, L. (1999) 'Introduction: defining democratic renewal', *Local Government Studies*, vol 25, no 4, pp 1-18.

Preuss, C.G. (1981) 'The effects of density and urban residence on voter turnout', *Population and Environment*, vol 4, no 4, pp 246-65.

Putnam, R. (1966) 'Political attitudes and the local community', *American Political Science Review*, vol 60, no 3, pp 640-54.

Rallings, C., Thrasher, M. and Downe, J. (1996) *Enhancing local electoral turnout – A guide to current practice and future reform*, York: Joseph Rowntree Foundation.

Rallings, C. and Thrasher, M. (1997) *Local elections in Britain*, London: Routledge.

Rallings, C., Temple M. and Thrasher, M. (1994) *Community identity and participation in local democracy*, CLD Report No 1, London: Commission for Local Democracy.

Rao, N. (1994) *The making and unmaking of local self-government*, Aldershot: Dartmouth.

Rao, N. (2000a) *Research Report to The Nuffield Foundation on the Political Representativeness of Councillors*, unpublished.

Rao, N. (2000b) *Options for change: Mayors, cabinets or the status quo?*, unpublished.

Rao, N. and Young, K. (1999) 'Revitalising local democracy', in R. Jowell, J. Curtice, A. Park, K. Thompson. with L. Jarvis, C. Bromely and N. Stratford (eds) *British Social Attitudes: The 19th report*, Aldershot: Ashgate.

Rao, N., Young, K., Lynn, P. and Hurrell, P. (1994) 'Place, personal characteristics and councillors' roles: a multi-variate analysis of survey data, *Policy & Politics*, vol 22, no 1, pp 31-41.

Read, D. (1964) *The English provinces: 1760-1960: A study in influence*, London: Edward Arnold.

Redcliffe-Maud (1969) *Royal Commission on Local Government in England: 1966-69, Report of the Commission*, Cmnd 4040, London: HMSO.

Redlich, J. and Hirst, F.W. (1972) *The history of local government in England* (2nd edn edited by B. Keith-Lucas), London: Macmillan.

Reiter, H.L. (1979) 'Why is turnout down?', *Public Opinion Quarterly*, vol 43, no 3, pp 297–311.

Rentoul, J. (1990) 'Individualism', in R. Jowell, S. Witherspoon and L. Brook, *British Social Attitudes: The seventh report*, Aldershot: Gower.

Rhodes, G. (1976) 'Local government finance, 1918-1966', in Department of the Environment, *Local Government Finance: Appendix 6 to the Report of the Committee of Inquiry under the Chairmanship of Sir Frank Layfield, QC: The relationship between central and local government: evidence and commissioned work*, London, HMSO, pp 102-73.

Richards, P.G. (1975) *The reformed local government system*, London: Allen and Unwin.

Richardson, A. (1983) *Participation*, London: Routledge and Kegan Paul.

Ridley, N. (1988) *The local right: Enabling not providing*, London: Centre for Policy Studies.

Ridley, N. (1991) *'My style of government': The Thatcher years*, London: Hutchinson.

Rose, R. (1973) *Governing without consensus*, London: Faber and Faber.

Rose, R. (1997) *Evaluating election turnout*, Glasgow: University of Strathclyde.

Royal Commission on Standards in Public Life (1976) *Report of the Commission*, Cmnd 6524, London: HMSO.

Royal Commission on the Constitution (1973) *Devolution and other aspects of government: An attitudes survey*, Research Papers 7, London: HMSO.

Rupeni, A. (1989) 'Improving local service quality: a response to new needs', in G. France (ed) *Local public services and crisis of the welfare state*, Rimini: Maggioli Editore.

Schwartz, D. (1969) 'Towards a theory of political recruitment', *Western Political Quarterly*, vol 22, September, pp 552-71.

SEU (Social Exclusion Unit) (1998) *Bringing Britain together: A national strategy for neighbourhood renewal*, Cm 4045, London: Cabinet Office.

Sharp, E. (1962) 'The future of local government', *Public Administration*, vol 40, pp 375-86.

Shields, T.G. and Goidel, R.K. (1997) 'Participation rates, socio-economic class biases and congressional elections: a cross validation', *American Journal of Political Science*, vol 41, no 2, pp 683-91.

Shils, E. (1955) 'The British intellectuals', *Encounter*, vol 4, no 4, pp 6-7.

Skeffington, A. (1969) *People and planning: Report of the Committee on Public Participation in Planning*, London: HMSO.

Slunge, W. (1989) 'Role and participation of citizens in the provision of collective services in Sweden', in G. France (ed) *Local public services and crisis of the welfare state*, Rimini: Maggioli Editore.

Snell, Lord (1935) 'The town council', in W.I. Jennings, H.J. Laski and W.A. Robson (eds) *A century of municipal progress: The last hundred years*, London: Allen and Unwin, pp 66-81.

Steele, J. (1995) *Public access to information: An evaluation of the Local Government (Access to Information) Act, 1995*, London: Policy Studies Institute/DoE.

Stewart, J.D., Kendall, E. and Coote, A. (1994) *Citizens' juries*, London: Institute for Public Policy Research.

Stewart, J.D. (1995a) *Innovation in democratic practice*, Birmingham: INLOGOV.

Stewart, J.D. (1995b) 'Appointed boards and local government', in F.F. Ridley and D.Wilson (eds) *The quango debate*, Oxford: Oxford University Press in association with The Hansard Society for Parliamentary Government, pp 48-63.

Stott, T. (1995) '"Snouts in the trough": the politics of quangos', in F.F. Ridley and D.Wilson (eds) *The quango debate*, Oxford: Oxford University Press in association with The Hansard Society for Parliamentary Government, pp 145-62.

Thatcher, M. (1993) *Downing Street years*, London: Harper Collins.

Thomas, H. (1959) 'The establishment and society' in H.Thomas (ed) *The establishment*, London: Anthony Blond, pp 9-20.

Thomas, H. (ed) (1959) *The establishment*, London: Anthony Blond.

Thompson, M., Ellis, R. and Wildavsky, A. (1990) *Cultural theory*, Boulder, CO: Westview Press.

Times, The (1973) 6 August.

Todd, J. and Butcher, B. (1981) *Electoral registration in 1981*, London: Office of Population Censuses and Surveys.

Travers, T. (1991) *The government of London*, London: London School of Economics, Greater London Group.

Travers, T. and Jones, G. (1997) *The new government of London*, York: Joseph Rowntree Foundation.

Tsouros, A. (1990) 'Healthy cities means community action', *Health Promotion International*, vol 5, no 3, pp 177-8.

Verba, S. and Nie, N. (1972) *Participation in America: Political democracy and social equality*, New York, NY: Harper and Row.

Wheatley, A. (1969) *Report of the Royal Commission on Local Government in Scotland*, Cmnd 4150, Edinburgh: HMSO.

Widdicombe, D. (1986a) *Committee of Inquiry into the Conduct of Local Authority Business, Report of the Committee*, Cmnd 9797, London: HMSO.

Widdicombe, D. (1986b) *Committee of Inquiry into the Conduct of Local Authority Business, Research Volume II: The local government councillor*, Cmnd 9799, London: HMSO.

Widdicombe, D. (1986c) *Committee of Inquiry into the Conduct of Local Authority Business, Research Volume III: The local government elector*, Cmnd 9799, London: HMSO.

Wolfinger, R. and Rosenstone, S. (1980) *Who votes?* New Haven, CT: Yale University Press.

Young, K. (1984) 'Political attitudes', in R. Jowell and C. Airey (eds) *British Social Attitudes: The 1984 report*, Aldershot: Gower, pp 11-37.

Young, K. (1989) 'Bright hopes and dark fears: the origins and expectations of the county councils', in K. Young (ed) *New directions for county government*, London: Association of County Councils, pp 4-21.

Young, K. and Rao, N. (1994) *Coming to terms with change: The local government councillor in 1993*, York: Joseph Rowntree Foundation.

Young, K. and Rao, N. (1995) 'Faith in local democracy', in R. Jowell , J. Curtice, A. Park, L. Brook and D. Ahrendt (eds) *British Social Attitudes: The twelfth report*, Aldershot: Dartmouth, pp 91-118.

Young, K. and Rao, N. (1997a) 'Public attitudes to local government', in *New perspectives on local governance: Reviewing the research evidence*, York: York Publishing, pp 118-57.

Young, K. and Rao, N. (1997b) *Local government since 1945*, Oxford: Blackwell.

Young, K. and Rhodes, G. (1972) 'Voting and elections', in G. Rhodes (ed) *The new government of London: The first five years*, London: Weidenfeld and Nicolson.

Young, K., Gosschalk, B. and Hatter, W. (1996) *In search of community identity*, York: Joseph Rowntree Foundation.

Appendix A:
The surveys

The survey results presented in this book are, for the most part, drawn from a range of studies in which the author was involved in either carrying out, or reporting on the research. In a number of cases, the data have not been previously published, and the purpose of this Appendix is to describe for the reader the basis on which they were undertaken.

The 1998 British Social Attitudes survey and multivariate analyses

The National Centre for Social Research (NCSR) (formerly Social and Community Planning Research [SCPR]) is Britain's leading social research institute. As an independent institute, its work is primarily funded by government departments, local authorities or quasi-governmental organisations to provide information on aspects of social or economic policy. The NCSR is responsible for undertaking the annual British Social Attitudes (BSA) survey series of the British public. The latest in the series, undertaken in 1998, included a module of questions on local government, designed to explore public perceptions of and attitudes to the Labour government's modernisation agenda.

The sampling strategy for each annual survey is designed to yield a representative sample of adults aged 18 or over. Since 1993, the sampling frame for the survey has been the Postcode Address File (PAF) – a list of residential addresses or postal delivery points compiled by the post office. A multi-stage design was adopted with three separate stages of selection: selection of 200 postal sectors; selection of 30 addresses in each of the sectors; and a random selection of individuals from those listed as living at the selected address. This produced a total of 6,000 addresses which, after excluding those addresses which were vacant, derelict or otherwise out of scope, left 5,323 addresses at which 3,146 productive interviews on a face-to-face basis were achieved – a response rate of 59% was obtained. The sample was divided into three tranches and three separate questionnaire modules – A, B and C – were developed; each address in each sector being allocated to one of the tranches. In addition to the face-to-face interview, each respondent was given a self-completion questionnaire which was similarly produced in three versions. Questions pertaining to local democracy were incorporated in versions A and B of both the interview schedule and the self-completion questionnaire. Of those interviewed, between 78% and 82% returned the self-completed questionnaire.

The results reported in Chapter Five arise from a logistic regression, based on the 1998 BSA survey dataset, and carried out on behalf of the author by Dr Stephen Almond of the Personal Social Services Research Unit (PSSRU) at the London School of Economics/University of Kent at Canterbury. This study, which involved a reanalysis of the 1998 BSA survey dataset, was undertaken in order to identify the most powerful influences on people's voting.

Dependent variables

The 1998 BSA survey included a number of questions about voting in local elections, of which one – whether or not the respondent voted in the local election held that May – is the most suitable for this study. There are trade-offs to be made in selecting this single variable as it captures only 870 of more than 3,000 individuals surveyed. However, despite the smaller number of cases, it is possible to be more confident in the analysis, which critically requires the dependent variable to relate to a single point in time. A second, and closely related, dependent variable was constructed from responses to a question put to non-voters (those who hadn't voted in 1998) asking why they had not done so. The eight possible reasons were: there was no one who I wanted to vote for; I was too busy; I/someone in my family was unwell; I was away from home on election day; I was not interested in the election; I was not registered to vote; I deliberately decided not to vote; and the polling station was too difficult to get to. These responses indicate whether or not the respondent may be considered a potential voter – as someone who might have voted had circumstances not prevented them – who may be distinguished from those respondents who actually chose not to vote through lack of interest or some other, deeper, disaffection. This new dependent variable with its three categories – voter, non-voter and potential voter – was used in the analysis.

Independent variables

A large number of independent variables – those that might be expected to drive voting behaviour – were used in the analyses. The first category relates to socioeconomic and demographic factors which include gender, age, education, tenure and household income. A second category included the region variable. The third category covered a range of attitudes to local government and included people's trust in politicians and faith in local democracy, as well as a composite score derived from respondents' positions on a range of the attitude questions described above. The fourth classification covered voting in the general election; the fifth a range of local authority issues including respondents' knowledge of their local councils, and their views of the council's performance in informing people about service provision.

The simplest form of results are the descriptive statistics for all the variables used in the regression models, as shown in Table A1.

The analyses

For the first dependent variable – *voted/did not vote* – a logistic regression was carried out. A feature of this technique is that it enables the 'odds ratio' of each explanatory variable to be calculated.

Variables were entered into the regression one at a time and in different combinations, to allow the effects of each upon the others to be observed. Those which are not significant or which have a high level of multi-collinearity were dropped from the equation in the interests of parsimony. On these grounds, party membership, employment status, respondents' income, interest in politics, television viewing and newspaper readership were among a large number of variables dropped. Other variables excluded in the interests of improving the model ranged from marital status to age bands (the continuous variable fitted better), views on the duty to vote, on whether government has too much power or confidence in parliament (missing values limited their utility), and trust in politicians or in government (trust in MPs proved a better measure). The ACORN measure of types of residential area was included in this dataset, but was found to have too many categories to be useful, and proportion of owner occupancy proved a better measure. Membership of a political party was not useful, as the great majority of respondents were not members. The exclusion of variables with a large number of missing values reduced the sample size from 870 to 551, although this reduction made little difference to the

Table A1: Descriptive statistics for variables used in multivariate analyses*

Variable	Mean	Std dev
Vote in local elections in England (0 = No, 1 = Yes)	0.45	0.50
Vote in local elections in England (1 = Yes, 2 = Potential, 3 = No)	1.95	0.91
Gender (1 = Male, 2 = Female)	1.58	0.50
Age (continuous)	48.9	18.66
Education (1 = Degree, 2 = A level/Higher, 3 = O level/CSE/Other, 4 = None)	2.86	0.98
Tenure – % of owner-occupied in region (continuous)	68.48	16.67
Household income (unequivalent, 0 = bottom quintile, 1 = Rest)	0.78	0.41
Party identification (0 = None, 1 = Very strong, 2 = Fairly strong, 3 = Not very strong)	2.17	1.02
Trust in MPs (1 = Just about always, 2 = Most of time, 3 = Some of time, 4 = Almost never)	3.38	0.66
Knowledge of who leader of largest party on council is (1 = Yes, 2 = No)	1.85	0.36
How well local council informs about service provision (1 = Very well, 2 = Fairly well, 3 = Not very well, 4 = Not at all well)	2.45	0.80
How well local council informs about things happening (Coding as for service provision)	2.53	0.80
Politics and government seem so complicated … cannot understand … (1 = Agree strongly, 2 = Agree, 3 = Indifferent, 4 = Disagree, 5 = Disagree strongly)	2.46	1.08
More likely to vote if local elections held at weekend … (1 = More likely, 2 = Makes no difference, 3 = Less likely)	1.92	0.47
Composite score on various opinions (derived from code as for politics and government above)	7.58	3.11
Voted at the previous General Election (1 = Voter, 2 = Potential voter, 3 = Non-voter)	1.36	0.75
Regional variable (1 = Northern, 2 = NW, 3 = Yorks & Humberside, 4 = West Midlands, 5 = East Midlands, 6 = East Anglia, 7 = SW, 8 = SE, 9 = London)	†	†

Notes:

* Full sample size (n = 3,146) is used for age, gender and region variables.

† Not appropriate statistic to be computed (purely categorical).

results when the main variable concerned – the composite measure of opinions on local democracy – was dropped.

Turning to the dichotomous variable *voted/did not vote*, the logistic regression model which ensued from the exclusion of the large number of variables as discussed in Chapter Five was:

> Vote (yes or no) = Constant + Age + Education + % Owner occupancy + Household income + Party identification + Trust in MP + Knowledge of local council leadership + Perception of information on services given by local authority + Perception of information on other matters that affect residents + Understanding government and politics + Views on weekend voting + General election voting behaviour + Composite score on opinions on local democracy + Regional identifier + error term.

The second analysis performed was a multinomial logistic regression – a change of modelling technique made to accommodate the move from a dichotomous dependent variable (voted/did not vote) to the three-fold category of *voter, non-voter* and *potential voter*. For this analysis, a second and closely related dependent variable was constructed from responses to a question put to non-voters (those who hadn't voted in 1998), asking why they had not done so.

The results of these analyses are shown in Tables A2 and A3 and are discussed in Chapter Five.

Table A2: Logistic regression to predict vote/did not vote at local elections in England

Variable	B	Sig	Odds ratio	95% CI
Gender	0.2056	0.3779	1.2282	0.7777-1.9397
Age	**0.0198**	**0.0134**	**1.0200**	**1.0041-1.0361**
Degree	0.1894	0.6907	1.2085	0.4755-3.0717
A level/higher education	−0.2094	0.5406	0.8110	0.4147-1.5862
O level/CSE/other	−0.2048	0.5304	0.8148	0.4298-1.5448
No qualifications	*	0.6996	–	-
Tenure – % owner-occupied	0.0133	0.0732	1.0134	0.9988-1.0282
Household income	−0.1474	0.6554	0.8629	0.4517-1.6488
No party identification	−0.7116	0.1214	0.4909	0.1995-1.2078
Very strong party identification	**1.0031**	**0.0209**	**2.7266**	**1.1641-6.3863**
Fairly strong party identification	**0.9584**	**0.0001**	**2.6075**	**1.5970-4.2576**
Not very strong party identification	*****	**0.0001**	**–**	**–**

Table A2: Logistic regression to predict vote/did not vote at local elections in England (continued)

Variable	B	Sig	Odds ratio	95% CI
Just about always trust MP	1.4121	0.3315	4.1048	0.2375-70.9571
Trust most of the time ...	−0.2695	0.5889	0.7637	0.2874-2.0298
Trust only some of the time ...	0.0445	0.8549	1.0455	0.6490-1.6842
Trust almost never...	*	0.7247	–	–
Know who leader of largest party...	**0.5902**	**0.0535**	**1.8044**	**0.9912-3.2847**
LA informs on services very well	−0.0362	0.9580	0.9644	0.2504-3.7150
LA informs on services fairly well	0.2034	0.6870	1.2255	0.4558-3.2952
LA informs ... not very well	−0.0138	0.9759	0.9863	0.4015-2.4225
LA informs ... not at all well	*	0.8778	–	–
LA informs on other things that affect you ... very well	0.7840	0.2773	2.1902	0.5324-9.0099
LA informs ... fairly well	−0.6026	0.2051	0.5474	0.2155-1.3902
LA informs ... not very well	−0.0046	0.9914	0.9954	0.4311-2.2981
LA informs ... not at all well	*	**0.0342**	–	–
Understanding government and politics – agree strongly	**−1.3815**	**0.0510**	**0.2512**	**0.0627-1.0058**
Understanding ... agree	**−1.3123**	**0.0507**	**0.2692**	**0.0722-1.0039**
Understanding ... neither agree nor disagree	**−1.7241**	**0.0233**	**0.1783**	**0.0402-0.7911**
Understanding ... disagree	**−1.2872**	**0.0549**	**0.2760**	**0.0742-1.0275**
Understanding ... disagree strongly	*	0.2611	–	–
Would vote if polls held at weekend – more likely	**−1.9428**	**0.0001**	**0.1433**	**0.0556-0.3693**
Would vote ... make no difference	−0.1527	0.6831	0.8584	0.4124-1.7868
Would vote ... less likely	*	**0.0000**	–	–
Score for selected opinions	**0.1741**	**0.0000**	**1.1902**	**1.0965-1.2919**
Voted at general election	**1.5605**	**0.0004**	**4.7610**	**2.0015-11.3253**
Potential voter at general election	**1.5345**	**0.0437**	**4.6389**	**1.0439-20.6131**
Non-voter at general election	*	**0.0019**	–	–
Northern region	**1.1413**	**0.0223**	**3.1308**	**1.1767-8.3302**
North West	0.1275	0.7438	1.1360	0.5287-2.4409
Yorks and Humberside	0.0432	0.9232	1.0441	0.4337-2.5136
West Midlands	−0.0219	0.9530	0.9783	0.4724-2.0260
East Midlands	0.5688	0.3560	1.7662	0.5278-5.9097
East Anglia	0.4941	0.3060	1.6390	0.6365-4.2206
South West	0.3222	0.5677	1.3802	0.4570-4.1680
South East	−0.1947	0.6031	0.8231	0.3950-1.7149
Greater London	*	0.3430	–	–
Constant	**−3.5182**	**0.0021**	–	–

Notes: (n = 551), significant coefficients in bold, * is reference category.

Table A3: Multinominal logistic regression – voter compared with non-voter coefficients

Variable	B	Sig	Odds ratio	95% CI
Gender	−0.146	0.570	0.864	0.523-1.430
Age	**0.026**	**0.004**	**1.026**	**1.008-1.045**
Degree	0.459	0.389	1.583	0.557-4.500
A level/higher education	−0.181	0.636	0.835	0.394-1.767
O level/CSE/other	−0.185	0.612	0.831	0.407-1.697
No qualifications	*	–	–	–
Tenure – % owner-occupied	**0.018**	**0.025**	**1.018**	**1.002-1.034**
Household income	0.496	0.185	1.642	0.789-3.418
No party identification	**−1.027**	**0.033**	**0.358**	**0.140-0.918**
Very strong party identification	**1.015**	**0.043**	**2.76**	**1.033-7.370**
Fairly strong party identification	**1.060**	**0.000**	**2.887**	**1.654-5.041**
Not very strong party identification	*	–	–	–
Just about always trust MP	0.634	0.667	1.886	0.105-33.846
Trust most of the time…	−0.414	0.447	0.661	0.227-1.923
Trust only some of the time …	0.129	0.630	1/138	0.673-1.923
Trust almost never…	*	–	–	–
Know who leader of largest party is…	0.605	0.078	1.831	0.934-3.589
LA informs on services very well	0.063	0.938	1.066	0.217-5.227
LA informs on services fairly well	0.099	0.857	1.105	0.374-3.267
LA informs … not very well	−0.188	0.709	0.829	0.309-2.222
LA informs … not at all well	*	–	–	–
LA informs on other things that affect you … very well	0.805	0.347	2.236	0.418-11.949
LA informs … fairly well	−0.815	0.117	0.443	0.160-1.225
LA informs … not very well	−0.008	0.985	0.991	0.398-2.468
LA informs … not at all well	*	–	–	–
Understanding government and politics – agree strongly	−1.313	0.112	0.269	0.053–1.359
Understanding … agree	−1.361	0.085	0.257	0.055-1.205
Understanding … neither agree nor disagree	**−1.708**	**0.053**	**0.181**	**0.032-1.023**
Understanding … disagree	**−1.607**	**0.041**	**0.201**	**0.043-0.938**
Understanding … disagree strongly	*	–	–	–
Would vote if polls held at weekend – more likely	**−2.234**	**0.000**	**0.107**	**0.037-0.309**
Would vote … make no difference	−0.427	0.333	0.653	0.275-1.550
Would vote … less likely	*	–	–	–

Table A3: Multinominal Logistic regression – voter compared with non-voter coefficients (continued)

Variable	B	Sig	Odds ratio	95% CI
Score for selected opinions ...	**0.215**	**0.000**	**1.239**	**1.130-1.359**
Voted at general election	**1.529**	**0.001**	**4.614**	**1.878-11.336**
Potential voter at general election	**1.804**	**0.036**	**6.072**	**1.127-32.701**
Non-voter at general election	*	–	–	–
Northern region	1.014	0.060	2.758	0.958-7.937
North West	–0.001	0.998	0.999	0.432-2.308
Yorks and Humberside	0.106	0.832	1.111	0.418-2.953
West Midlands	–0.241	0.559	0.786	0.351-1.762
East Midlands	0.184	0.782	1.202	0.326-4.431
East Anglia	0.390	0.461	1.477	0.524-4.165
South West	0.195	0.765	1.215	0.339-4.360
South East	–0.105	0.803	0.900	0.394-2.055
Greater London	*	–	–	–
Constant	**–3.236**	**0.011**	–	–

Notes: n = 551, significant variables in bold, * is reference category.

Joseph Rowntree Foundation survey of councillors, 1993

This survey was based on a 10% sample of elected members in the local authorities of England, Wales and Scotland. There were, at that time, 513 authorities with the number of councillors totalling 24,420. The authorities were stratified by country and type and a systematic random sample of authorities was drawn to give a total of 54 authorities. All councillors in these authorities – a total of 2,496 – were sent questionnaires for self-completion. A response rate of 67% was achieved, with a return of 1,665 completed questionnaires. Questions covered included councillors characteristics, their council work, their views on and satisfaction with the committee system, member information and support, and councillors' views on the changing management of local government.

SCPR surveys of working and non-working councillors, 1997 and 1999

The first of these two studies was carried out in 1997 and intended to explore both councillors' experiences of combining employment with their public duties, and employer practices and views. Funded by the

DETR, it investigated the characteristics of employed councillors, along with the practices of their employers with regard to time off for public service (Courtenay et al, 1998).

In order to identify councillors' employers, a two stage research design was adopted. A representative sample of 5,772 councillors was drawn and telephone contact made to establish their working status. Non-working councillors were screened out, while those in employment were interviewed to collect information about their personal characteristics, work, council duties and time off arrangements. A total of 1,849 councillors (35% of those screened) were eligible for interview. The employers of a subset of these were then identified for the main stage of the survey. As a result of this procedure, the team gathered detailed information on the occupation, social class, age and gender of the minority of councillors who are employed. However, no such detailed information was collected for the large majority of councillors who were retired, unemployed, looking after a home or not working for other reasons.

The second survey was funded by the Nuffield Foundation (Rao, 2000a) and took forward that investigation to include *non-working* councillors (by far the larger proportion) so as to achieve, in combination, a representative sample. A sample of 1,336 of the 3,404 councillors who were earlier screened out on grounds of their not being in work at the time of the survey was drawn, stratified by council type and by whether the councillors were self-employed or not working. Councillors were selected systematically, with a random start. They were contacted by letter and invited to participate in a second telephone interview.

An outline of the information to be sought in the interview was sent to respondents in advance to enable respondents to refresh their memories. This was important for, in order for the data from both surveys to be comparable, the questions in the second interview had to refer to the councillor's experience or circumstances as they were in April 1997. By this means, a total of 1,011 responses were received giving a response rate of 78%. For the purpose of the final analysis, and to enable comparison of working and non-working councillors, the responses from the second survey were combined with the 1,849 from the first survey to give a total of 2,860 cases. These were then weighted to give a representative sample.

The author's 1999 survey of councillors

This survey was funded by Goldsmiths College and intended to update the data collected in the 1993 Joseph Rowntree Foundation study (Young and Rao, 1994). The primary purpose of the survey was to explore councillors' views of the proposed changes to local authority decision-making structures. In this study, a sample of councillors in all English authorities was drawn to give a 10% sample of councillors. The reason for this change of design was to attain a comprehensive coverage of responses to the Blair government's modernisation agenda, which was expected to be received very differently in authorities of different types. Non-participation rate was found to be higher among Labour-controlled authorities – a small number of which explicitly declined to cooperate. An overall response rate of 60% was obtained, with 1,242 completed questionnaires returned. Questions covered included much the same ground as the 1993 study, replicating some questions, but specifically focused on councillors' responses to the proposed new management structures. The questionnaire also covered some questions from the 1998 BSA survey to enable a comparison to be made between councillors' attitudes to elected mayors and cabinets, and those of the public. The report is yet to be published.

1999 National Centre for Social Research survey of attitudes to local finance and public consultation

This study was commissioned by the Department of the Environment, Transport and the Regions to discover the extent to which people living in England were actively engaged with and informed about their local authorities, about financial issues in particular. Respondents were asked questions to assess their basic knowledge and understanding of local government systems, satisfaction with services and the provision of information, and attitudes to public consultation. This last section covered people's experiences of, and willingness to take part in, local consultative initiatives. A random sample of the English adult population was drawn and 2,047 interviews were conducted in the period March–April 1999. The overall response rate was 65%. The results were published in March 2000 (Bromley et al, 2000).

Appendix B: The legislation

The Labour government's modernisation agenda was set out in a series of consultation documents and Green Papers before being incorporated in a series of Bills – all but one of which, at the time of writing, has passed into the statute book.

2000 Representation of the People Act

The government has already moved to reform electoral practices and maximise voter registration by maintaining rolling registers, encouraging participation in elections and improving access for people with disabilities under the 2000 Representation of the People Act. Local authorities are permitted to experiment in electoral practice, including electronic voting, mobile polling stations, voting at different hours, on different days, or over a number of days; holding elections entirely by postal vote.

2000 Greater London Authority Act

The 2000 Greater London Authority Act establishes, for the first time, the office of executive mayor for Greater London which, together with a Greater London Assembly, constitutes the new Greater London Authority (GLA). This body covers the same area as the former Greater London Council, but has differently constituted powers. Its establishment marks a new beginning for London government, after a period of 14 years in which there has been no overall strategic authority. Elected with a manifesto commitment to establish such a body after first holding a referendum, New Labour acted swiftly to ensure that the new bodies would assume their powers within three years of the government taking office.

Under the 2000 Greater London Authority Act, the elections for the mayor and the Greater London Assembly took place in May 2000, and the mayor and Assembly members took office on 3 July. Ken Livingstone, running as an independent candidate, secured a convincing victory in the mayoral election, while no party secured an overall majority in the Assembly.

1999 Local Government Bill

The consultation paper, *Local leadership, local choice* (DETR, 1999), presented the government's proposals on new executive arrangements for local government in the form of Part I of the draft Local Government (Organisation and Standards) Bill. The draft bill was scrutinised by a Joint Select Committee, which expressed doubt about the proposed separation of executive and scrutiny roles. The Committee highlighted the extent of ministers' powers to determine the important matters by regulation, and expressed concern at the lack of criteria for their application. The Committee expressed the view, contrary to that of the government, that in some councils the traditional committee system worked well, meeting the fundamental principles of transparency, accountability and efficiency – local choice and locally appropriate arrangements would be ensured if the adoption of new executive arrangements were left optional, rather than made compulsory. The government responded to their report in December 1999, shortly after the introduction of the 1999 Local Government Bill in which Part I dealt with the new duty to promote local well-being (as foreshadowed in *Modern local government: In touch with the people,* DETR, 1998), and Part II the introduction of new executive structures.

The arrangements set out in Part II – a leader with cabinet; an executive mayor; an executive mayor with a council manager – provided for changes to local government arrangements to bring these structures into place, and made requirements for referendums on proposals to introduce elected mayors. Despite criticisms, the government insisted on compelling these new forms of local governance to be submitted to local referendums with a view to ensuring the adoption of one or another pattern by all authorities. The Bill was introduced in the House of Lords, and on 9 March 2000 the government was defeated on the core issue – whether the proposed executive arrangements were a requirement and on whether councils should have a discretion to adopt them (if they chose not to do so, Part II of the Act would not apply to them). The opposition, which prevailed on this occasion, took their stand on the different needs of rural and urban authorities, the limited role proposed for non-executive members, the need for local choice and the circumstances of councils with no overall majority. There was also support for a 'fourth option', an alternative approach to forming an executive outside the proposals of the government.

The government indicated that it would not accept the amendments, but would seek to reverse them in the House of Commons. This it duly did, although the government conceded that 'additional forms of executive' would be accepted, leaving it to the Secretary of State to make regulation defining just what these might be. The intention, however, was to find executive forms that would best suit local needs, thus meeting the widespread criticism of the bill.

When the bill returned to the Lords there was a risk that the upper house would reinstate their earlier amendments leaving the government unable to use the Parliament Act to enforce its view, as the bill had originally been introduced in the Lords. Instead, an agreement was made to accept an amendment proposed by the Liberal Democrat peers, which would introduce an opt-out provision for smaller district councils. This would apply to district councils with a population of less than 85,000. Such authorities would be able to eschew any form of executive providing they accepted a modernised forms of committee structures including some form of scrutiny arrangements.

This escape clause covers about 40% of district councils raising the prospect that, if they were so minded, the majority of English authorities could retain a committee based system of decision making. The Secretary of State is empowered to extend the range of authorities falling in this category. As to Wales, the National Assembly has been given wide-ranging power to define the exempted category.

Index

R

Rebuilding trust 64-5
Redcliffe-Maud, Lord John *see*
  Committee on the Management of
  Local Government; Royal
  Commission on Local Government
referendums 138-9, 176, 177, 178
regeneration *see* urban regeneration
regulation, of local government 131-2
remuneration, of councillors *see*
  expenses
Representation of the People Act
  (2000) 225
representativeness
  of councillors 88-91, 165-70
  of government 16
  of local government 11-13
  and party politics 192-4
residence, length of
  and electoral turnout 104
  and local government involvement
  84-5, 150-1
Royal Commission on Local
  Government 42, 43, 47-8, 135, 164,
  167
Royal Commission on Local
  Government in Greater London 41
Royal Commission on Local
  Government in Scotland 38-9
rural areas *see* counties

S

salaries, for councillors 37, 38-9, 169
School Standards and Framework Act
  (1998) 124-5
schools 60-1, 124-5
  see also education
Scotland, Royal Commission on Local
  Government 38-9
SCPR surveys of working and non-
  working councillors 222-3
  see also National Centre for Social
  Research
scrutiny committees 170, 172-3, 176,
  178, 180

selection in schools, New Labour
  policies 125
service provision, by local government
  19-28, 58-61, 62-3
sex *see* gender
shops, voting in 159, 160
social change, and cultural revolution
  70-2, 73-4
social class
  of councillors 168
  and electoral turnout 104-5
  and willingness to participate 81
  see also middle classes; working classes
social diversification 51-2, 70
social housing *see* housing
social services 50, 123
  see also health services
suffrage *see* franchise

T

Thatcher, Margaret
  and centralisation 53-4
  and cultural change 75
third way politics 119-21
time commitments, of councillors
  36-7, 53, 168-9
trades unions *see* industrial democracy
trust
  in councillors 88, 90, 143
  and participation 77
  see also government, loss of confidence
  in; local government, confidence in

U

United States
  electoral turnout 94, 95, 104, 105, 106
  participation in local government 122
urban regeneration, New Labour
  policies 126-7

V

voters
  characteristics 107, 108-17
  registration 97-8, 155